START & RUN A LANDSCAPING BUSINESS

Joel LaRusic

Self-Counsel Press
(a division of)
International Self-Counsel Press Ltd.
USA   Canada

Self-Counsel Press acknowledges the financial support of the Government of Canada through the Book Publishing Industry Development Program (BPIDP) for our publishing activities.

Printed in Canada.

First edition: 2005

Library and Archives Canada Cataloguing in Publication

LaRusic, Joel
    Start & run a landscaping business / Joel LaRusic. — 1st ed.

    (Self-counsel business series)
    ISBN 1-55180-605-3

1. Landscaping industry—Management. 2. New business enterprises—Management. I. Title.
II. Title: Start and run a landscaping business. III. Series.

SB472.5.L37 2005   712'.068   C2005-900266-2

Self-Counsel Press
(a division of)
International Self-Counsel Press Ltd.

1704 North State Street	1481 Charlotte Road
Bellingham, WA 98225	North Vancouver, BC V7J 1H1
USA	Canada

CONTENTS

ACKNOWLEDGMENTS

Many thanks go to the cast of exceptional people who helped make this book a reality.

To Self-Counsel Press for giving me this opportunity, especially to the editors — Ruth Wilson, Audrey McClellan, and Barbara Kuhne — who helped to shape my collection of useful information into something worthy of publication.

For their professional expertise I would like to acknowledge and thank Gail Hetherington, my long-time accountant and guiding light in business matters. Also, from Northwest Mower & Supply, Dana Nicholson, the best small engine repair guy in the world (and thanks to Keith for making him available). Finally to Bruce Avery of Westgro Sales Inc. for the expertise he contributed on fertilizers and pesticides.

I am deeply indebted to Mum and Dad, Adam and Glenn, Roger and Rudy, who provided much-needed encouragement. Also to my right-hand man, Mark, and everyone else who made Dirty Deeds successful. Special thanks to my wife, Kelli, for tolerating my marathon writing sessions and for the love and support she always shows to me and my bird-brained schemes.

Lastly, I dedicate this book to an age-old institution — one where ideas flourish uninhibited, encouragement stokes the imagination, and challenges are raised high up with our pints. This one is to "the boys." Cheers!

PREFACE

Because you've taken the initiative to pick up this book and start reading, I assume you have thought about a career working in the fresh outdoors. You are interested in a job that brings you close to nature, that is satisfying, that is healthy. You also want a job that pays you well for your hard work. Perhaps you already work in such a rewarding field, but now you want to be your own boss. Or perhaps you would love to run your own business or take advantage of the tax benefits that go along with a home-based business.

A career as a self-employed gardener and/or lawn care expert can give you all of this and more. To achieve that end, this book will help you get started in the fascinating business of landscape maintenance and will help shorten the learning curve ahead of you. You will be able to avoid costly mistakes and you'll learn tricks of the trade that may take months and years to pick up on your own. If such a book had been available when I started my lawn care business in 1990, it would have saved me countless headaches, not to mention dollars.

I begin with the assumption that you know nothing or very little about running a landscaping business. I explain each step in easy-to-understand terms and include what to consider before you start, how to set up your business, how to keep it running profitably, and everything in between. I also provide basic information on plant and lawn care to help you get started.

This book assumes that you are motivated and a self-starter. You like to work hard and you take great pride in what you have accomplished. You love the natural world around you: the vast variety of flowers, shrubs, and trees, and the exquisiteness of a beautifully manicured lawn. And you definitely don't mind getting your hands dirty!

If this describes you, then this book is for you. Following the steps contained in these pages will allow you to realize a profit in the satisfying work of landscape maintenance.

INTRODUCTION

1. WHY THE LANDSCAPING BUSINESS?

The smell of a freshly cut lawn. The pleasing look of a well-trimmed hedge. The sweet fragrance of a flowering lilac shrub. The stunning beauty of a hundred colorful tulips bursting forth in unison. The tranquil feeling of watching ferns and hostas unfurl each spring.

Your foray into the world of landscape maintenance encompasses all these things and so much more. Working outdoors, helping to beautify someone's property, is both rewarding and satisfying. Consider the advantages of running your own lawn care and gardening business:

- *You will work in a fascinating field.* The variety of yard and garden work is staggering. When you work on beautifying lawns and gardens with ornamental shrubs and plants, there is no

end to what you can learn. Those who work in the field often become passionate about it.

- *It offers a healthy lifestyle.* Gardening and yard work are great outdoor exercise. That's not to say that every day and every job will be a test of your physical fitness and endurance (although you will experience such a test on some days). But even simple jobs such as pushing a mower, bending to pull weeds, or planting flowers provide a great workout. It is a very active lifestyle. After a good day's work, you'll sleep well.

- *The job is satisfying.* There is little more rewarding than being able to see what you have accomplished with your own hands at the end of the day. You may be dirty, you may be wet, and your muscles may ache. But nothing can take away that feeling of satisfaction as you look over your handiwork. It's a wonderful feeling that will make you feel good inside.

🌶 *The landscaping industry is booming.* There has never been a better time to enter the business. The lawn and garden industry is huge now and it is growing. Baby boomers, the largest demographic, are starting to retire. They love their gardens and they love *to* garden — and they are going to need some help. In a 1998 survey, the National Home Center reported that in the United States, baby boomers account for half the business in the multibillion-dollar-a-year lawn and garden industry. The Professional Lawn Care Association estimates that the service portion accounts for about 10 percent of the industry as a whole. In Canada, the numbers are smaller, but the proportion is the same, if not larger.

🌶 *You can be your own boss.* Working for yourself allows you great freedom. You can be as busy as you want to be. You can grow your company to a comfortable level and make an excellent living, or you can expand your business and make even more! If you want to take two months off in the winter, it's up to you. You will have complete control of your business.

🌶 *The start-up costs are low.* Compared to many other businesses, there is little capital needed to start a landscape maintenance business. This is a home-based business, so you won't incur costs such as rent. You'll also benefit from the many tax benefits of having your office at home. You'll need some basic equipment, but you can begin work with just a few items and then expand as the money starts coming in.

2. HOW THIS BOOK WILL HELP YOU

This book has been designed to tell you everything you need to know to start and run your own successful landscape maintenance business. It will teach you the basics of lawn care and gardening and will provide advice on many aspects of running any business. Once you've read this book, you'll be able to hang out your shingle and get to work.

As you move along in your career, you may want to add to your knowledge base by doing some self-directed study or by taking a course. Many continuing education departments offer evening courses on plant and lawn care, and some colleges offer one- and two-year programs dedicated to the field of landscape maintenance. Part-time programs are sometimes available, allowing you to continue to run your business while studying to increase your expertise.

The book is divided into three parts, which cover all aspects of starting and running a landscaping business:

🌶 *Part 1: Starting Your Business.* Here you'll learn all about what happens before you open the doors to your business. This section covers important issues you should consider before committing to this business and advises on how to start planning for it. Once you are sure that the landscaping business is for you, you'll move on to information describing how to set up your office, your shop, and your truck, and what equipment you will need to buy. You'll also find many practical ideas about how to organize, how to accessorize, and how to computerize your new business.

❧ *Part 2: Running Your Business.* You won't be successful if you don't spend time on the business end of your business! This section covers marketing and managing your business, including keeping records, working with employees, and staying organized. A highlight of this section is the three chapters that take you through a typical job from start to finish — from the point of first contact right through to pricing, scheduling, and follow-up.

❧ *Part 3: The Services You Offer.* This section covers all the "how-to" aspects of the actual work you will do. It includes a crash course in how to cut a lawn, when to mulch (and when not to), when to power rake and aerate, and how to prune and trim plants. You'll also learn a few "green industry" essentials, such as the best fertilizers to use and tips on other services you might offer, including off-season work.

In writing this book, I have drawn on the experience I gained running my own landscaping business for ten years. I include sample letters and forms that I have used successfully, including letters to announce price increases, quotation worksheets, routing sheets, newsletters, and advertising samples. I also include tips and tricks of the trade that only experience can teach. Of course, not every pearl of wisdom offered

will apply or appeal to you, but many will, and I hope they help ease your road to success.

The CD-ROM that accompanies this book includes a list of recommended websites and books that you can refer to when you're ready to learn and study more. It also includes checklists, worksheets, templates for letters, a detailed sample business plan, and a sample company InfoPack.

3. A NOTE ON EXPERIENCE

If you already have some experience in the field of landscape maintenance, you have an advantage, though I think you will still benefit from reading this book to pick up some pointers and learn new techniques.

If you are completely new to the industry, you have a lot to learn. Not to worry though; you are well on your way by relying on this book. To quote the old adage, "The longest journey begins with a single step." Don't be intimidated by focusing on the entire journey — just look ahead to the next step and enjoy the ride!

The instructions offered in this book will greatly reduce the learning curve that you have ahead of you, but they will not replace actual experience. To help you get started on the right foot, consider the following ideas:

❧ *Get some on-the-job training.* Consider working for someone else for a year or so to learn the ropes of landscape maintenance. Alternatively, if you know someone who already works in the field, ask if he or she would be willing to spend some time with you. At the very least, try "spying" on some experienced gardeners. Watch their techniques, their systems, their routines. Take notes. Learn.

Keep to the middle of the road. For the first year at least, do not head to the most prestigious neighborhoods, where the lawns are all kept in mint condition, and say "no" to large or complex jobs that come your way before you are ready for them. Stick to middle-class areas where the occasional error will not be grounds for cutting off your services! These jobs may not pay as well, but they provide a great starting point. Once you have more experience, you can choose whether to stay in this market or move on to a different clientele.

 Practice! You can practice in your own yard, in your parents' yard, or even at a good friend's yard. But practice, practice, practice!

PART 1
STARTING YOUR BUSINESS

You've done well! You have done more than just think about being your own boss in the landscaping business; you have also taken the initiative to start reading this book. You have already shown that you have at least one quality that is needed to be successful in this business — motivation! However, other qualities are also desirable if you expect to last long. The chapters in this section will help you decide if you have what it takes to run a business. You'll also have an opportunity to look more closely at the business to be sure this is a career you want. If you decide to move on, you'll learn how to complete your business plan — the necessary first step to starting up. After that, you can begin to think about setting up shop by buying equipment and organizing your home office.

1
SIZING UP THE BUSINESS: WHAT YOU NEED TO KNOW BEFORE YOU BEGIN

1. IS THIS BUSINESS FOR YOU?

Gardening is many people's favorite pastime. They love to putter in the garden, snipping back a few daisies, turning over the soil in the bed here and there, cutting the lawn at a nice leisurely pace. Who wouldn't want to do that for a living?

Well, this business is a lot of things, but puttering is not one of them! In my ten years in the business, I don't think I have puttered even once. Instead, I'm usually on the go. It is a job that requires a lot of energy and a lot of motivation, and before you invest too much time and money in starting your own business, you should take a step back and assess whether it is right for you.

Worksheet 1 will help you identify your strengths and weaknesses for starting a landscaping business. You can use the results to determine if your expectations are realistic and if there are areas you need to work on to ensure your success. Take the time to complete Worksheet 1 now.

2. YOUR PERSONAL IMPROVEMENT PLAN

It's important to assess yourself as accurately as possible. If your answer to any questions in the first six sections of Worksheet 1 was "no," you should consider carefully if you are cut out to run your own landscaping business. The traits identified in those sections are *required*, not suggested, for success. If you don't possess several of these traits, it's better to find out now, before you have spent money on a truck and equipment and advertised for your first customers. If you answered "no" to just one or two questions in these sections, and if you really think you can work on those points, then you should carry on with the exercise.

3

WORKSHEET 1
SKILLS SELF-ASSESSMENT

Answer all of the following questions by checking "Yes" if you feel the answer is mostly yes and by checking "No" if the answer is mostly no. Take a good, introspective look at yourself and answer as honestly as you can. If you plan to go into business with a partner, make a copy of the assessment and ask him or her to complete it as well so that you can evaluate how the two of you may complement each other.

		Yes	No
Work ethic	You enjoy hard work?	☐	☐
	You work conscientiously?	☐	☐
	You prefer to do a thorough job?	☐	☐
	You maintain high standards?	☐	☐
Physical strength	You are in good physical health?	☐	☐
	You can lift 60 pounds?	☐	☐
	You can walk all day?	☐	☐
	You don't mind getting your hands dirty?	☐	☐
Plant knowledge	You love plants?	☐	☐
	You love to learn about plants?	☐	☐
	You want to learn a lot of plant names?	☐	☐
	You like to have the best-looking lawn?	☐	☐
Motivation	You are a self-starter?	☐	☐
	You work well without a boss?	☐	☐
	You get out of bed easily?	☐	☐
	You want to run a lawn care company?	☐	☐
People skills	You enjoy meeting new people?	☐	☐
	You can manage people?	☐	☐
	You tolerate different religions and races?	☐	☐
	You can handle difficult people?	☐	☐

		Yes	No
Positive attitude	You have an easy smile?	☐	☐
	You usually see the cup as being half full?	☐	☐
	Setbacks are challenges to you?	☐	☐
	You prefer a happy work environment?	☐	☐
Integrity	You are honest?	☐	☐
	You stand by your word?	☐	☐
	You treat people fairly?	☐	☐
	You will go back to fix a job?	☐	☐
Communication	You think before you speak?	☐	☐
	You speak clearly?	☐	☐
	You are a good listener?	☐	☐
	You can write good letters?	☐	☐
Organization	You prefer to be organized?	☐	☐
	You like record keeping and bookkeeping?	☐	☐
	You can use a daytimer?	☐	☐
	You like to make and use checklists?	☐	☐
Diplomacy	You seldom lose your temper?	☐	☐
	You can accept constructive criticism?	☐	☐
	You prefer to make peace?	☐	☐
	You know how to say "no"?	☐	☐
Creativity	You like to create?	☐	☐
	You try to think of new ways to do things?	☐	☐
	You like working with colors?	☐	☐
	You like to be creative in marketing?	☐	☐

If you answered "no" to questions in the final five sections, you have identified some areas in which you need to improve. You can start by using Worksheet 2 to make your own action plan based on the answers to your self-assessment. Place a check mark in the column beside each of the questions you answered "no" to on Worksheet 1. Then read the comments, which explain why that particular characteristic is important. In the last column, fill in your action plan for improvement. Again, your candid answers will help you in the long run, so be honest with yourself.

When considering your action plan, think of what you might do to improve that particular skill. For example, if you answered "no" to the question "You can lift 60 pounds?" you might write, "Work out in gym until I am able to lift 60 pounds into my truck." Or if you aren't confident about writing letters, you might write, "Read books on writing successful business letters. Practice."

Make it a personal goal to follow through on *all* of your action items. Make these goals important to you because they will help you succeed in your business.

3. RESOURCES FOR FURTHER HELP

As you go through your self-assessment and think about how you can improve on those areas in which you may need help, remember that you are not alone. There are thousands of other people in the landscaping business. Some, like you, are starting out. Others are long-term veterans. Most are willing to share their experience with you if you only ask.

Landscaping associations give you the chance to network with other business-people. Doing so benefits everyone, as you will learn from other people's experiences and they can learn from yours. The industry as a whole is bettered. Associations can also be your voice in government and keep you abreast of laws and bylaws in your area that may affect your business.

Such associations often offer certification programs, and I recommend that you complete such a program. If and when you have staff, support them in becoming certified too. If you are certified, you can display the certification logo on your advertising material, proving that you have met certain criteria and possess certain competencies.

You usually have to pay an annual fee to become a member of an association or similar organization. This money is well spent. As a member, you will be offered direct savings such as fuel discounts. Also, your membership may win you customers. Belonging to these organizations will not make your phone ring off the hook, but if you are competing head-to-head with a nonmember, you are more likely to come out on top.

- In the United States, contact the Professional Lawn Care Association of America (PLCAA) <www.plcaa.org/home>. Each state has a chapter.

- In Canada, contact the Canadian Nursery Landscape Association (CNLA) <www.canadanursery.com>. Each province has a chapter.

There may be other organizations and associations in your area, such as the local chamber of commerce, that can be helpful and provide good networking opportunities.

Ask if the member list is available so you can review how many people are involved and what they do for a living. This may help you determine if the cost and time investment are worth the potential new business you might secure.

Another good source of information is the Internet. If you do not have a computer and an Internet connection, I would highly recommend getting both. There is a universe of information at your fingertips when you are online. Sometimes you must sort through a lot of fluff to get some quality information, but once you have found some good sites, you can visit them again and again.

For a start, check out my own website <www.MowBoy.com>. It provides a bulletin-board-style forum so you can talk to other lawn care operators and ask questions. There are many tips on horticulture and business, as well as a number of links to other quality sites. Finally, I also offer business consulting services, in case you need a little help getting your business up and growing.

WORKSHEET 2
MY ACTION PLAN

Statement	Comments	Answered No?	My plan to improve
Work ethic			
You enjoy hard work?	If you feel good after a hard day's work, you're on the right path. If you are afraid of a little sweat, this may not be the job for you.		_____ _____ _____ _____
You work conscientiously?	Conscientious means diligent, thorough, consistent in application or attention, persistent. This is a key to your success.		_____ _____ _____
You prefer to do a thorough job?	If you always like to be thorough, then this is a perfect job for you. The details matter a great deal in this business.		_____ _____ _____
You maintain high standards?	Sloppiness does not win bids. You must set stringent standards for yourself and your employees from the beginning.		_____ _____ _____

Statement	Comments	Answered No?	My plan to improve
Physical strength			
You are in good physical health?	This is a very active lifestyle. Are you up to it? If you are not sure, try working for someone else for a year to find out.		_____ _____ _____
You can lift 60 pounds?	If you work smart, you can avoid situations that require strenuous lifting, but sometimes you won't be able to get away from it.		_____ _____ _____
You can walk all day?	You need endurance. You may be walking miles a day with either a mower or a weed whacker in front of you.		_____ _____ _____
You don't mind getting your hands dirty?	Not just your hands, either. Your arms, legs, and face may also get dirty. If that idea bothers you, consider carefully whether you want to take on this career.		_____ _____ _____
Plant knowledge			
You love plants?	You need to enjoy the plants you take care of to do your best work. Do you like to stop and smell the roses? Do you sometimes stand in awe of the marvels of creation?		_____ _____ _____
You love to learn about plants?	What you learn will help you in your business. People will take you seriously when they know you are an expert.		_____ _____ _____
You want to learn a lot of plant names?	Telling your customers you are going to prune "that shrub" will not impress them. You need to know the names of the most common plants, at least (Latin names too).		_____ _____ _____
You like to have the best-looking lawn?	There is a certain pride that goes with having (or looking after) the nicest lawns on the block. If you feel this, you will do well.		_____ _____ _____

WORKSHEET 2 — Continued

Statement	Comments	Answered No?	My plan to improve
Motivation			
You are a self-starter?	The fact that you have come this far suggests that you meet this requirement ... and a requirement it is. Success will evade you without it.		_____ _____ _____ _____ _____
You work well without a boss?	You may enjoy having no one to tell you what to do next or how to handle a crisis, but on the other hand, *you* will need to know what to do next or how to handle a crisis.		_____ _____ _____ _____ _____
You get out of bed easily?	If you need someone to push you out of bed each morning, this is something you'll want to work on.		_____ _____ _____
You want to run a lawn care company?	If you don't have the basic desire, you won't have what it takes to keep going.		_____
People skills			
You enjoy meeting new people?	You don't have to love everyone you meet, but you really should enjoy meeting and working with new people. It will make your job more enjoyable.		_____ _____ _____ _____
You can manage people?	Being able to manage people is a valuable skill, but it is something that can be learned.		_____ _____
You tolerate different religions and races?	You will be dealing with folks of all races, creeds, and religions. Be tolerant. Prejudice will hamper your efforts to serve people.		_____ _____ _____
You can handle difficult people?	There will be times when difficult people cause you grief. Will you be able to handle it professionally?		_____ _____ _____

WORKSHEET 2 — Continued

Statement	Comments	Answered No?	My plan to improve

Positive attitude

You have an easy smile? — Most folks expect a gardener to have a sunny disposition. You don't have to beam like the sun all day, but at least greet people with a smile and a wave or a nod.

_____
_____
_____
_____

You usually see the cup as being half full? — You must be able to look on the bright side of things. Problems will come up. There will be bad days. Can you endure?

_____
_____
_____

Setbacks are challenges to you? — It helps if you can break a problem down into small, manageable chunks, turn obstacles into challenges, and convert weaknesses to opportunities for improvement.

_____
_____
_____
_____

You prefer a happy work environment? — Not too many people would answer "no" to this question. If you aren't happy in your job, you're in the wrong place!

_____
_____
_____

Integrity

You are honest? — Dealing with people in a dishonest way will catch up with you and ruin your reputation. The opposite is true too; word of an honest company offering honest deals gets around.

_____
_____
_____
_____

You stand by your word? — If you promise something, you must stick to it, even if it costs you. It will cost you a lot more in the long run if you come across as inconsistent.

_____
_____
_____
_____

You treat people fairly? — Deep down, you should want to treat people with fairness all the time. You may encounter so-called opportunities to take advantage of people and make money. Don't fall prey to them!

_____
_____
_____
_____

Statement	Comments	Answered No?	My plan to improve
You will go back to fix a job?	If the job is not done right, you'll need to go back and fix it. It will lower your profit, but it will probably make your customer happy. Happy clients are your future.		_____ _____ _____ _____

Communication

Statement	Comments	Answered No?	My plan to improve
You think before you speak?	Once the words are out of your mouth, you cannot take them back. A good business owner will think before he or she speaks.		_____ _____ _____
You speak clearly?	Your command of English should be very good. If English is your second language, work on improving your skills so you can communicate clearly with your clients.		_____ _____ _____ _____
You are a good listener?	The most important part of a conversation is the listening. Listen carefully to your customers to understand their needs.		_____ _____ _____
You can write good letters?	You will need to write a lot of letters in this business, but this is a skill that can be learned.		_____ _____

Organization

Statement	Comments	Answered No?	My plan to improve
You prefer to be organized?	The more organized you are, the easier your business life will be. Keeping on top of your paperwork and client needs will improve your profit margin.		_____ _____ _____ _____
You like record keeping and bookkeeping?	Bookkeeping is an important part of being self-employed. Not all the business is taken care of outdoors. There are plenty of books and software packages to help you — or, if you can afford it, you can hire someone.		_____ _____ _____ _____ _____
You can use a daytimer?	Daytimers are excellent tools for running your small business. Learn how to use one if you do not know how already.		_____ _____ _____

Statement	Comments	Answered No?	My plan to improve
You like to make and use checklists?	Checklists are excellent ways to develop systems and procedures that bring consistency and stability to your business. Use them!		_____ _____ _____
Diplomacy			
You seldom lose your temper?	Are you a hothead? There's no room for anger when working for customers.		_____ _____
You can accept constructive criticism?	Don't take criticism personally. Learn from it. Thank people for their feedback and try to take their advice to better your business.		_____ _____ _____
You prefer to make peace?	Gardeners have a reputation as peace-loving people. An easygoing nature works well in this business.		_____ _____ _____
You know how to say "no"?	While you may be peace-loving, that does not mean you are a pushover. Sometimes you will need to say "no."		_____ _____ _____
Creativity			
You like to create?	Creativity is a huge advantage in this business. You can use creativity to help make gardens more beautiful, to design a marketing flyer, and to solve problems.		_____ _____ _____ _____
You try to think of new ways to do things?	If you are always thinking of better, faster, more efficient ways of doing things, your business will be an exciting one.		_____ _____ _____
You like working with colors?	You're not alone if you aren't sure how well you work with colors. You can learn the basics from any garden design book.		_____ _____ _____
You like to be creative in marketing?	Creative marketing will help your business tremendously. Read the chapter on marketing carefully and then read more books. Be creative, be exciting.		_____ _____ _____ _____

2
MAKING YOUR BUSINESS LEGAL

If you've decided you have what it takes, it's time to think about what you need to do to make your business legal — from choosing a name to ensuring you have the proper licenses and permits. This chapter outlines what you need to know generally. It's not possible for me to provide specifics for every jurisdiction, so you will have to look into the particular regulations for your area.

1. CHOOSING A BUSINESS NAME

Many expectant parents spend hours choosing the right name for their baby. They know it is a name that will be with them for a long time and will be used many times each day. Your new lawn care business is much the same. It's your baby. What will you call it?

My own experience illustrates the importance of the business name. When I started out, I came up with the name Dirty Deeds Landscaping. It was catchy, and I received positive comments daily. It was not until a few years later that I realized how this name was working against me. Think about it: If you wanted to hire someone to come in and beautify your lawn and garden, who would you call first? Dirty Deeds or a company named something like Beautiful Lawns? On the other hand, if it is June, you have not cut your lawn yet, and your dog has been doing his business in the long grass, who will you call to give it that first cut? In that case, Dirty Deeds probably sounds just right. Dirty Deeds served me well for the first couple of years, when I was willing to take almost any job that came along, and I did get a lot of calls. Later, when I could be choosier about my work and had moved on to a narrower market, it required a lot of marketing to convince the public that the company was all about beautifying.

The moral of the story? Choose a name that represents what you want to do. And don't forget about resale value in case you ever want to sell your business. A name like Johnny's Lawn Care will work against you if your potential buyer is not named Johnny.

You should register your business name with the government department that handles business registration in your jurisdiction. Note that in many areas, registering your name does not secure it, but it does let you know if there is a company with a similar name operating in the area. To secure the name and prevent others from using it, you often must incorporate (see section **2.3**). Check with the government department for the rules in your area.

2. CHOOSING A BUSINESS STRUCTURE

You will need to choose a business structure that best suits your needs. A business can be formed as a sole proprietorship, a partnership, or a corporation. There are pros and cons to each of the structures, and there are important tax implications. You should obtain legal and tax advice before making your final decision.

2.1 Sole proprietorship

By far the easiest and cheapest form of business setup is the sole proprietorship, and it is what I recommend you start out with. A sole proprietorship is simply a business owned and operated by one person. You and the business are one and the same. You have full decision-making control over the business and you get all the profit, which is recorded on your personal income tax statement.

On the other hand, since the business is legally considered an extension of you, you have no protection against creditors. You assume all responsibility and liability for your business. Sole proprietorships lack the tax flexibility that an incorporated company offers. As well, if you need financial backing for your start-up, you may have more difficulty attracting it than you would with a legally incorporated company. Finally, if you are seriously injured or die, there will be no one to carry on the business. You or your survivors will lose that source of income.

2.2 Partnership

Like a proprietorship, a partnership has the advantage of low start-up costs, and you may enjoy sharing the responsibility of owning a business with someone else. But be careful before entering into this form of business structure. Most discussions of partnerships are rife with warnings and horror stories. Incompatibility between partners can lead to the breakdown of the business, as well as the end of any personal relationship you may have had with your partner or partners.

If you are considering a partnership, reflect on these points:

- A partnership works best when the people involved have complementary skills and attributes.

- Equal partnerships are most likely to fail due to deadlocked situations. There is nothing saying that a partnership has to be equal. Consider making one of the partners the "leader" and grant that partner a greater share of the business, even if it is just one percent more. If you cannot decide on who will be leader, take warning. It may be a glimpse of things to come.

🔊 Be aware that in most partnerships, one partner may be responsible for the other partners' liabilities if something happens to them.

If you choose to run your business as a partnership, seek legal and financial counsel first. Be sure to draw up a partnership agreement that includes explicit directives for the graceful termination of the partnership should it become necessary.

2.3 Incorporation

A limited, or incorporated, company is a separate legal entity. One benefit to incorporating is that your liability is limited to your investment in the company, hence the name "limited liability company." (Note, however, that being incorporated only protects you from liability up to a point. For example, you may be protected if you were sued, but most creditors will insist on a personal guarantee if you purchase items on credit, especially if you are just starting out.) There may be tax advantages to incorporation as well, but you should investigate local statutes and talk to a financial advisor to find out if and how you would realize them.

Since the limited company is expensive to set up and administer (you have to pay annual fees), requires a lot of work to maintain (forms must be filled out, records kept, income tax statements prepared by accountants, etc.), and is usually overkill for a small start-up company, I don't recommend it unless your financial advisor offers compelling reasons to go this route.

3. LICENSES AND PERMITS

To legally operate a business, you must take care of the obligatory bureaucratic red tape. Consult with municipal and state or provincial authorities to make sure you have all the necessary licenses and permits. Here are some of the considerations that generally apply:

🔊 *Business license.* You will have to register and pay an annual fee for a business license. You may also need a special permit to run your business from your house.

🔊 *Fictitious business name registration.* Most jurisdictions require that you register a "fictitious" business name (that is, a company name that does not include your surname or the names of your partners).

🔊 *Vehicle permit.* Check to see if you must have special commercial vehicle permits in your area.

🔊 *Contractor's license.* In the United States, you may need to have a separate license if you decide to expand beyond general maintenance (lawn care and gardening) into landscaping. This is not the kind of license that requires you fill out a form and hand over some cash. Instead, it involves a test that generally requires you to show that you have worked in the field for a number of years. (This is not a requirement in Canada.)

🔊 *State/provincial tax registration.* In the United States, tax laws vary from state to state and even within a state. Check with the tax department or an accountant. In Canada, you will likely not have to register for provincial tax unless you become a reseller of goods. Services are not taxed at the provincial level.

❧ *Federal tax registration.* In the United States, as a sole proprietor you probably don't need to register federally (unless you have employees). If you do have employees, you may need an Employer Identification Number (EIN). Check the IRS website <www.irs.gov> for more information. In Canada, most businesses must register for the GST. Contact your local tax office for all the instructions.

❧ *Employee taxation.* If you have employees, you will be responsible for withholding and remitting applicable deductions. Once you hire employees, you definitely should get professional advice to be sure you are complying with all existing regulations. The penalties for non-compliance can be severe, and ignorance is no excuse.

❧ *Workers' compensation.* If you have employees, you must register with workers' compensation in your area and pay a percentage of wages to cover employees if they are hurt on the job. If you have no employees and are running a sole proprietorship, you usually can choose whether or not you want workers' compensation. You may want to compare workers' compensation rates with those of private insurance companies, which provide coverage 24 hours a day, not just on the job. This is the kind of coverage you need if you are self-employed and your business relies on you.

4. BYLAWS AND ZONING

You need to ensure that you are legally allowed to operate your business from your home. Some jurisdictions have restrictions on what kind of business may be home-based. For example, there may be a limit on the number of employees you can have.

Even if bylaws do permit you to operate your business from your home, you should always be considerate of your neighbors. If you have large crews showing up at your home at 7:00 a.m., starting and cleaning equipment and leaving trucks idling for long periods, you won't win any friends in your neighborhood.

Also check out the noise bylaws in the areas where you will be working. Some places restrict the use of portable equipment, such as backpack leaf blowers, because they are often overused or used inappropriately. (See section **4.2** of chapter 12 for more information on using a backpack blower without being a nuisance.) Most jurisdictions also have rules about what time of day you can start working outside (e.g., not before 8:00 a.m. on weekends).

5. INSURANCE

Stuff happens, as they say, and insurance can protect you when that stuff happens. Be sure to speak to a professional about the type and amount of insurance you need. An oversight can be expensive. It may even cost you your business. Here are some of the types of insurance you'll need to consider when you work for yourself:

❧ *Vehicle insurance.* It's a given that you need vehicle insurance, but will you need special coverage? Who will drive the vehicle (just you, or staff members as well)? Do you require special commercial plates on the vehicle? Do you qualify for fleet insurance (when your business gets a little larger)? Note that in most cases only items that are "attached" to the vehicle are covered. Your vehicle insurance will likely not cover damage or theft of your equipment (see the paragraph on equipment insurance below).

🖦 *Liability insurance.* When you start bidding on commercial properties, you will be asked to prove you have sufficient coverage to protect against things like injuries to bystanders and property damage.

🖦 *Equipment insurance.* Your power equipment should be covered for loss by theft or fire. You may find it more difficult to find an insurer for your portable equipment because it's so easy to steal. Keep looking, though, because such insurers are available. Consider saving money by having a high deductible (around $500). If you have a single piece of equipment stolen, don't tarnish your record by claiming it; just buy a new one. On the other hand, if all of your portable equipment disappears, then $500 is a small price to pay to replace it.

🖦 *Personal disability insurance.* In many small businesses, if the owner is out of action, the money stops coming in. You should have enough personal disability insurance to cover your business overhead and perhaps the cost of hiring a replacement so the work can

go on. In most areas you can opt to have workers' compensation coverage, but this will not apply if you are injured off the job.

🖦 *Life insurance.* You probably already have life insurance, but you might want to review your coverage now that you plan to be self-employed. If you are supporting others, how will they be supported if you die prematurely?

🖦 *Medical insurance.* Availability of supplemental medical insurance varies by jurisdiction. Be sure you are adequately covered.

🖦 *Home office insurance.* Check to ensure that your current home insurance (theft, fire, etc.) will cover your home office. There may be a specific rider that excludes it.

🖦 *Business interruption insurance.* This is designed to cover you for a period of time to allow recovery from disasters such as loss of premises or files.

🖦 *Employee benefits.* Group insurance is available for even small companies. It is a great benefit and worth investigating.

6. USING PROFESSIONAL ADVISORS

It's wise to rely on the advice of professionals early in the planning of your business. It isn't possible for an individual to stay on top of all the changing regulations, bylaws, and requirements for small business, so don't be afraid to contact a lawyer or accountant whenever you need help.

Professional accountants will usually be well versed in local law and taxation regulations, since they deal mostly with small and medium-sized businesses. In the United States look for the designation CPA (certified public accountant) and in Canada look for CGA (certified general accountant) or CA (chartered accountant).

You may require the services of a lawyer if you plan to incorporate or sign a partnership agreement. The best way to find a lawyer is through referral. If you have friends in business, ask them who they use and if they are pleased with the services provided.

Finally, your local insurance agency should be able to offer further advice on the amount and kind of insurance you need for your business.

3
MONEY MATTERS

Let's face it: Starting a business takes money. And while it is true that you don't have to buy everything for your landscaping business right away, ideally you'll have enough basic equipment to cover a variety of jobs. Without sufficient capital at the start, running your business may quickly become tiresome and stressful. You need to consider funding sources and develop your business plan.

1. FINANCING OPTIONS

The money you need for your business can come from a variety of sources. Keep in mind, though, that you should always be careful of debt and work hard to keep it under control. If you borrow, borrow only what you need and when you need it.

1.1 The bank of Mom and Pop

If you are just starting out in the world of business, your best bet for securing needed funds may be your parents, other relatives, or friends. Use good judgment when borrowing from family and friends. Friends are forever, but money can be gone tomorrow, and if it's not paid back, it can wreck your relationship. If you do borrow, prepare a promissory note that details the terms and conditions of your arrangement.

1.2 Personal loans

If close relatives are not an option and you have decided (probably wisely) not to borrow money from your friends, a personal loan from the bank may be your answer. Good credit is required, as is collateral. Your lawn care equipment will probably not be sufficient for collateral (unless you have some particularly large and costly pieces of equipment), but vehicles are good collateral if you own them, as are stocks, bonds, and other assets that can be liquidated. Equity in your home is like gold.

1.3 Business loans

A business loan is another option, but bear in mind that banks do not loan money based on a great idea, no matter how well documented it is. Like a personal loan, a bank loan must be secured somehow. The bank will want you to provide your business forecast, business plan, cash flow summary, list of assets, and more. After that, it is still going to want to see collateral, and it will ask you to prove your commitment to the project by supplying a significant portion of the required investment. For these reasons, I recommend that you ask for a personal loan instead of going through the hoops for a business loan.

If you have incorporated your business and are planning to apply for a loan in the name of the business because you are "protected," you may want to reconsider. The bank will ask you to personally guarantee the loan, and you'll have to jump through many hoops to get the money you want. Again, you're probably better off seeking a personal loan.

On the other hand, if you have been in business for a while and have built up a reputation, business assets, and some healthy and steady receivables, then a business loan may be just the thing you need when you are ready to expand or buy the next piece of equipment.

1.4 Help from the government

If the bank won't come to your assistance, you should check out government departments and agencies that support small business. These organizations will require paperwork too, but not as much as the banks. They tend to be more sympathetic to

small business and are worth investigating. Even if you don't get financing, they offer a lot of information that can help you in other ways.

- ❧ In the United States, go to the Small Business Administration <www.sba. gov/>. Its stated mandate is to help small businesses succeed.

- ❧ In Canada, check out the Business Development Bank of Canada at <www.bdc.ca>. It was established by the federal government specifically to help companies that were having trouble securing financing for their operations.

In either case, be prepared with your well-thought-out business plan.

2. YOUR BUSINESS PLAN

To decide how much money you need now and in the future, you have to do some planning, and that entails writing a business plan. You probably don't want to do this work because you're raring to get moving. As well, you may believe you already have a plan in your head, but that is not enough. I can't overemphasize the importance of having a written business plan. Too many would-be entrepreneurs overlook this step.

Having a business plan is particularly important if you plan to get outside financing for any part of your business. Your business plan will answer questions such as:

- ❧ How much money do you need and what do you intend to spend it on?

- ❧ When do you expect to start making a profit in your company?

- ❧ Will the company be able to afford loan payments?

Even if you do not require outside financing, the business plan will provide much-needed direction and focus. It will force you to think objectively and critically about the future of your company. For example, you should answer questions such as:

- What services will I choose to offer?

- How big do I want to grow my company?

- What are the keys to the success of my business?

By stating clear goals in a business plan, you will be able to measure your success and make changes as necessary. Without the goals, you will have no way to measure how your business is progressing or determine when to make changes. Many businesses fail due to poor planning; don't let yours be one of them.

Writing out your plan will provide a stimulus for further creativity. You'll likely discover areas of your business that you have not thought about yet. Developing your plan will compel you to think ahead, think deeper, imagine different scenarios, and visualize your dream. The end result will be a sharper focus, a clearer sense of direction, and increased determination.

A complete sample business plan is provided on the CD-ROM. Review it before writing your own. Then put pen to paper and start on your own plan, making sure you include the sections described below.

2.1 Executive summary

The executive summary is the overview. It contains three important subsections:

- *Mission statement*. The mission statement should define what kind of business you are in, set out goals relating to the quality of your service, and perhaps briefly summarize your competitive advantage.

- *Objectives*. You should list three or four measurable items that you feel are the objectives of your company. These points will give you and your employees a focus as you grow.

- *Keys to success*. These points spell out how you will ensure that you meet your objectives. If one of your objectives is to provide exceptional customer service, then one of the keys to success will indicate how you intend to do this.

2.2 Company overview

In this section you summarize the "five Ws" of your business: the who, what, where, why, and when. Start-up companies should also list what resources they will be starting with.

- *Company summary*. What is your company's name? When did it start and why? Where is your home base? Where will you do your work? What services will you provide and to whom? Will you specialize in anything or are you going to mow, blow, and go? These are the types of questions you need to answer in the Company Summary. It may be a paragraph or it may be a full page or more.

- *Company ownership*. Here you describe the business structure you have decided on and explain the specifics of how your business will be organized. If you are a sole proprietor, this would likely be a single paragraph. If there are several owners and you have decided to incorporate, you would need more explanation to introduce all the people involved and their roles in the company.

2.3 Start-up summary

In the first part of this section you explain how much money you will need to spend to start your company, how much you already have, how much you still need, where the money is coming from, and what exactly you will be spending it on.

In the second part of this section you follow up your written summary with a spreadsheet that neatly lists all the financial information to do with your start-up. See the example in the business plan on the CD-ROM for a suggested format. It is important to note that all the items in this table are items that come into play *before* your first day of business. Do not include revenue figures or ongoing monthly expenses at this stage.

Although the spreadsheet follows the written summary in the plan, it is probably easier to complete the spreadsheet first.

2.4 Management summary

Your readers met the owners of your business in the company summary. Now you need to provide a little more information about each person. If there are key people involved in the business who are not owners, include them in this section, too. If you will be sharing your business plan with potential investors, this is where you really want to sell yourself and your team. What is your background? Why do you want to start a business? Why landscaping? List qualifications, experience, passions, and anything

else that will prove your dedication to your business. Complete this section even if you are not looking for external financing. It will give you a comprehensive record of your (or your team's) assets. It may also reveal areas that need improvement. Make a note of these insufficiencies on a separate personal list, not on the business plan. You are trying to sell your competence as a business owner here. This is no place for modesty!

2.5 Products and services

In this section you want to tell readers what services you will offer and what products you will sell, if any. List all the services you plan on offering now or in the near future. Be specific, listing specialties or areas that you are most interested in growing. Include any innovative ideas you have about your offerings. For example, in my business, many of my full-service programs end in November. However, I offer an extra visit right before Christmas to clean up the last of the leaves and debris that may have blown around. People appreciate this small extra, as it shows I am interested in their property.

Will you sell products? To keep things simple, you should consider the application of products, such as fertilizer, as a service. But if you sell something to your customers without a service attached (e.g., summer annuals for customers to plant themselves), then you would list product sales as part of your plan.

2.6 Your market

In this section, describe your target customers, your competition, and any peculiarities about the marketplace. All of the information in this section can be extracted from your marketing plan (see chapter 6), which should be prepared first.

2.7 Your financial plan

This is where you deal with the nitty-gritty of your business plan — the numbers. Do not skip this section, even if you are only completing a business plan for your own benefit. It is important for tracking your company's progress, or lack thereof.

To produce a financial plan, you need to complete three worksheets:

- The pro forma profit and loss statement (forecast)
- The balance sheet (current snapshot)
- Cash flow projections

Examples of these three worksheets are contained in the sample business plan included on the CD-ROM.

2.7a The pro forma profit and loss statement

At the very least, you should try to estimate your income and expenses for one year ahead of time, but I recommend trying to look ahead two years. It's difficult to project any longer than that, especially when you are starting out, because you don't know the industry well and you can't anticipate what modifications you might make over time that could throw long-term projections out the door. For example, you may plan to pursue multi-dwelling property (such as condos and townhomes) contracts in your third year of business, but discover after two years that you are happy and profitable doing residential work only.

First-year forecasting can be challenging. How do you estimate what you simply don't know? How much fertilizer or equipment fuel will you use? How many customers will you attract? How fast will your business grow? The bottom line is this: You make an educated guess and you do the best you can. After that, you will test your business savvy and your confidence in yourself and your new enterprise as you project yourself into the future and think about how you want your business to grow. You will probably be surprised at how close your estimates are if you put some thought into them.

The profit and loss statement is your guide to your business projections. (If you are new to record keeping and accounting, you may want to pause here and read chapter 7 on record keeping before proceeding.)

The first item to consider is income. As you think about your income projections, ask yourself key questions about how much work you will do. How much are you going to work each month? Will you work full time or part time? Will you work by yourself or will you have a helper or even a second crew? How much are you going to advertise? Are you going to blitz certain areas? Are you planning to use many different marketing techniques or just a couple? Over what time period will you advertise — in the spring or all through the season? Also, how motivated are you to get work? If you have a small contingency fund to get by with as you get your business started, you will be more motivated than if you have a large surplus of cash after start-up expenses. What are your financial obligations? A mortgage, car payment, and kids to support are strong motivators to turn a coin in this business!

Depending on where you live, certain months will be slower than others. No matter where you live, spring and fall will be busy. An old saying in the gardening business is that if you are not busy in the spring and fall, you're doing something wrong. Summer can be slower if you don't have regular maintenance customers; you may not have many in your first year, so expect to hustle. Winter revenue depends largely on where you live and if you will be offering snow-clearing services.

Set a goal for the number of regular maintenance customers you want in your first and second years. Are you starting from scratch? Perhaps set a goal of generating $1,000 per month in regular cuts by May. Regular maintenance customers are a beautiful thing because they are as close to a steady paycheck as you get working for yourself. You can count on this money each month. Will you buy any maintenance contracts (see section **3.4** in chapter 6)? Prices may vary from place to place, but a general rule of thumb is that a good residential client is worth one month's revenue. Do you have friends in the business who may throw you a bone as they move on to bigger and better customers? Take these things into account as you forecast your revenue.

In the sample business plan on the CD-ROM, the owners of Greener Grass Lawn and Garden Company have set revenue goals for the area they live in, the Pacific Northwest. They expect strong spring and fall seasons because they know there will be a lot of work. The summer will be slower and they'll have to hustle for work. In the winter they may do a little snow clearing and cleanups, but they don't expect to be really busy during these months. Their projections are on the modest side because the company is

starting out and has no history to refer to. They hope to do a little better than what is forecast, and in the second year, with the benefit of one year under their belt, they may make more accurate projections.

After calculating income, you need to estimate your first year's expenses. The usual expense items are listed in the sample business plan provided on the CD-ROM. You may not use all categories listed in your first year.

You can develop your own profit and loss statement using the form provided in your accounting software package (see chapter 7 for more information). Then every month you can compare your projections to your *actual* monthly totals. Don't wait for the whole year to go by before you analyze how your projections/goals compare to your actual totals. Check how you are doing each month to see if you are meeting your goals, and take action if you are not.

2.7b The balance sheet

You need to include your current balance sheet as part of your business plan (see chapter 7 for more information on balance sheets). If you are preparing your business plan for an investor, you should also include a pro forma balance sheet that projects where your company will be in one year.

2.7c Cash flow projections

The cash flow projection is probably one of the most overlooked aspects of business planning. Although you have estimated, in your profit and loss statement, what your revenue and expenses are going to be, it is even more crucial to know *when* you will receive and spend that money.

The Importance of Cash Flow

I learned the lesson of cash flow the hard way when I started out. December was my favorite month at one time. Not because of Christmas, but because I was so busy in November, finishing up the fall cleanup and getting people's lawns ready for winter. I made a lot of money in November, but that money had a 30-day lag since I usually billed at the end of the month and received checks throughout the following month. December, on the other hand, was slow, so I did not have to spend the money I received to buy supplies, pay staff, and so on. This created the impression that I had a lot of extra disposable income. March, on the other hand, was the opposite. I was busy, running full crews, buying lime and fertilizer and all sorts of other spring supplies, but because February was slow, I had little money coming into the business. Had I analyzed my cash flow in the early days, I would have saved myself some grief by making sure I planned for these types of situations.

Using the tool of a cash flow projection worksheet, you will be able to see trouble spots ahead of time, such as March and April when expenses are high and income may be low. Take a look at the cash flow projection worksheet included in the sample business plan on the CD-ROM. You will notice that the worksheet is split into three different sections: estimated receipts, estimated expenditures, and total expenditures.

Total estimated sales for the month (from the pro forma profit and loss statement) are listed by category: cash sales and term sales. When you think about your own cash flow projection, ask yourself how much of total sales is jobs that you bill (and get paid for) when the job is done. A general rule that I use is that *regular* maintenance customers (i.e., those who receive scheduled weekly or biweekly visits) are entitled to the privilege of getting a single invoice at the end of the month with "net 20" payment terms, but non-regular customers are expected to pay at the completion of the job. You need to estimate how you will split the

cash sales and term sales. In the example on the CD-ROM, it has been assumed that 70 percent of total sales will be cash sales, and the remaining 30 percent will be term sales.

For term sales, you need to determine how much you expect to see in the following month (that is, how many people will pay on time). The best way to estimate is from historical data, but if you don't have any history, try using a formula. Take your total term sales for the month and assume that you will receive 80 percent in the next month. Of the remaining 20 percent, assume that 15 percent will come in during the second month and the final 5 percent will finally roll in during the third month. If you stay on top of receivables and let your customers know that prompt payment is important to you, then an 80/15/5 breakdown will work for you in these projections.

You can apply similar logic in figuring out expenditures. Use your pro forma statement to see what expenditures you expect, then break them into one of two groups: cash expenditures and term expenditures. If you expect to cut a check for the purchase at the time you buy it, that would be a cash expenditure. If, however, you decide to take advantage of terms offered by your vendors and buy goods on credit, put these in the term expenditures line.

What you do next is up to you, but it is best to be committed to maintaining good credit with all of your suppliers, which means you should pay all expenditures in the next month, when they are due (assuming you get "net 30" terms from your suppliers). In the sample cash flow projections shown in the business plan on the CD-ROM, the assumption is that the company will pay 40 percent of all expenditures in the month they are incurred, and the remaining 60 percent in the following month.

The key line in a cash flow projection worksheet is "Net Cash Flow." If the number in this line is positive, it means you have enough money coming in during that particular month to cover your expenses. If the number is negative, you do not have enough money and you will need to resort to cash that you have retained from more lucrative months.

Finding yourself short on a given month is a hassle. It will cost you in money and reputation because you may not have enough cash to pay your creditors on time. It may cost you again in the same fashion as you cut checks with little room for error, struggling hard to stay on top of things. Sooner or later you will make an error and those checks will start bouncing back to you. However, by using the valuable information in your cash flow projection worksheet, you can plan how you will spend the money that comes in from your business so that you do not find yourself short.

4

CHOOSING THE RIGHT EQUIPMENT FOR THE JOB

You are a landscaping professional, so it is important that you select equipment made for professionals. First of all, you want to look the part of a lawn care expert. Would an expert show up at a jobsite with a tiny, 0.5 horsepower, electric weed whacker? No. Leave that for the kid next door, who will cut your lawn for five bucks. To separate yourself from that kid-next-door image, you must purchase professional equipment.

Second, you're going to be giving your equipment a thorough workout day after day, which means you need commercial-quality equipment. The equipment made for the average homeowner will simply not stand up to this use and in the long run will end up costing you more money, more frustration, and more downtime.

You may not need all the equipment listed in this chapter for your own business; what you need will depend on what services you are planning to offer. As well, you may not have the cash to buy everything you want right away. However, I wanted to provide information on all the essentials, as well as advice on which items can wait until you have cash coming in regularly.

You will notice that I recommend specific brand names for many of the tools of the trade. Generally these are the biggest manufacturers of each of the major pieces of equipment. That is not to say there are no other reputable companies from which you can buy, but the names supplied will help you get started. Check out the companies' websites to see what they offer. Then, when you visit your local dealer, you will have an idea of what you need and what you are talking about.

Choosing a Dealer

Become familiar with your local equipment dealers. If possible, talk to other landscapers and see where they shop. As you investigate equipment suppliers, ask yourself the following questions:

- What lines of equipment manufacturers do they carry? Do they specialize in one line of equipment or do they offer you a choice?

- What type of clientele do they have? Do they deal strictly with commercial companies or are they also a retail outlet? They will probably be more helpful to you if they specialize in commercial equipment.

- Do they service equipment as well as sell it? Do they have loaner equipment that you can use if yours is in the shop? (This may not necessarily be a free service, but it is a useful one.)

- If a shop has a service department, talk to the mechanics. Are they experienced? A good mechanic will know the equipment inside and out and will be able to tell you technical pros and cons of different models, what types tend to be higher maintenance than others, and what breaks down the most. Your mechanic can be an excellent source of time- and money-saving advice, so put a high priority on choosing a good one.

- Was the staff helpful in advising you on what equipment to buy? Do they offer demo models so that you can test an item before committing to the purchase?

1. YOUR VEHICLE

The ideal vehicle for a landscaping business is a pickup truck, although some people do manage with a station wagon or minivan. If you have no other way to start out, then, of course, make do with what you have, but you will find that a pickup makes your business run more smoothly.

Pickups are sized according to how much weight they are designed to carry. For example, a half-ton truck can carry half a ton of soil (or other load), while a three-quarter-ton truck, often called a full-sized pickup, is a more heavy-duty option. One-ton trucks, even larger, are generally six-wheeled, flatbed vehicles.

The size you choose will depend on what services you plan to offer. If you will be delivering soil or other materials, if you are going to tow a trailer, or if you plan on having a large crew (four or more people), then you should consider purchasing a full-sized three-quarter-ton pickup. An alternative, if you already have a half-ton truck, is to install a reinforced suspension, which is not as difficult or expensive as you might think.

Don't feel you need to spend the money on a brand-new truck. Most of all you want a vehicle you can count on and that suits your particular needs. Do some research and make your purchase as you would for any other vehicle.

2. TRAILER OPTIONS

I was in business for five years before I bought a trailer. Once I did, I wondered how I ever managed without one.

While there are a multitude of different trailers you can choose from, there are two basic types that you should consider: fully enclosed and open.

2.1 Fully enclosed trailer

A fully enclosed trailer has four sides and a roof. If it is nicely painted with your business name and logo, it presents a classier and more professional look than an open trailer. It also has several practical advantages:

- You can keep your day-to-day equipment in the trailer and lock it up each night, saving you the trouble of loading and unloading everything each day.

- You can keep your equipment secure on the jobsite by locking the trailer.

- You can protect your gear from the environment. For example, you can keep weather-sensitive supplies, such as fertilizer and lime, in the trailer and not worry that they will be rained on.

- The trailer can provide a bit of shelter for you, too. For example, if it is rainy or windy you can step inside the trailer to fill your fertilizer spreader or your chemical applicator.

If you're in the market for a fully enclosed trailer, be sure to check out the following options. They should be available at purchase or can be installed professionally once you've got your trailer.

- *Floor tie-downs.* You will need a few tie-downs to help secure your equipment while you are moving.

- *Wall tie-downs.* These may be as simple as perforated metal strips (similar to shelving tracks) running along the length of both sides of the trailer. Ideally there will be two or three parallel tie-downs to provide plenty of anchor points for securing all of your equipment. Alternatively, you can install special wall mounts, similar to the floor mounts.

- *Rear ramp door.* A ramp door requires more room to open but makes unloading and loading much easier.

- *Dome light.* A simple dome light is helpful if you are loading or unloading at night.

There are some disadvantages to the closed-style trailer. Keeping dirty equipment in the trailer can create a stench, and if there is no airflow in the trailer, mold will quickly develop. However, you can solve or avoid these problems by choosing a trailer with a rooftop vent and side vents. Leave the rooftop vent open when you park the trailer overnight. The side vents provide airflow while you are moving. (The rooftop vent should be closed for traveling to prevent it from being damaged by the wind.) With a good venting system, your trailer still won't smell like springtime roses, but it won't be offensive either.

2.2 Open trailer

An open or flatbed trailer has several advantages. It is generally a lot lighter than an enclosed one, which means you will spend less on fuel pulling it around. It is also likely less expensive to buy. Open trailers are generally easier to modify with racks for your tools (there are plenty of aftermarket kits you can buy and install yourself), and proper airflow is definitely not an issue. If protection from the elements is not a concern for you, an open trailer is probably your best bet.

Regardless of which type of trailer you use, don't forget to think about security. If the trailer is attached to your truck, lock the hitch so that the trailer cannot be removed. If the trailer is detached, lock the hitch in the closed position so that it will not fit onto a corresponding ball hitch.

For tips on how to organize your trailer, see chapter 5.

> **TIP:**
> Wells Cargo builds sturdy, great-looking trailers, both enclosed and open. Check out the website <www.wellscargo.com>.

3. CHOOSING THE RIGHT LAWN MOWER

You are a lawn care expert (or will be soon enough), so your choice of mower is an important one.

There are three types of rotary mowers to consider: a push mower, a commercial walk-behind (midsized), and a rider. Reel mowers, or cylinder mowers, are different machines completely, and although you will not likely want to start out with one of them, they are also discussed below to give you a full range of options.

3.1 Push mowers

Unless you are starting out with some big commercial properties or large residential lawns, you will want to begin with a push mower. The name says it all. You push, the machine mows. When selecting your push mower, consider the following features.

Cutting width: Expect a 21-inch cutting width on almost all commercial push mowers.

Horsepower: Look for at least 5 horsepower. Newer models boast 6.5 and more.

Blade brake clutch (BBC): All new mowers must have this important safety feature, which ensures that if you lose control of your mower, the blade immediately stops spinning. There are two variations. In the first, the blade *and* the engine stop. In the second, the blade stops, but the engine keeps running. The latter option is better as it will save you time, energy, and your pull start cord too, since you will be able to safely empty bags, clean the chute, and drive over sidewalks without shutting the motor off each time.

Self-propelled drive: As you may be cutting miles of lawn each day, having a self-propelled drive is well worth the extra cost. It is also useful to have a variable speed setting, which allows you to adjust the mower's speed to your walking pace for different lawn conditions.

Two-cycle or four-cycle: Many mowers come with a choice of two-cycle or four-cycle engines. The two-cycle requires that you put a mixture of gas and oil in the tank. Since the oil is burned with the gas, and because a two-cycle engine burns twice as much gas as a four-cycle, this is not the most environmentally sound choice. I recommend the four-cycle. It involves a little more maintenance (changing the oil), but boasts more power. I'd make an exception to this advice if you will be cutting steep slopes. Four-cycle engines have difficulty circulating oil on steep slopes.

Mowing height adjustment: There should be at least five settings for mowing height, ranging from about one to three inches.

Bagging: Avoid mowers with a side bag; rear bagging is the only way to go. A better mower will have some sort of spring-loaded hatch in the back so that if you choose not to bag (e.g., if you are mulching), you can simply remove the bag and the hatch will cover the hole where the grass would normally come out. Other models may have a detachable cover that must be manually removed and replaced each time you switch from bagging to mulching. In any case, make sure you have the option to not use the bag.

Best names: Toro, Honda, John Deere, Ariens.

Author's recommendation: Toro Proline 21-inch Model 22172 (6.0 hp) or 22177 (6.5 hp). Both are four-cycle, have variable speed self-propelled drive, and feature BBC that does not stop the engine.

3.2 Commercial walk-behind mowers and riders

If you work on larger commercial properties, you will want to consider a larger mower. Even if you restrict your bsuiness to residential properties, once you build up a lot of customers or have a number of clients with large lawns, a commercial mower might be a good choice.

There are so many brands and varieties of commercial walk-behind mowers and riders that it is difficult to recommend anything specific; your choice will depend largely on what you will be using your mower for. The best bet is to visit your local dealer and take a look at what is available. As well, check out the websites of the name brands listed below for ideas on what they offer. Here are a few general tips on what to look for in these types of mowers.

Cutting width: There is a lot of variation within this class of mower. You can get deck sizes from 32 inches up to 60 inches. The best rule of thumb: Get as big a mower as will fit in your properties.

Horsepower: Expect at least a 15 horsepower engine on your midsized mower. Higher horsepower options are available.

Fixed or floating deck: Floating decks are suspended from the frame of the mower and allow more independent deck movement. Fixed decks are firmly attached to the mower. Floating decks offer easier mowing height adjustment than fixed decks. They also cost more, so if you cut mostly level lawns and don't need to adjust the height of the mower from jobsite to jobsite, you may want to choose the fixed-deck style. However, fixed-deck mowers are not as forgiving on bumpy lawns and can scalp the grass. This becomes an issue with the larger-width models, so if you are getting something wider than 36 inches, you should choose a floating deck.

Sulkey/velke: These are cool little attachments for walk-behind mowers, designed like a trailer for the person doing the mowing. You sit on a sulkey and you stand on a velke. Jump on the jointed foot plate or mini-seat with wheels and let the mower pull you around as you cut.

Striping kit: Customers love that striped look on their lawn. A striping kit is a roller that flattens the grass a little after it's been cut to give it a more pronounced nap.

Other attachments: There are a number of attachments available for commercial walk-behind and riding mowers, including leaf-bagging vacuum systems, large-capacity bags, sun shades, deluxe seats for maximum comfort, fertilizer spreaders, and more.

Best names: Exmark (a division of Toro), Bunton, Bobcat, Bad Boy, Scag, Husqvarna, Wright, Hustler.

Author's recommendation: Exmark is the biggest name in this market, and many people rave about its products. Check out the newcomer Bad Boy Mowers.

3.3 Reel mowers

The reel mower is a specialty item. They are expensive, require more knowledge and skill to use, and are finely calibrated, high-maintenance pieces of equipment. For these reasons it is not a good idea to start out with a reel mower if you have never used one before.

Reel mowers are often used on golf course putting greens. The precision of the cut is exquisite, and you may find that as your business grows and you take on higher-end clients, they may request their lawn be cut with this style of mower. If you do purchase one, make sure the dealer has the expertise in-house to sharpen and calibrate the mower properly.

Cutting width: From 20 to 27 inches cutting width on standard walk-behinds.

Number of blades: There are usually either five or seven blades on the cutting reel. The more blades, the better the cut.

Best names: California Trimmer, Tru-Cut.

Author's recommendation: Tru-Cut C25H7 (25 inch) or C27H7 (27 inch).

How to Sharpen Your Lawn Mower Blade:

- A dull mower blade can slow you down significantly and, in serious cases, can also distract from an otherwise beautifully kept lawn. You can tell if the blade needs sharpening by looking closely at the grass. If the ends are rough and turn brown after a day or two, you are using a dull blade. As a professional mower, you should sharpen your blades daily. You will need a bench grinder, a crescent wrench, and a socket wrench or similar tool to remove bolts.

- Safety first! Remove the spark plug wire from the spark plug.

- Remove the blade. You may need a squirt or two of WD-40 or other oil to loosen it up. Use a blade holder, a block of wood, or, if nothing else, your foot to stop the blade from moving as you remove the bolt(s) that hold the blade on.

- Note the angle of the blade. You'll want to try and maintain that angle. If the angle is too sharp, you'll get a great cut for the first cut or two, but it will quickly dull. If the angle is not sharp enough, your cut will suffer, although the blade will wear more slowly.

- Check the blade for straightness. A bent blade cannot be repaired, and using it could be dangerous. If you think the blade is bent, throw it out.

- Start up your grinder and move the blade back and forth lightly on the grinding wheel. The first inch on either side of the blade does most of the work, so work particularly on those areas. Try to maintain the original angle. Don't press the blade too heavily onto the wheel. Don't stay in the same spot on the blade for too long. If the blade gets too hot, it will lose its hardness.

- Don't try to grind all the nicks and cuts out of the blade; a few nicks are acceptable. If there are many nicks or actual gouges, the blade should be replaced.

- Use a simple cone-shaped blade balancer to see if the blade is weighted properly. If it doesn't balance, take a little more metal off the heavy side and try again. An unbalanced blade causes excessive vibration and unpleasant cutting.

- Use a wire brush or a file to remove any excess burrs or slivers. Then reinstall the blade.

4. POWER EQUIPMENT

4.1 Line Edgers

One of my favorite magazine ads showed a man driving in his pickup truck. His dog was in the box of the truck and in the passenger seat was a Shindaiwa T-27 trimmer. That ad pretty well sums up the kind of relationship you can expect to have with your line edger.

Keep the following points in mind as you select a line edger, also known as a string trimmer, line trimmer, weed whacker, or weedeater.

Power and size: You should consider power and size together because they are directly related. Powerful line edgers are great when you need them, but if you are trimming for four hours out of the day, you may want to trade off a little power for less weight and less fatigue. The ideal, and your eventual goal, is to have both a heavy-duty

and a light-duty edger available for whatever job comes along.

The more powerful line edgers put out about 1.5 to 1.8 horsepower and weigh 12 or 13 pounds. Lighter commercial edgers weigh in at about 9 pounds, at the cost of 0.5 horsepower or so. If you want a heavy-duty model and are concerned about the weight, use a shoulder harness to reduce the load.

Shaft: Avoid curved shafts (also called flex shafts). They are not designed to be used for long periods (you will feel it in your back). Look for the straight-shaft models.

Head: Different brands use different names to describe their heads (the business end of your line edger). Variations of "tap and go" are the most common and probably the best. With this style, the line comes out only when you tap the head on the ground while it is spinning. There are also intelligent or "smart heads" that automatically give you more line when the edger senses, based on centrifugal force, that the line is short.

Best names: Shindaiwa, Echo, Redmax, Stihl, Husqvarna.

Author's recommendation: Shindaiwa T-27, 1.5 horsepower, 12.3 pounds.

4.2 Blade Edgers

A blade edger, also known as a stick edger, is used for trimming along sidewalks and possibly garden beds.

Power and size: Blade edgers come in a variety of sizes. The unit weight goes up with the horsepower. If you are blade edging regularly, a lighter model is suitable. You will need a heavy-duty model if you take on jobs where sidewalks have not been edged in some time or if blade edging is a service that you offer less frequently (i.e., monthly or quarterly). In these situations, the accumulation of grass and soil along the sidewalk may require a little more horsepower to cut through.

Consider getting a multi-head tool for maximum versatility, allowing you to use one machine as a blade edger, a hedge trimmer, a pole saw, and a line edger. Each head is sold separately.

Best names: Shindaiwa, Echo, Redmax, Stihl, Husqvarna.

Author's recommendation: Redmax EXZ2500S-BC multi-head system.

4.3 Blowers

It is possible to get by without a blower for a while. You can use a broom instead, but the investment in a blower will pay off quickly in saved time.

You can get a handheld or a backpack blower. A handheld blower is light duty; it will suffice if you will be using it just to blow grass off sidewalks. However, you will likely want to use your blower for much more than that, in which case you will want the backpack style.

There are many blowers on the market, and while each has its own nuances, they are all pretty much the same. As you shop for a blower, keep in mind the following options:

Power: There are heavy-duty blowers available that pack a bit more punch if you feel you will need it.

Trigger: A locking throttle trigger is important. If you have to hold the throttle in position all the time, it will cause finger and wrist fatigue.

Ergonomics: All new mowers have a handle on the blower tube. If you have an old one without a handle, you should be able to buy a kit to install one. Wrist fatigue will set in fast without this option.

Best names: Shindaiwa, Echo, Redmax, Stihl, Husqvarna.

Author's recommendation: Redmax EB7000.

4.4 Hedge Trimmers

A power hedge trimmer falls into the "nice to have" category, as you can certainly get by with shears when you are first starting your business. Make some room in your budget as soon as you can, though, as a hedge trimmer is a real time saver.

There are a few different options to consider when you make your purchase:

Length: You can choose a cutting blade from 18 to 40 inches long. The longer blades require more skill to use, so if you are just starting out, stick with 30 inches or less.

The easy-reach model has a long shaft and looks like a line edger with a hedge trimmer attachment (in fact, you can buy a multi-head unit with both hedge trimmer and line edger attachments). This style is indispensable for trimming high hedges or shrubs. It comes with a cutting blade between 20 and 25 inches long.

Single- or double-sided blades: Double-sided cutting blades can be useful, but many people prefer a single blade. The choice is yours; try out both styles if you are not sure which is right for you.

Articulating blade: This is only an option with the easy-reach models. Depending on the model, you can change the angle of the blade from 0 to 150 degrees to accommodate what you are cutting.

Best names: Shindaiwa, Echo, Redmax, Stihl, Husqvarna.

Author's recommendation: Shindaiwa AH230 articulated, double-sided, easy reach.

4.5 Power Rakes

A power rake is not essential for start-up, but is a useful tool if you think you will offer power raking services as your business grows. Power rakes are also called vertical mowers or dethatchers. They have rotating tines that cut into the lawn to remove moss and thatch. If you are planning to purchase a power rake, consider the following features:

Independent or attachment: Power rakes can be purchased as independent units or as attachments to your mower. The attachments don't stand up well to commercial use, and they don't do as thorough a job as the actual power rakes, although they are more productive (faster) and much cheaper, too. If your customer wants to reduce the thatch level in the lawn a little, then the attachment may suffice. If you will be completing a lawn renovation or rejuvenation, you should choose a full power rake.

Reel types: There are three types of reels available for power rakes: spring tines, flail blades, and slicing blades. The type you choose will depend on your application. Flail blades have square teeth that basically flail the lawn and remove anything not firmly planted (i.e., moss and thatch). These do by far the best job for both moss and thatch removal. Spring tines are similar to flail blades, except they have skinnier, lighter-duty tines. Slicing blades are not useful for removing moss and thatch and are discussed in section **4.6** on overseeders.

Best Names: Ryan, Bluebird, Classen, Billy Goat.

Author's recommendation: Ryan Ren-o-Thin Power Rake.

4.6 Overseeders

While the best overseeding method is to first top-dress the lawn with sand or soil and then spread seed, this may not be practical for larger lawns due to the labor-intensive nature of top-dressing. This is why you may want to invest in an overseeder.

Overseeders are similar to power rakes, but they have two main differences:

🔌 The reels are different. Overseeders have slicing blades that are in a fixed position and rotate vertically, cutting into the ground. They do a good job of preparing the soil for planting grass seed because they create little grooves for the seed to fall into.

- Overseeders have a hopper in which you put the seed. The seed is then dropped gradually onto the ground as you move along.

If you plan on buying an overseeder, look for one that you can convert into a power rake by changing the reel.

Best names: Ryan, Bluebird, Classen, Billy Goat.

Author's recommendation: Billy Goat OS Overseeder (converts to a power rake by changing the reel to flail blades and removing the seed hopper).

4.7 Aerators

Core aerators are used for aerating or coring lawns. Aerating is a great little profit-making service, so at some point you may want to purchase your own aerator.

The most common type of aerator has a rotating reel under the deck, with hollow aeration tines that are pushed into the ground by the weight of the machine (most have detachable weights that can be added or removed as needed). As the machine drives itself along, cores are ejected through the end of the tines as new cores enter. While there are subtle differences between the various brands, any of these types will serve you well in the residential market.

The Ryan LA-28 aerator, however, is in a class by itself. It differs fundamentally from the common aerator in that the tines are driven into the ground with piston action force, not simply by the weight of the

machine. As well, it has independent drive and aerating functionality and a tricycle front end that allows for a zero turning radius and nonstop aerating. It also boasts 12 holes per square foot on the first pass, which is more than any other walk-behind aerator.

There are also trailer aerators, which you would probably only consider if you chose aerating as a specialty and were planning on aerating acres of lawn.

Best names: Ryan, Bluebird, Classen, Billy Goat.

Author's recommendation: Ryan LA-28 if you plan to aggressively market your aerating services; otherwise the Ryan Lawnaire IV.

4.8 Other Power Equipment

There is other power equipment that you may need depending on where you live and what services you will be offering your customers.

- *Chain saw.* Even though you are likely not an arborist, a chain saw comes in handy for pruning medium and larger limbs of trees and cutting landscape ties.

- *Pole saw.* This is a telescopic pole with a small (6- to 12-inch) chain-saw blade on the end. If you will be pruning trees, this is a good investment. Remember, if you purchase a multi-head tool for line edging and/or blade edging, you may be able to get a pole saw attachment as well.

- *Pressure washer.* This is a valuable tool for both you and your customers. You can generate income with it by offering pressure-washing services to your customers, and you can also use it to keep your own truck clean.

🪶 *Rototiller.* Earn extra money by offering to till people's gardens each year.

5. HAND TOOLS

5.1 Fertilizer Spreaders

Fertilizer and lime/sulfur applications are a good way to generate extra revenue and offer your customers full lawn care service.

There are essentially two types of spreaders: the drop spreader and the broadcast spreader (also known as a rotary spreader). The drop spreader offers maximum control of material distribution, but it takes much longer to spread. Unless you are looking after golf courses or higher-end lawns, the drop spreader is more than you need.

Broadcast spreaders come in a variety of sizes and qualities, and you will find that you get what you pay for. In the $100 range you will find good-quality spreaders, but don't expect more than a year or two of service out of them. In the $300 range you get a product that will last a number of years. You can also buy broadcast spreaders that will attach to your rider mower.

Look for these signs of quality in the push models:

Pneumatic tires (as opposed to plastic): The bigger the better for use on the roughest terrain.

Adjustable settings: You want to control how much fertilizer comes out of the spreader. The better models allow finely tuned calibration.

Side baffle: Controlling where your fertilizer goes is the biggest challenge with broadcast spreaders. A side baffle allows you to cruise along a sidewalk and have the material distributed only on the grass side.

Adjustable throwing ports: This option is useful to adjust the spread pattern based on the type of material you are spreading and the size of the area.

Hopper: The hopper holds the material you are spreading. A large hopper has obvious benefits. Plastic breaks down and becomes weaker in the sun, but fiberglass does not. Stainless steel is another good option.

Rain cover: An indispensable option for rainy areas.

5.2 Hand Pruning Equipment

It is wise to invest in all the proper tools you need for trimming and pruning; using the wrong tool makes the job longer and will shorten the tool's life. For example, using your hand snips to lop off a 1½-inch branch will take its toll, and you will soon be in need of new snips.

🪶 *Hand pruners.* The fancy and most correct name is "secateurs," but you can call them hand pruners or, simply, snips. A gardener without snips is like a carpenter without a hammer. You are not complete without them. Buy a pouch (scabbard/holster) for your pruners and wear it at all times. Felco is the king of professional pruners, and there are as many models as you can imagine uses. Your supplier should carry a number of models and can provide assistance in selecting one that suits you. Visit the Felco website for more information <www.felco.ch>.

- *Loppers.* These are long-handled, heavy-duty snips for cutting larger material than your handheld snips can handle.

- *Hand saw.* Make quick work of medium-sized branches with a hand saw. A folding model allows for easy portability as you can put it in your pocket or pouch.

- *Shears.* Even if you have power pruners, you will find that there are certain things that look better when cut with shears. Shears are also good for smaller jobs. Long-handled shears can come in handy.

- *Pole pruners.* These are like loppers on a telescopic pole. It is good to have them in your truck in case you need to reach something a little higher.

5.3 Rakes

Rakes are like golf clubs. They look much the same, but there are small variations that make them very different. As you become more experienced, you will learn which rake is best to use in which situations. Here are a few tips:

- *Fan rake.* This is a must-have. The generic variety has metal tines and is a multipurpose tool. There are so many different types; the one you choose will depend on your personal preferences.

- *Lawn rake.* This rake is plastic with wide tines and is great for rough-raking lawns (i.e., after power raking) and raking leaves on the lawn. It also works well on pavement and curbs.

- *Leaf rake.* This is much like the lawn rake except it's huge. If the leaves are dry and plentiful, a leaf rake is a good choice.

- *Hard rake.* It is good to have a hard rake for miscellaneous tasks. As with the fan rake, there are many varieties of hard rake with subtle differences.

- *Landscape rake.* This is basically a wide hard rake and is used to level soil in preparation for lawn installation.

- *Top-dressing rake.* A top-dressing rake is invaluable if you will be doing lawn renos or top-dressing.

5.4 Other Hand Tools

Here are a few other hand tools that you may find useful in your work:

- *Scoop.* Use a scoop to pick up the debris you have raked. A scoop is also good for fanning out top dressing.

- *Cultivator/hoe.* Use a hook, a claw, or some type of hoe to freshen up garden beds.

- *Shovels and spades.* At the very least you will need a pointy shovel for digging holes and a flat shovel (spade) for edging garden beds.

- *Litter picker-upper.* This is a handy little tool if you offer litter control as a service. The long-handled pincers save you from bending down constantly, and your back will thank you.

6. LADDERS

The best type of ladder for landscape maintenance is a tripod or orchard ladder. These are much like a stepladder, except on one side there is just a single pole. This makes them maneuverable, as they can be put inside and over trees, shrubs, and hedges.

7. SNOWBLOWERS

If you live in an area where it snows a lot, you might consider clearing snow as a way to make money in the winter. You will first want a snowblower; then, as you build your business, you may consider adding a blade to your truck so that you can get bigger snow-clearing jobs (e.g., parking lots, roads, etc.).

The snowblower (sometimes called a snow thrower) is a walk-behind machine and is ideal for residential walkways and short driveways. There are various sizes with differing degrees of power. The equipment dealer from whom you purchase your lawn care equipment will probably be able to help you select a snowblower too. Once again, use the Internet to investigate what is out there so you can make an intelligent decision when you talk to your dealer. Consider these options:

Size and power: The size of the machine (the width of the auger) and the amount of power you want will depend on where you live and how much snow you expect to move. Choose from 24- to 36-inch blowers ranging from 7 to 13 horsepower.

Single or dual stage: Single-stage snowblowers, with an auger that shoots the snow directly out the discharge shoot, are not for professionals. The auger in dual-stage blowers ingests the snow from the walkway and then tosses it against a rotating impeller, which drives it out the discharge chute. Definitely choose a dual-stage blower.

Propelling method: All dual-stage snowblowers are self-propelled. Some offer tracks instead of wheels for demanding snow conditions.

Auger type: Consider a serrated auger if you think you will be tackling compacted snow and ice.

Best names: Toro, Honda, Ariens, John Deere.

There is a multitude of truck-mounted blades to choose from, depending on the application you have in mind. For example, there are light-duty plows that will work nicely on a smaller pickup truck (4x4 drive is strongly suggested for any truck-mounted plow). There are also heavy-duty commercial plows that must be mounted on full-sized 4x4 pickups or larger one-ton trucks.

To choose the right blade, your best bet is to investigate the offerings of the major suppliers by browsing their websites or visiting local dealers.

Best names: Fisher Snow Plows, Blizzard Plows, Western Plows, Meyer/Diamond.

8. EQUIPMENT MAINTENANCE

Would you like your lawn mower to last one year or three or more years? Would you like your equipment to start easily each morning, or do you prefer to break a sweat yanking the pull start? Do you mind unexpected downtime as you rush to your mechanic in the middle of the day for a quick fix? Your answers to these questions should be obvious.

To keep your equipment running well, you need to treat it well and implement a regular maintenance program. Weekly checks and preventive maintenance will greatly increase your equipment's longevity. Owners' manuals don't make the most exciting reading, but it is important to refer to them; at least read the parts about how to maintain your equipment properly.

Here are some other tips to get the most out of your equipment:

- Sharpen blades every day. Keep a lot of spare blades so that you have a healthy rotation. Do your actual sharpening once a week so you have a fresh supply of blades always ready to go. Keep one or two in the truck in case you damage one on the road.

- Change oil often on four-cycle engines. Check the manual, but plan on doing it at least weekly. Check the oil daily to make sure there are no nasty surprises. If the equipment has an oil filter, don't forget to replace that from time to time too. Dispose of old oil responsibly.

- Clean air filters in all equipment that has them. Foam air filters should be saturated with clean oil after cleaning. Pleated paper filters can be tapped gently to remove loose dirt. If either type is damaged, replace it. It's a good idea to buy extra filters and keep them in your shop.

- Change spark plugs periodically. Check manufacturers' recommendations for frequency of replacement.

- Grease all the nipples. Check the manual to see how often you should do this, but generally it doesn't hurt to pump a little grease in. If it's full,

it'll leak out. Hopefully you'll see it leaking out and stop pumping. If not, keep on pumping until you finally see it leaking out somewhere. Next time you'll know where to look to see if it's leaking out.

- Keep key components such as carburetors and drive mechanisms clean. Use a clean rag to remove heavy buildup of oil and grease (remember — don't use a degreaser).

- Tighten parts periodically. Check all nuts and screws, and keep them tight. A few loose nuts can cause increased vibration, which in turn will loosen other nuts — until one day your blower bursts into 100 pieces.

- Check starter ropes for wear. This probably won't prolong your equipment, but it will help you avoid the agony of watching your pull cord disappear inside the engine while you are on site one day. Your downtime will be 15 to 30 minutes depending on how handy you are with tools (add an hour if you don't have the spare parts or tools to fix it).

- Have a special fuel container for mixed gas. Do not mix oil and gas in the gas tank of the equipment you are using. Mixtures that are too rich or too lean will harm the engine in the long run. Make sure your mixed gas tank is easily distinguishable from your straight gas tank. Putting non-mixed gas in a two-cycle engine will wreck it.

- Don't pressure wash your equipment. There are seals, bearings, and other sensitive parts that will be obliterated by 2,000 lbs. of water pressure.

🍃 Store your equipment properly at night. Do not store it in the truck in puddles of water or underneath a half-ton of debris. Improper storage is the most common reason equipment ends up in the shop.

🍃 Properly store your equipment for the winter (see sidebar).

How to Winterize Your Equipment

Improper storage is a leading cause of downed equipment. Here are some steps, ideas, and suggestions for winterizing your equipment.

- Store your equipment in a dry place. If you have heated accommodation, that is best. Moisture wreaks havoc on all equipment.

- For four-cycle engines (with straight gas), add gasoline stabilizer to the tank and then fill it up (or mix it up a little if it was already full). Start the engine and run it for 5 to 10 minutes so that the stabilized gas circulates through the engine. The stabilizer will prevent gummy deposits from forming as the gas deteriorates.

- For two-cycle engines (with mixed gas), do not use stabilizer. Instead, empty out the gas (you can use it in your car; that little bit of oil won't hurt a thing). Run the piece of equipment until it dies.

- Change the oil and oil filter in your four-cycle equipment.

- Remove air filters and spark plugs, and spray fogging oil into both the carburetor and the cylinders (about five-second blasts should do). Pull the starter rope a few times to lubricate the pistons and rings.

- If your equipment has a battery, remove it, clean it, and store it in a cool, dry place.

- Clean off any large deposits of oil and dirt, as well as excess grass, in the engine area.

- Lubricate any parts that need lubrication.

- Spray exposed metal parts with WD-40 to protect against rust.

PART 2
RUNNING YOUR BUSINESS

Well done! You have made it through the planning stages of your business and you are still raring to go. Now it's time to consider a few business basics that will be invaluable in the successful operation of your business. Here we look at how to make marketing your business fun and creative, what you need to know about record keeping, and some secrets to hiring and managing employees. After that, I'll show you how to plan the work-flow of a job, from first contact to job completion. Good luck!

5
SETTING UP SHOP: YOUR HOME OFFICE

One of the advantages of running a landscaping business is that you don't need to rent commercial space for your office. As most of your work is done on the job, outside, all you need is a small, organized space in which to keep your records and do your paperwork — and a home office fits the bill. You'll also need to set aside some space where you can store your tools and supplies (e.g., fertilizer, off-season equipment that you don't want to carry in your truck or trailer). This space, too, will ideally be at your own home. Finally, you need to consider your vehicle an extension of your office and establish systems to keep any on-the-road paperwork organized and close at hand.

1. THE HOME OFFICE: REWARDS AND CHALLENGES

You can probably easily list many advantages to running your business out of your home. No congestion or road rage during your commute. Snack time is when you say it's snack time. Nap time is when you say it's nap time. The dress code is whatever you want, even your housecoat and slippers. The resulting tax deduction can save you money.

It's true. Having a home office is wonderful, but it's only wonderful if you recognize that certain challenges can arise and if you are disciplined enough to organize your space to run your business efficiently. A little forethought and planning are prudent because once you're set up, it can be difficult to move. To use the carpenter's old adage: Measure twice and cut once.

1.1 Cultivating self-discipline

Many people report that the greatest challenge in working out of a home office is self-discipline. If you work all day in the field and only spend time in the office during the evening, this may not be a big problem for you. However, prepare yourself by thinking about potential conflicts. Is the evening usually when you spend time with your family or friends? Is it when you watch TV? If you like computer gaming, are you strong enough to stay focused on work and not start playing? The best way to deal with this challenge is to set a certain time every day after work for doing specific tasks in the office. This could be an hour or two right after work, after dinner, or later in the evening. If there is a certain time you know you'll be in the office, it leaves the rest of your after-work time free for more enjoyable activities.

TIP:

If you are tempted by computer games, as I am, take away the temptation. Uninstall or delete all games from your work computer. It will be the best productivity move you ever make. It was for me!

1.2 Handling distractions

Handling distractions goes hand in hand with cultivating self-discipline, since you may need self-discipline to overcome distractions. If you can anticipate some of the distractions that will come your way, you'll be better prepared to deal with them.

The main distraction you will face in a home office is your family. Will your spouse and children respect your need for undisturbed time to work? Or will they be running in and out of your office, borrowing your stapler, using your photocopier, and generally interrupting you?

You need to set limits on your time in the office and on your family's inclination to disturb you when you are working. The entire family needs to understand that your work contributes to the household income. Set the rules early so everyone knows what to expect. For example, once you have decided when you'll do your office work, let everyone know that you can't be disturbed during this time. Think now about how you will combat the challenge of distractions, and be sure to include your family in your discussions.

Other distractions abound in the home, from the lure of television to the temptation to work all night. The key is to examine your situation, anticipate possible distractions, and work out a plan for keeping on task.

2. WHERE TO PUT YOUR OFFICE

You can have your office anywhere it's possible to carve out some space to organize your records and paperwork. The ideal is a self-contained room, perhaps a spare bedroom or a den. But if you don't have a spare room, take a creative look at the space in your home. Is there a large closet you can convert? What about the end of a hallway, or another nook or cranny? Maybe you can use the corner of an existing room. Wherever you set up, try to keep your space free from distractions or ensure you are going to be able to manage them. If at all possible, choose a spot that has a door you can close to keep the rest of your home life separate from your office.

If you are starved for space in your home — if, for example, you live in an apartment — a corner of your bedroom can be your office. There are nifty ways to hide your work area.

Workspace armoires are great as they fold up inconspicuously. When open, they provide desk area and storage space. Think about disguising your work area with a decorative screen or lots of plants.

You'll need enough room for a desk and chair, working space, your computer, and a filing cabinet. You'll also need adequate power to run your computer and any other electric equipment you might use, as well as a phone jack for your phone and fax. If you are hooked up to the Internet and subscribe to a cable service, you'll need a cable outlet. If you have dial-up or ADSL connection, you'll need another phone jack.

Think about lighting, too. Does the space you've chosen have enough lighting for you to work comfortably? You may need to purchase a lamp or install some task lighting (natural light is the best; florescent is the worst). And don't forget about noise. You want a relatively quiet area in which you can concentrate. Try to find a space removed from the sounds of daily family traffic. Possible inexpensive quick fixes for a noisy office could be weather-stripping the windows or replacing hollow doors with solid ones. Some people find playing recorded background noise, such as chirping birds or crashing waves, a helpful way to filter out the more distracting noises.

Finally, don't be shortsighted when choosing your office space. What may be large enough today may be too small next year. Make sure you leave yourself room to grow. On the other hand, if you anticipate that your smaller office quarters will be temporary, don't waste your time and money on extravagant room improvements and/or renovations.

3. THE MOST ESSENTIAL ITEM: YOUR BUSINESS COMPUTER

If you don't already own a computer that you can use for your business, you need to buy one as soon as possible. These days, a computer is a business necessity, not a luxury. If you don't know how to use a computer, learn. It seems that every community offers some sort of introductory course on computers. You can also learn from a book, video, or tutorial CD-ROM available at your local bookstore or library. You can even look for help over the Internet to learn virtually anything you want. However you do it, you *must* learn how to use a computer!

3.1 How your computer can promote business success

Here are ten ways that computers can help you with your business.

1. *Computerized accounting.* Since the advent of computers and consumer accounting software packages, it has become possible for the average person to look after his or her own accounting records without a lot of training. Once you are set up, you will find these programs save you hours of work compared to the antiquated manual entry method of bookkeeping. While a solid understanding of bookkeeping basics is essential whether you are using a computer or not, accounting software packages today hide many of the technical details to create a more user-friendly interface that even the numerically challenged can manage. (See chapter 7 for more information on setting up an accounting system.)

2. *Internet access.* Numerous reputable websites on running a business, landscaping, garden maintenance, and more will prove invaluable as you start and grow your business. You can also use the Internet to investigate the competition, check the weather forecast before you head out for a job, and buy and sell equipment. You might even develop your own website to use as a marketing device. (See recommended websites on the CD-ROM that accompanies this book.)

3. *Industry-specific software.* There are software programs designed especially for you, the lawn care operator/professional gardener. Features vary from package to package, but all give you a database in which to store your customer information; a system for tracking receivables, invoicing, routing, and scheduling; and much more. I highly recommend using one of them. (See section **3.3** on software for details on three specific programs.)

4. *Printing invoices and checks.* You will appear more professional if your invoices are printed off your computer. You can also print your own checks, saving you a lot of time, if you buy blanks that fit your printer.

5. *Communications.* E-mail allows you to communicate instantly whenever you need to. You can send quotes, estimates, and schedules by e-mail. You could even explore the possibility of using an instant messaging program to talk to your clients, perhaps setting aside an hour or two a day when you are available for questions.

6. *Promotions.* Desktop publishing software can help the most inexperienced users create professional-looking documents. Create your own flyers, brochures, presentations, or advertisements. Most software packages contain templates you can work with to create amazing documents.

7. *Creating documents and spreadsheets.* Two must-haves for your computer are a word-processing package and a spreadsheet program. Use a word processor (such as Microsoft Word or Corel WordPerfect) to write your introductory letters, thank-you notes, notices of price increases, and so on. Use a spreadsheet program (such as MS Excel or Corel Quattro Pro) to create anything from a simple customer list to a more complex job-costing worksheet or a what-if scenario for next year's forecasting.

8. *Plant encyclopedias.* Plant encyclopedias are available for sale as CD-ROMs, which you can install on your computer for reference. You will also find an abundance of information on the Internet. Use these resources to help you select the right plants for your clients and to learn more about the plants you are working with.

9. *Managing contacts and tasks.* Use your computer to store contact information for friends and family, clients, suppliers, and other key people. Use the calendar to record to-do lists, tasks, appointments, etc.

10. *Personal digital assistants* (PDAS), such as Palm Pilots or Blackberries, are great

because you can download information (such as contacts and appointments) from your home PC to the PDA and have that information handy wherever you are. There are many programs for palm-sized computers that will improve your effectiveness in business.

Get a Guru

Do you need a logo? A website? A newsletter design? Some advertising copy? Check out <guru.com>, a great resource for people running a small business. You post your proposed project on the site, explaining in your own words what you want. Once it is posted, experts from all over the world can bid on your project. You select the one you like, and he or she completes the entire project over the Internet. You agree on a price and payment terms before the expert starts working, and sign a contract to confirm it (for smaller projects, you should expect to pay upon satisfactory completion of the project). It is not in the interest of the freelancing pros you hire to renege on an agreement or cross you in any way, as they would then lose their access to the website.

3.2 Buying a computer

Buying a computer has never been easier or cheaper. The hardest part is deciding how many bells and whistles you want or need. If you are familiar with computers, all you need to do is visit a few computer vendors and compare prices. Have a written list of what you need so you don't forget anything while you're shopping, and make sure you get enough space for all your word-processing and spreadsheet programs and other business applications. Think about what kind of printer you want. You'll appreciate a higher-quality (probably color) printer if you plan to design your own marketing flyers and announcements.

If you aren't familiar with computers, think carefully about what you want to use your business computer for, do some research, and ask a more computer-savvy friend or colleague for help. After that, it is as simple as making a trip to the local computer retailer or, even easier, buying from one of the big companies (Dell or HP). You can order from their websites or via the phone and have your computer delivered to your door.

Should you buy used? With the price of brand-new computers falling to less than $500 (with monitor), it is difficult to justify buying used. If buying new means holding off a month or two to save your pennies, I suggest that route. Computers become obsolete within one or two years, so you don't want to limit yourself by buying yesterday's model. Even though logic tells you that the computer should be able to run the same programs today that it ran two years ago, the reality is that new software you buy today may demand newer hardware. If you do decide to buy a used computer, get one that comes with some kind of warranty, even if it is only for 30 days, so you can make sure it all works.

Other computer options you might consider are laptops and PDAs. A laptop, also called a notebook, is portable and may be attractive because you can take it with you in your truck. However, laptops are much more expensive than desktop computers and are often targets for thieves. You may find the advantage of having your computer with you is not worth the risk. On the other hand, a personal digital assistant (PDA) is small enough to keep in your pocket at all times. You can upload information from your PDA to your home computer, ensuring that any information you enter during the day is saved. You may find the features offered on various models help you stay organized on the job.

3.3 Software

Whatever computer you buy will come with the software necessary to run it, and may also contain a word-processing program, an Internet browser, and an e-mail program. Once you know what is included with your computer purchase and what isn't, consider other software applications you might need or find useful.

- *Virus protection.* Virus protection programs are generally available as a renewable one-year subscription that provides continual updates. Check out Symantec's Norton Antivirus <www.symantec.com> and McAfee VirusScan <www.mcafee.com>. If you have an Internet connection, both a firewall and virus protection are essential. Firewalls can be purchased as a package with your virus protection. If you have more than one computer at home and use a router to share your Internet connection, that router will likely have an effective, built-in firewall. If you have neither a router nor virus protection, consider a fully functional free firewall called Zone Alarm <www.zonealarm.com>.

- *Backup software.* You will want to back up your data often (e.g., weekly). To do so, you will need a CD burner or some other removable storage media for the job. You can do backups manually by copying the important data to your CD, but it's more convenient to use a backup utility that runs automatically, say in the middle of the night, to regularly back up your important files. There are many programs available, and some offer free trials. There are also backup subscription services that let you back up your data to an off-site location via the Internet.

- *Office suite.* While office programs can be purchased independently, they are most often packaged as a suite. The advantage of buying the suite is that it's cheaper than buying each program separately, and the products are integrated so that they work well together. An office suite would include an advanced word processor for creating letters and other documents, a spreadsheet program for creating worksheets, a database program for creating your own databases, a presentation program for designing presentations, and possibly other programs such as website designers, drawing/illustration programs, or project management programs. The most popular suite is Microsoft Office <office.microsoft .com>. Corel also offers an office suite <www.corel.com>, and there are many others. Consider using Open Office <www.openoffice.org>, which is a quality open source product — and it's free!

- *Accounting software.* I highly recommend that you use one of the excellent accounting software programs to ease your record-keeping burden. See chapter 7 for a review of some of the accounting packages available.

- *Lawn company operator software.* There are a few programs that are specifically designed for lawn care company operators and professional gardeners. These programs are useful because they integrate your customer database, job history, billing, routing, scheduling, and job costing. All three of the programs reviewed in the sidebar offer these core features. Each has a different look and offers other features that you can research by visiting the websites. All three offer free trials, so you can try out the programs before making a decision.

- *Graphic design software.* If you want to create your own newsletters, ads, brochures, and so forth, there are powerful programs available. The learning curve on these programs is steep, but if this aspect of the business appeals to you and you are up for the challenge, you can do amazing things with them.

Software for Lawn Care Companies

Prices mentioned are in us dollars and were correct at time of writing. Check for current pricing.

Groundskeeper Pro <www.adkad.com> comes in two sizes, Pro and Lite. The Lite version does not limit the number of customers you are allowed to have, as other programs do (it allows up to 10,000), but it does exclude what I would consider essential features such as scheduling and job costing. Therefore, I recommend the Pro version, which lets you track expenses as well as revenue, a useful option if you are not going to be doing your own bookkeeping. With this program you can track your revenue and expenses throughout the year and then give everything to your accountant at year-end. Cost: Pro $380; Lite $260.

Gopher Software <www.gophersoftware.com> comes in three versions. Basic includes all the core features, Plus includes more advanced features and some integration with QuickBooks, and Professional includes employee-scheduling features and lets you track equipment usage and chemical applications. If you want to start with one of the more basic versions, you can upgrade to advanced versions at any time. If you plan to use an accounting package, the integration to QuickBooks is a great feature. Also useful is the Palm module, which lets you list daily jobs on your Palm Pilot, enter the start and stop times for the jobs, and have them automatically synced up to your computer each night. Gopher also offers a service that allows customers to receive invoices via e-mail as well as view recent jobs, payments, or quotes online. You can download a free trial from the site. Cost: Basic $200; Plus $300; Professional $400.

CLIP: <www.clip.com>, the Computerized Lawn Industry Program, boasts the best integration with QuickBooks. It also offers live, wireless, scheduling options using web-enabled phones and integration with GPS devices to provide real-time tracking of your crews. You may not need these options when you first start up, but as your business grows, you can consider their benefits. CLIP offers a package for small companies, CLIP Classic Visual 50, which limits you to 50 customers. The next step up is CLIP Classic Visual Small Business Solution, which has no integration but allows you more customers. Cost: Classic Visual 50 $400; Classic Visual Small Business Solution $800.

4. OTHER OFFICE ESSENTIALS

4.1 Telephone

You will need a business phone in your home office. The monthly cost of a business line will usually get you a simple listing in the Yellow Pages, and having a dedicated business line will ensure that your company isn't competing with your family for the use of the phone.

Consider using a hands-free headset for your office so you can work and talk on the phone without straining your neck. Speakerphones also allow you to have your hands free, but they can be annoying for the person on the other end. Another option is a cordless phone, which lets you leave your office while you talk. These are particularly useful if you want to carry on a business conversation when it is inconvenient to be sitting at your desk.

Be sure to invest in an answering machine or voice mail feature so customers can leave messages for you if you are out or on the line with someone else. Remember to return the calls promptly. If a customer can't reach you, or if you don't return a call, you risk losing that customer completely.

It may be convenient for you to have a cell phone because you are away from your office most of the day. However, when shopping for a cell phone plan, compare deals carefully. If your customers call you regularly on your cell phone, you may find that your monthly bill is beyond your budget. Be selective about who you give your cell number to. There is a fine line between great customer service (which includes being easily accessible) and being interrupted in your work because your cell phone is constantly ringing.

4.2 Fax

A fax machine is a must for your home office. If you have the right software, your computer can double as a fax machine. In some cases that's the best way to go. If your fax is integrated with your computer, you can fax a document from your computer without having to print it out. On the other hand, if you want to fax a document that is not on your computer, you will first have to scan the document and then fax it. Think about how you are going to use your fax machine and then make the best purchase for your needs. Today there are good options on multi-function machines. For $300 to $500 you can get an all-in-one printer, copier, scanner, and fax machine.

4.3 Daily planner

As the proud owner of a new business, you will find yourself wearing many hats. One of those is the project manager hat, which requires strong organizational skills. The key to staying organized is to break up large jobs and objectives into smaller, bite-sized tasks. Even after you are up and running, you will benefit greatly if you employ this technique.

Your most important tool as a project manager is the daily planner or organizer. You can purchase software varieties of organizers, but I recommend starting out with the real thing, an actual book or binder. Your daily planner will be your mobile office. In it you keep your schedule, your business cards, your contacts, general notes, and more. There is a wide variety of daily planners available, and you can find them at any office supply store. You can also check online at <www.dayminder.com> or <www.daytimer.com>.

Organizers, if used correctly, are not so much calendars as they are *systems*. The good ones come with a recommended system, or you can devise your own. This tool will not only help you get your business started, it will also be invaluable in the everyday running of your business.

The Daily Drop File

Using a "daily drop file" is an excellent way to keep track of things that might otherwise slip through the cracks. Go to the office supply store and purchase an accordion-style file holder with 31 file slots, one for each day of the month. Then each time you have a "to do" for another day, simply drop it into the appropriate slot in your file holder. If this system is going to work, you must check the file holder every day to retrieve your list of things to do. Make a habit of checking it in the morning before you leave for work and then again at night.

4.4 Some necessities and niceties

Here are some other items that will make your home office more organized and appealing:

- A good supply of basic office materials such as pens, pencils, ruler, stapler, paper clips (assorted sizes), sticky tape, printer paper, scratch pads, sticky notes, and 3" x 5" index cards

- An invoice pad (for handwritten invoices you might prepare on the road or, in a pinch, in your office)

- Blank floppy disks and CD writable disks for your computer

- Hanging file folders and the files to go in them

- Dry erase boards and bulletin boards (good for notes, reminders, sketches, etc.)

- Wall map of the area you intend to work in, with pushpins showing where your customers are located

- Rubber stamp with your business name, address, and phone number

(You might also want a stamp with "deposit only to" and your bank account number for depositing checks.)

5. SETTING UP A SHOP

Along with your home office, you are also going to need some space in which to store supplies, such as fertilizers and equipment, when you are not using them. Ideally, you can organize part of your garage or outside shed for this purpose. If you don't have a garage or shed, I recommend you buy or build a small tool shed in your yard. If you don't have room in your yard, or if you live in an apartment, you might have to rent space for this purpose.

Wherever you set up, be sure to include these items in the shop:

- *Tool kit.* At least in the beginning, you will be doing most equipment maintenance yourself. Keep a basic tool kit that includes a wrench set or socket set (with deep sockets for spark plugs), screwdriver set, crescent wrench, Allen wrenches, hammer, pliers (needle nose and adjustable), rags, and WD-40.

- *Grinder.* Mower blades need to be kept sharp. You can do this yourself with a grinder. (See the sidebar in chapter 4 for tips on sharpening your own blades.)

- *Shelving.* Some shelving from your local hardware store will prove helpful for storing fertilizers and other supplies.

- *Safety equipment.* For safety's sake, keep a first-aid kit and a fire extinguisher in the shop.

- *Extra parts.* Buy extra heads for your line edgers. Have a couple of pre-loaded heads ready to go in a pinch. Keep spare blades for lawn mowers and edgers. Have two or three times more lawn mower blades than you need for your equipment so you can swap out blades, sharpen them later, and then add them back into the rotation.

6. SETTING UP YOUR TRUCK AND TRAILER

Your truck is an extension of your home office, and it needs to be supplied in much the same way to be ready to serve your customers. Be sure to have the following items handy in your truck or trailer at all times:

- *Tool kit.* The same tools that you keep in your shop (see section **5**) should also be in your truck. You may scale down the collection once you get to know your equipment. For example, you may not need an entire socket set, but just a few common sockets that you know fit your equipment.

- *Raingear.* You'll need raingear that you and any employees can put on if it starts raining partway through the day. Wet workers look unhappy, and that won't do your business any good. If you plan on working in the rain, make sure that everyone who works with you knows they must wear raingear.

- *Ratchet tie-down straps.* These are great for cinching down even the biggest loads. I have had more than one green employee say, "You'll never get that all on the truck." I just smile and retort, "Pay attention, you might learn something." Ratchet tie-downs are the key.

🍃 *Pruning hand tools.* Keep snips, shears, loppers, and a hand saw in the truck.

🍃 *Tarps and buckets.* You will use either tarps or buckets to collect debris. If you use tarps, keep a healthy supply. Reuse them if you can, but once they get holes in them they are not worth the hassle and should be replaced. Smaller five-gallon buckets are useful for litter control, minor weeding, or smaller piles of debris.

🍃 *Extra clothing.* You'll want extra socks, shirts, and sweats in case you get wet, overly dirty, or cold. A few towels come in handy too.

🍃 *Miscellaneous tools.* You'll need motor oil, two-cycle oil, gasoline (straight and mixed in different containers), chemicals (if you use them), extra blades for mower and edger, preloaded head(s) for line edgers, assorted bungee cords, tools for repairing and changing tires, eye protection, ear protection, first-aid kit, ASA or ibuprofen, fire extinguisher, flashlight, an orange cone or two, a florescent safety vest, duct tape, rags, a grease gun, and water to drink on hot, dry days.

🍃 *Ready-for-business supplies.* Are you ready to make new customers while you work? Make sure you stock the truck with business cards, flyers, paper and pen, invoice book, blank quotation sheets, and information packs that describe your services (see chapter 6). A measuring wheel for doing quotes, a phone book for reference, and maps to find new customers are also handy things to have with you.

Once you have all the equipment and supplies you need, you must decide how to organize them in your truck or trailer. Here is one suggestion based on hauling everything in a truck with an enclosed trailer (5' x 8.5').

Generally, keep your tools in the trailer and reserve the truck for debris. The one exception to this rule is gasoline. Put that in a milk crate or similar box and place it in the back corner of the truck, behind the wheel well. It is important to secure the gas containers so they don't bounce around. If you have an open trailer, you can put the gas on the trailer, but do not keep it in an enclosed trailer.

You'll find that your orchard ladder fits well in the back of the truck. You may not need it each day, but when you do, it ties down nicely whether the truck is full or empty — just throw it on top and cinch it all down.

In the cab of the truck you should have a box to store all your paperwork (e.g., maps, invoices, etc). Raingear and some hand pruning tools can go behind the seat.

In the trailer, it is helpful to have a bench type of storage area in the back, closest to the trailer hitch. It should open on the top so that you can store things such as blades, trimmer heads, tools, and chemicals (secured tightly like the gas). Next, push your lawn mowers to the very end of the trailer, right up to the bench, one on each side. Or put a mower on one side and something like an aerator on the other side. Secure these with floor or wall tie-downs and put triangle wedges behind the wheels.

Line and blade edgers and trimmers can go on either wall of the trailer with the proper fixtures to hold them. Secure them with bungee cords or with whatever built-in system came with the trailer. Hand tools such as rakes and shovels can slide in near the ceiling of the trailer once you have modified it for this. This leaves some room in the trailer for whatever else you are hauling.

An organized truck and trailer will make you a happy and effective worker. In the arrangement described above, I assume that the trailer has been modified with fixtures and tie-downs. You can customize your own trailer by buying specialty products (visit <www.greentouch.com> for some great ideas), or you can hire a mechanic, body shop, or welder to do what you want (for example, install roof and side air vents). Think about what will work for you, then visit your local mechanic or welder and work with him or her to create your dream machine!

<www.MowBoy.com>

This site deserves special attention, and not just because it is run by the author of this book! Communicate with pros from around North America via an online forum. There are tips and tricks of the trade, frequently asked questions, business and industry articles, free buy-and-sell classifieds, links to other great sites, contests and competitions, consulting services, and much more. Come on by!

6
MARKETING YOUR BUSINESS

All your shiny new equipment, your fully equipped home office, and your passionate desire to do the best job you can will not make your phone ring. For that, you must tell people what you have to offer. Welcome to marketing!

Many people think that marketing is just advertising, but advertising is only one small part of your total marketing effort. Marketing covers everything to do with designing a product or service that the public needs or wants, making people aware of it, making them want it, and finally selling it to them. Marketing is how you will represent yourself to the public. It is integrated into everything you do. Marketing includes how you answer your phone, how quickly you respond to quotes and requests for service, how you and your employees dress, the appearance of your work truck, how you act while on the jobsite, and how you follow up after the job.

At its simplest, marketing is getting people to try your business and then getting those people to keep using your business. Each component requires different methods and strategies, and if they are well implemented, you will soon find your new equipment earning you money, your home office churning into life, and your passion for the business taking you as far as your dreams will allow.

To put a solid marketing plan in place requires forethought and careful planning. It also provides a wonderful avenue for your creativity and it does not have to cost a lot of money.

1. DEVELOPING YOUR MARKETING PLAN

What chance would a blindfolded boxer have in the ring? Obviously not much.

Without being able to see, the boxer wouldn't be able to direct any blows.

This analogy stresses the importance of having a plan. Without one, you will be randomly punching into the air. It's much better to direct your blows so they achieve the maximum effect.

Get your pen and paper out again. The first part of developing your marketing plan is to *position yourself in the marketplace.* To do so you must ask yourself the following questions and write down your answers as thoughtfully as you can:

1. **Who is your target market?** What group will you primarily sell your services to? Your answer could be defined by age groups (e.g., baby boomers), geographical area, neighborhood, or occupation (e.g., busy professionals). Or you might specify people with certain values, such as environmental integrity. It will certainly be people who share economic similarities (e.g., homeowners rather than renters). You may target more than one group. You should also have a good idea of why you've identified the markets you have. For example, if you identify professionals as a target market, you might write, "Professional people tend to have little free time to spend in the garden. They are more likely to be able to afford to hire a lawn care/gardening company."

2. **What are the benefits of your offerings?** Why will people buy your service? Will it save homeowners valuable time? Provide expertise to those who don't have it?

3. **What is your competitive advantage?** What sets you apart from other similar companies? Is it next-day service? Diligent attention to detail? Reasonable prices? Organic programs? After you have been in business for a few years, you can add "experience" to this list of advantages, but for now you must find a strength to help you stand out from the others.

4. **What are your weaknesses?** Some weaknesses are short term. For example, if you are just starting out, you would list your inexperience as a weakness (but see the sidebar on strategies to overcome a lack of experience). Another weakness may be that you can only run your business part time at the start, and you have obligations on certain days of the week that may affect your response time. Think hard and list all the things that may have a negative effect on your business.

5. **Who is your competition?** There are likely too many landscaping companies in your area to list. Concentrate on the ones that you perceive to be your direct competition in whatever area you are focused on. Check the Yellow Pages to identify some of the bigger outfits. Watch for these and take notes. If they are doing something good, copy them.

6. **What trends that relate to your service are apparent in the economy?** What are the needs of your market? List any peculiarities or special notes about the marketplace that will affect your business. Are there

any other factors that will influence people's buying? For example, is having a gardener a status symbol in a certain area? Is the contrary true in another area with a lot of do-it-yourselfers? Are there any interesting demographics, like a high proportion of a specific nationality or age group in some area? You can learn more about the demographics of your target market by visiting your local library and asking for community statistics or using the Internet at home to do the research. You should be able to identify average income, number of homeowners, family size, and much more. Check out the demographics in your area before you start your marketing campaigns. What you learn will help you direct your marketing efforts and make them fully effective.

7. **What is your identity?** Your marketing is your image, your identity; it is how you would like potential customers to see you. If this image is out of line with what you really are, this inconsistency will catch up with you in the long run, and it will cost you. For example, if your marketing presents the image of a professional and friendly company, but you are rude to your customers and leave a mess behind, you're not living up to your marketing image. You want to build your identity with the highest ideals of hard work, integrity, and honesty. Write down how you would like to be perceived in the marketplace, and then stand by your plan.

Use Worksheet 3 to answer these questions for yourself and your business. Write as much as you want about each question, using more paper if you need it. (The worksheet is also included on the CD-ROM that came with this book.)

Ten Strategies to Overcome a Lack of Experience

There is no way around it — if you are just starting out, you are at a disadvantage. But remember that every day you will know a little more than you did the day before and be a little better at your job. Before you know it, you'll be a pro. Here are some tips to help you overcome your disadvantage.

1. **Pay close attention to instructions:** Learn from your clients by listening. As they explain to you what work they want done, take note of any plant types they name — they may know more than you at this point.

2. **Don't be afraid to ask questions:** If you are not sure about something, ask for clarification. You will expose your lack of experience, but how much worse will it be if you ruin someone's plants and/or lawn? Asking questions will *not* make you look stupid. Instead, you will appear professional and careful.

3. **Focus on your strengths:** In your marketing, highlight what you do best. Perhaps you work harder, try harder, go the extra mile, provide better customer service and a faster response time.

4. **Your size is a strength:** When you are starting out, you can sell your small size as a strength. Customers know that they will get the best service when the president of the company shows up to do the job. (Be careful with this tactic, however, because once you hire employees, you will have to ensure that the company's standards do not drop when you are no longer on the crew.)

5. **Don't miss opportunities:** Use the flexibility of time you have in the early days of your business to sell your services at every opportunity. If a prospective client calls and asks for a quote, offer to go immediately to his or her house and assess the job instead of making a date for later in the week. You will likely impress your prospect by your prompt service.

6. **Play the emotional card:** You are a small business. Small business drives our economy. You are a self-motivated person trying to raise your family. People relate to these attributes, so don't be afraid to use them in your marketing. This is a difficult message to convey in print, but you can do it easily in person. Let clients know in your words and actions that you are a motivated businessperson who works hard to provide for yourself and your family. Be personable and likable.

7. **Advertise cumulative experience:** If you have more than one person working with you, advertise your cumulative years of experience (e.g., "Backed by 12 years of experience"). Having said that, don't proactively advertise experience, cumulative or otherwise, until you have more than 10 years under your belt.

8. **Look professional:** Have a smart, sensible uniform. Create a catchy logo and use it on your truck and/or trailer, your uniforms, your invoices, and so on. Act big. Be consistent with the delivery of your service. Don't let your six-year-old answer your business phone. Don't arrive at a job in a truck with a broken muffler so the whole block hears you backfiring down the road.

9. **Try to get "face time":** If you are just starting out and don't have much experience, you probably have more time on your hands than a large, busy company does. Take advantage of this by trying to meet people face to face. When customers call you, set an appointment when they are home so you can meet them. After completing a job, canvass a few houses in the area to introduce yourself and let people know what you do.

10. **Use systems:** Create systems for maintenance visits, quoting and invoicing, maintaining your equipment, and more. Your customers may not see your systems at work, but they will see the results as your company will run smoothly.

WORKSHEET 3
TARGETING YOUR MARKET

1. Who is your target market?

   _____

   _____

2. What are the benefits of your offerings?

   _____

   _____

3. What is your competitive advantage?

   _____

   _____

4. What are your weaknesses?

   _____

   _____

5. Who is your competition?

   _____

   _____

6. What trends that relate to your service are apparent in the economy?

   _____

   _____

7. What is your identity?

   _____

   _____

2. YOUR CORE STATEMENT

By answering the questions in Worksheet 3, you have strategically placed yourself in the marketplace with your competitors. No doubt there are some points that make you stand out from them. Now it's time to condense what you have to say into one or two sentences. This will be your core message or statement, which will sum up what your business is about and will be the cornerstone of your marketing effort. Everyone who works in your company must know and believe in this statement.

Look specifically at your answers to questions 1, 2, 3, and 7 on Worksheet 3. Use this information to write your core statement. For example, you might write:

My Company will promote time-saving, environmentally friendly solutions as we work hard and conscientiously for homeowners in My City.

Or

At My Company, our attention to detail will be second to none as we serve homeowners in select areas of My City. Our trademarks will be our hard work, honesty, and integrity.

Once you are happy with your core statement, stick with it. Commit to it. Your marketing *must* be consistent. Inconsistency will lower confidence and this, in turn, will lower sales. Broadcast your core statement and have a strong, unified front as you face the public eye.

3. SPECIFIC MARKETING STRATEGIES

The methods described below are mostly used to attract new business, but you can also use them to persuade existing customers to keep using your services. As you review these strategies, think how you might use them in your own business.

3.1 Branding

Branding means making your company known by giving it a specific form of identification such as a logo, a slogan, a jingle, or a sign. Most often it is your logo. For example, when people see the Golden Arches, they need no further information to know that it means McDonald's. I recognize a Home Depot commercial on the radio before a word is spoken because of the jingle. That is the power of branding. While branding your company takes time, it is something that must start from the beginning. Create a logo, have a slogan or catchphrase, and use it in your advertising and on your truck, business cards, stationery, etc. (The CD-ROM lists books you can read to learn how to brand your company.)

The most important thing to remember about branding yourself and your company is that you must be committed to providing exceptional service or branding will certainly backfire on you — the logo or slogan will produce a bad feeling in people instead of a good one.

3.2 Networking

Getting out and meeting people in your community is an excellent marketing tool. Join relevant associations and take in industry trade shows. Talk to your suppliers; they are an excellent source of knowledge, and you may be surprised what they will share. Whenever you meet people and the opportunity presents itself, give them your business card and talk about what you do. Ask for other people's cards, too, and don't be afraid to drop them an e-mail or give them a call to ask a simple question. In short, extend yourself, get known.

3.3 Buddy businesses

Think about the businesses in your neighborhood that offer services which complement yours — for example, window washing, gutter cleaning/repairs, or pressure washing (unless you offer any of these services yourself). Introduce yourself to the business owner and suggest you become "buddy businesses." You could share your customer lists, enclose each other's advertising in your billing envelopes, recommend each other to your existing clients, and help each other out in myriad ways. You might enjoy a wonderful and long, symbiotic relationship!

3.4 Buying customers

There are often opportunities to buy customers from existing lawn companies. Companies sell customers for a number of reasons. Perhaps they are downsizing or moving to commercial maintenance and dropping residential clients. Maybe they are selling their entire company, customers and all. Whatever the reason, the best way to learn about these opportunities is to network. Talk to your suppliers, other business owners, and the guy who fixes your mower. Look for posted notices in the places where you do your business. Check the "Business Opportunities" section of the classifieds. Use the Internet, as companies selling customers may also post notices on lawn care forums, such as the ones listed under websites on the CD-ROM.

If you discover an opportunity, the next question is: How much is it worth? The general rule of thumb is that maintenance contracts are worth one month's worth of revenue, but it may be more or less based on the following variables:

- Is there a signed contract in place? If so, is it for more than one year? The cost of the customer will go up with the length of the contract.

- Does the agreement cover extras or is it for lawn cutting only? Does the customer historically spend money on extra services? The more the customer spends, the more expensive the contract.

- Is the customer in a high-end neighborhood?

- How long has the selling company had the customer? The longer it has served the customer, the more likely the customer will trust that he or she is being treated fairly — not as a commodity — and will accept you as the new contractor. If the company is selling a brand-new customer, that customer may shop around instead of agreeing to the sale of his or her contract.

Be wise when buying customers and do some research to make sure you get your money's worth.

- Ask the seller to provide job costing information for the customers. How much time is being spent on site and is the account profitable?

- Ask for a complete account history. Does the customer pay on time?

- Put it in writing. Record customer names, addresses, revenue, and costs. Make sure the company that you are buying from agrees to assist you with a smooth transition, and document this too.

Consult your accountant. If the purchase is sizable, talk to a lawyer as well.

3.5 Using business cards

We've mentioned business cards as part of your branding effort, but there are other ways to use this simple and effective tool.

There are two philosophies about business cards. The first, which I personally subscribe to, is that your business card should be a veritable brochure containing as much information as possible. I use a folding card, with my color logo and contact information on the front. Inside is information on the services I offer and a catchphrase. Even the back of the card has information on it.

The other school of thought is "keep it simple," and that can work too. If you prefer this philosophy, you'll have a thoughtfully designed card that highlights your name, your logo and catchphrase, and your contact information. The beauty is in the uncluttered simplicity.

3.6 Word of mouth

Word-of-mouth advertising is both the cheapest and the most effective form of marketing there is. Don't forget that it works both ways. Unhappy customers talk as much as, often more than, happy customers.

The absolute best way to generate positive word-of-mouth feedback is to exceed expectations that you have set for your customer. This is a twofold task. First, and most obvious, you should attempt to go the extra mile for your customer. Brainstorm and think creatively about how you can set yourself apart from your competition (see sidebar). The second part of exceeding expectations is to not oversell yourself when trying to get new customers. This is more likely to produce the opposite result: your customer will be disappointed.

Ten Ways to Exceed Expectations (or How to Get People to Keep Using Your Business)

1. **Know your customer:** Learn the names of everyone in the family, including the pets. If possible, find out their occupations and hobbies. Know their property, their plant material, their landscaping challenges, and their pet peeves. Don't just file this information in your head. Write it down and use this knowledge to improve your service.

2. **Send thank-you cards:** Let your clients know that you appreciate their business by sending thank-you cards. Make sure the card is original, not generic. Consider having cards professionally printed, perhaps with a picture of your crew. If you don't have the funds for specialized printing, you can create a custom card on your computer.

3. **Offer free advice:** Take some time at each jobsite to look around for anything that might need attention. This is a good opportunity to sell an extra service or recommend another local company to do a job that is outside the realm of your experience. You might even suggest something the homeowner can do himself or herself. Your customers will appreciate the interest you show in their lawn and garden.

4. **Give gifts:** An inexpensive gift can go a long way to promote loyalty and exceed the expectations of your clients. For example, when you sign up new customers, ask what their favorite flower or plant is. Then, in your service delivery, surprise them with a free plant. Attach a card saying: "Compliments of My Company."

5. **Follow up regularly:** You have to make your customers feel important. If you lose a customer and you don't know why, it may be because the customer did not feel important. People complain in different ways. Consider yourself lucky if you get a call and the customer yells your ear off. That's feedback; it gives you something you can work on. Some customers complain silently. Make sure your customers know that you value their feedback and opinions. Ask them questions. Whether you do this directly or in the form of a survey, be sure to make the questions pointed and specific. For example, don't ask, "How are we doing?" Instead ask, "Are you happy with the way the lawn looks?" And don't forget to listen. Act on suggestions from your customers and maintain communication throughout the year, not just when you finish a job.

6. **Make communication easy:** Make it easy for clients to reach you. Tell them they can always leave a message for you on your business line, and consider developing a website on which they can leave messages. Take a few minutes and talk to them face to face if you see them while you're working. When you complete a job, leave a notice stating what you've done and giving any special instructions for the client. Be open and available.

7. **Be knowledgeable:** One of the simplest and most effective ways to make your customers feel important is to know your trade. Strive to continue learning about lawn care, plants, general horticulture, and the gardening industry. Clients will be much happier dealing with a knowledgeable person instead of someone who just pushes a mower and appears to have no real interest in the job. Keep learning!

8. **Be proactive, not reactive:** Try to anticipate what your customers want. Don't wait for them to ask you for a quote on trimming the hedge or power raking the lawn. Pay attention, notice that the hedge needs trimming and that there is a lot of moss and/or thatch in the lawn, and give them a quote for the work.

9. **Set reasonable expectations:** There is a fine line between selling yourself to your customers by telling them how great you are and setting expectations so high that you have no chance of exceeding them. Find that line and stay behind it. That doesn't mean you shouldn't claim to offer great service; you should. However, leave a few "tricks" (such as the suggestions in this list) hidden away to use as customer service "extras" rather than offering them as standard service.

10. **Be honest when you make a mistake:** It's not nice to think about, but you will have to deal with errors from time to time. When it happens, be upfront and ready to propose a solution when you talk to the customer. Fixing the problem may cost you money, but you'll keep your customers happy and they'll call you again. Most people realize that mistakes can happen and will react reasonably if you give them a prompt, honest response to the problem.

3.7 Referral bonus

Word of mouth works wonderfully, but sometimes people need a little incentive to get them to spread the word. Try offering a few dollars off to *both* parties if a referral is made. You could go a little further by increasing the discount based on the number of people involved. For example, say you charge $69 for aeration of an average-sized lawn. Offer $5 off to both parties if a referral is made to someone in a nearby neighborhood, and $10 off for all three if a third neighbor is included. How far you go will depend on your circumstances and how close the neighbors are. Be sure to draw the line somewhere or you'll be working for free.

3.8 Flyers

If you are starting a brand-new company, you probably have no clients and not much money to spend on advertising. However, flyers can be produced cheaply and can be delivered by you (and perhaps some loyal friends or family).

The best jobs to start out with are general cleanups. Make this the focal point of your first flyer (see Sample 1). Of course, you want to mention that you offer other services (such as weekly lawn and garden maintenance), but most folks will be hesitant about committing to a lot of work without knowing your reputation or seeing you in action. A cleanup is a good way to show your customer what you are made of.

One advantage of delivering flyers is that it gives you an opportunity to assess the lawns and yards in a neighborhood. Target those neighborhoods where people own their homes (renters generally do not want to spend money on their landlord's house). Leave your flyers at each house, even if everything looks great (you may be pleasantly surprised if these people call). When you come across a home that you can see needs some work, knock on the door and introduce yourself to the homeowner. I cannot stress enough what an impact this has on a potential customer. You are showing that you are motivated and excited about your work. Offer to give them a quote for the work right now. Often they will accept it on the spot!

Delivering flyers is an effective and efficient means of marketing if you are targeting a specific neighborhood for lawn care services. You can focus on one area, and once you get your first customer on a block, you can then deliver special flyers to everyone else on the block (not just once, but once per month), mentioning that you are currently working on the block and that you are accepting new customers (see Sample 2).

Note: Never give the address of existing customers on a flyer without their express consent.

You can also post some of your flyers on community bulletin boards. If you choose this method of advertising, you must be diligent about replacing the flyers periodically. You'll also want to have some tear-off tabs with your name and phone number that potential clients can take away with them. Tear off a couple of the tabs before you post your flyer so people think you've already attracted other customers. Most people don't want to think they are the only one interested.

FALL CLEANUPS
by
TUXEDO PROPERTY MAINTENANCE COMPANY

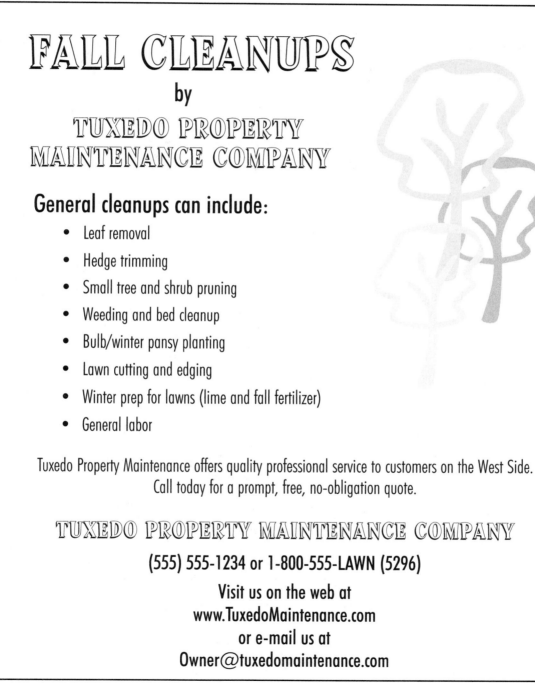

General cleanups can include:

- Leaf removal
- Hedge trimming
- Small tree and shrub pruning
- Weeding and bed cleanup
- Bulb/winter pansy planting
- Lawn cutting and edging
- Winter prep for lawns (lime and fall fertilizer)
- General labor

Tuxedo Property Maintenance offers quality professional service to customers on the West Side. Call today for a prompt, free, no-obligation quote.

TUXEDO PROPERTY MAINTENANCE COMPANY

(555) 555-1234 or 1-800-555-LAWN (5296)

Visit us on the web at
www.TuxedoMaintenance.com
or e-mail us at
Owner@tuxedomaintenance.com

Since We're in the Neighborhood...
Please Accept Our Invitation

TUXEDO PROPERTY MAINTENANCE COMPANY

is providing the following professional services to many of your neighbors:

- Lawn cutting and edging
- Bed and plant maintenance
- Lawn fertilizer programs
- Lawn weed control
- Trimming and pruning
- Planting and bed design
- Cleanups
- And more!

Your first regular maintenance visit is free with any multi-month lawn care program!

Tuxedo Maintenance offers top-quality lawn care and gardening services to customers on the West Side. Call today for a prompt, free, no-obligation quote.

TUXEDO PROPERTY MAINTENANCE COMPANY

(555) 555-1234 or 1-800-555-LAWN (5296)

www.TuxedoMaintenance.com
Owner@tuxedomaintenance.com

3.9 Door hangers

You can use door hangers the same way you do flyers. They are a step up: a little prettier to look at and a classier form of advertising. However, they are also more expensive. If you can afford it, you may find door hangers are more effective than flyers.

3.10 Newspaper classifieds

Advertising in the classified section of your local newspaper can be effective. The key is consistency. As with all advertising, you build consumer confidence each time a customer sees your name. If you are going to use classifieds, sign up for a regular weekly spot. If the paper comes out more than once a week and your budget does not permit putting an ad in each issue, then at least have a regular ad in the weekend edition. Most people will need to see your name many, many times before they call you.

You can insert a simple small ad, saying something like: "Spring cleanups. Hard workers, professional standards, reasonable rates. Satisfaction guaranteed. Ask about lawn care services too. Call for prompt attention. 555-555-5555."

Consider posting the ad in more than one section. For example, there may be separate classified sections for lawn care, gardening, and landscaping.

3.11 Display ads

A display ad makes a bigger statement and is more likely to be found by the casual reader who is not necessarily looking for lawn care services. However, you pay dearly for this privilege. As a result, display ads are not a good idea when you're starting out, but keep them in mind as your business develops.

3.12 Yellow Pages

The best thing about the Yellow Pages is that prospects who go there are actually looking for you! The bad news is that you are placing yourself in amongst all your competition. Still, there is no denying that Yellow Pages make the phone ring.

In most cities, if you buy a business telephone line you get a regular listing in the Yellow Pages. Anything more than that — bold printing, an extra line, or a display ad — will cost extra, and the price may be prohibitive when you are starting up. As you gain experience and have a bigger advertising budget, you can consider a bigger ad.

The Yellow Pages organization may offer you a slight discount on an ad if you display a truck sign that reads: "Find me in the Yellow Pages." I don't recommend this scheme. If your customers are already exposed to you (through your truck signs), why introduce them to your competition?

3.13 Direct mail

Direct mail involves mailing your advertisement to select groups. Often your ad is part of a package with material from other local businesses. This, too, is an effective way to get the phone to ring, but it is another expensive venture. Once you are established, you may want to consider direct mail, as you can focus your mailing so it only goes to your preferred demographic (e.g., home owners). Sample 3 shows a direct mail ad. The original was printed on two sides and in two colours to be eye-catching.

Don't underestimate the power of direct mail. If you do choose to go this route, make sure you are ready for the response.

SAMPLE 3
DIRECT MAIL AD (2 SIDED)

Roving reporter Hort I. Culture has the word from the grass...

"Dirty Deeds can punch holes in me anytime. It helps me grow in my poor soil base and when they're done I feel like I can lift 100 pounds."
—*Mrs. Clay Soil of Richmond*

"I've been living with moss for years and they're really quite greedy, always trying to take over. And every time my owners remove them, they're back in no time. The slit seeder is going to give me a lot of new friends and together we can conquer that moss... and weeds too!"
— *Mr. Moss Nomore of North Vancouver*

"Our caretakers have been pretty good by renting an aerating machine each year. Although I love the relief, I'm still a little cramped with just 6 or 7 holes per square foot, I heard Dirty Deeds gives most lawns 12. WOW! And I'm secretly hoping they'll do me again in the fall."
— *The Needlove Family of West Vancouver*

"I Love Dirty Deeds! They show my owner how to look after me in a way that's totally environmentally friendly. I even heard they'll be offering organic fertilizers. I hope they have a spring special so more of the people can see this."
— *Mr. & Mrs. Nochem of Vancouver.*

SPRING SPECIALS

$15 Value

FREE
LAWN CONDITIONER
APPLICATION
with lawn aeration service

Most Front & Back yards aerated for **$68**

* We use quality Dolomite Lime

Lawn Overseeding Services

$30 off

With Slit Seeding we can offer the finest:
• Power Rakes • Lawn Renovations
• Lawn Rejuvenations
• Inexpensive New Lawns
Prices vary - Please call for free quotation

SEE HOW AERATION HELPS YOUR LAWN

POOR TURF COMPACTED SOIL — AERATION - COMPACTION RELIEVED — DEEP ROOTING BEGINS — THICK, HEALTHY TURF

Day 1   Day 10   Day 20

Listen to your lawn and call Dirty Deeds today
Dirty Deeds — Lawn Aeration & Overseeding Specialists
Just mention this ad to qualify for savings!

CALL **987-6639** OR **941-1496**

Urgent Press Release to Lawns and Turfgrass!

Local Company Brings Magic of Slit Seeding to Lower Mainland Lawns

We Offer the Best Quality Aeration Too!

Lawns everywhere are overjoyed this week as Dirty Deeds, a lawn care company serving the lower mainland for five years were the first to declare "We are the lawn aerating and overseeding specialists".

Overseeding is the process of adding seed to your lawn without damaging the existing turf. Slit seeding offers the benefit of installing the seed into the ground at just the right depth for fast germination. Word has it that slit seeding will take Vancouver by storm. Latest reports tell us that shock had turned to elation as

thousands of lawns are rejoicing and looking forward to coming out of dormancy in the hope that their caretakers have heard the news.

Inside sources report that Dirty Deeds also offers the finest quality core aeration, an important and mostly over looked aspect of lawn care. Not only does it relieve compaction and allow water, fertilizer and oxygen direct access to roots, it also reduces thatch and improves the turf's strength.

Dirty Deeds Lawn Aeration

Call 987-6639 or 941-1496

3.14 Outdoor signs

Outdoor signs can be effective if they are tasteful and placed carefully. Your job is to beautify, so you don't want to litter the landscape with an ugly or badly situated sign. Some customers may let you post a small sign on their lawn for a limited time, but you may have to offer a small amount of money for the privilege.

3.15 Telemarketing

There are times when marketing by phone can be effective. Once people know that you are a local small business owner and not a typical telemarketer, they will be surprisingly accommodating. Use a reverse phone book (with listings by phone number rather than name) from the library to target neighborhoods.

The key is to keep your presentation short and to the point. For example, you could say: "Hi, my name is Johnny Professional and I'm calling from Johnny's Professional Lawn Care Services. We will be in your neighborhood next week doing lawn aeration and fertilizer applications. Since we will be in your area already, we are offering a $10 discount off our regular price of $69 for average-sized lawns. Would you be interested in taking advantage of this opportunity?"

The best time to reach people is between 6:00 p.m. and 8:00 p.m., but be aware that you might be interrupting people at their evening meal.

3.16 Local newspaper article

Community newspapers often publish special editions on home improvement and/or repair. Call your local paper and ask if they have one coming up and if they accept informational articles. If they do, write an article on whatever gardening topic you feel most knowledgeable about. Keep the article informative, telling homeowners how they can do the task themselves, and also telling them how they would go about hiring a professional to do it. List questions they should ask the professional and what they should look for when hiring someone.

Next, place a display ad, offering the type of service that you have detailed, within a few pages of the article. Then sit back and wait for the phone to ring. When it does, you will be ready to answer all the questions that you've told them to ask!

3.17 Cause-related marketing

When businesses affiliate themselves with charities or causes to provide mutual benefits, they are doing cause-related marketing. If there's a charity you believe in supporting, have a promotion and let customers know that your business will put aside a certain percentage of income for that charity. When you choose this method of marketing, be sure to keep it up so your customers understand that you truly believe in helping others and are not just doing it to attract attention. Of course you get attention, and there is nothing wrong with that, but it should not be the primary reason for doing it.

3.18 Volunteer opportunities

An excellent way to set your company apart from others is to volunteer some time to a community project. It may be a community garden or perhaps sponsoring litter removal on a stretch of road. A sign describing the project, with your company name on it, provides good advertising.

3.19 Newsletters

Create and distribute a newsletter for existing clients and prospects. This will help upsell existing clients and let prospects know you are a professional. The newsletter could feature specials of the month, an informative article or two about gardening and lawn care, some fun items such as a gardening-related crossword or word search, and, of course, a blurb about your company. You can create a simple one- or two-page newsletter on your computer.

4. YOUR MARKETING CALENDAR

Now it's time to create your own personal marketing calendar. This is where you plan your marketing efforts for at least one year in advance.

Go through all the specific marketing ideas discussed in this chapter and make a note of those you would like to use in your business. Think about how you can adapt them to your own situation and when is the best time of year to use each method you have selected. Don't forget to consider how much each will cost. Your budget will dictate much of your marketing calendar.

Sample 4 shows a typical marketing calendar for a small landscaping business.

SAMPLE 4
MARKETING CALENDAR

Marketing Method	Planned Start Date	Duration in Weeks	Cost	Description
Business Cards	Jan 1/2005	N/A	$84	5,000 business cards — full color, brochure style
T-Shirts	Jan 2/2005	N/A	$120	5 @ $24 with logo
Spring Flyers	Feb 15/2005	4	$80	2,000 flyers for spring specials; distributed to select neighborhoods
Local Paper Classified Ad	Mar 15/2005	10	$600	Advertise for new lawn cuts; $60/week for three editions of the paper each week
Bulletin Boards	Mar 15/2005	12	$-	Post flyer at four known bulletin boards
Free Gifts	Apr 1/2005	2	$40	Flat of lilies to give to new customers
Glossy Flyer	Apr 1/2005	4	$60	200 glossy flyers to promote summer planting; mostly for existing customers
Summer Survey	Jun 1/2005	1	$-	Design our own survey to see how we're doing; for all existing customers
Local Paper Classified Ad	Jun 1/2005	12	$300	Move to once per week only throughout the summer; $25/week, paid monthly
Fall Flyers	Sep 1/2005	4	$80	2,000 flyers for fall cleanups and other specials; distributed to select neighborhoods
Local Paper Classified Ad	Sep 1/2005	8	$480	Move back to three times per week for classified advertising; $60/week, paid monthly
Original Thank-You Cards	Nov 15/2005	1	$-	Create our own original thank-you cards (handwritten on the inside) for all customers

7
THE IMPORTANCE OF RECORD KEEPING

For many people, record keeping is a frightening task, a necessary evil that goes along with running a business. Some of you, like me, relish the thought of keeping your own books. You can consider yourself fortunate. You others, take heart: while record keeping is important to the health of your business, it doesn't have to be an onerous task, reconciling bank statements and meticulously entering expense transactions into the wee hours. If you follow the advice in this chapter, your bookkeeping will take all of 15 minutes per day (excluding year-end adjustments, of course).

For now, you only have to understand the basics:

- ✒ The difference between debits and credits and how they relate to your different categories of accounts (assets, liabilities, etc.)

- ✒ The principles of double-entry accrual accounting

- ✒ The difference between an income statement and a balance sheet and how to read them and identify critical profitability issues or problems with your company

Some of this information is included in this chapter, but if you are new to accounting, think about taking a night course to help you learn the basics. Once you've mastered the basics, set a goal of learning more to ensure your business runs smoothly.

1. THREE PRINCIPLES OF RECORD KEEPING

1. As an entrepreneur, make it part of your job to understand the numbers.

One of the keys to business success, well documented by successful business people and authors, is your ability to scrutinize and understand the numbers behind your business. How will you know if you are making money if you don't record your income and expenses and review summary reports? How will you know if you are meeting your goals? How will you know how much money you owe to people and, perhaps more importantly, how much people owe you? Don't view the books as something you have to do to keep the government happy; consider them a key to your success.

2. Use an accountant. The value of an accountant goes much deeper than his or her ability to record transactions. Your accountant can and should help you before you set up your new business or make your first sale. Once your company is up and running, an accountant will know how to interpret the numbers that come from your business and offer you practical advice that will assist you in growth, protect you from taxation ignorance, and help you increase your take-home money. Make your accountant part of your management team.

3. Buy an accounting software package, learn it, and use it. You do not need your accountant to complete the day-to-day transactions. It is obviously cheaper to do it yourself, and it's a good way for you to keep an eye on how you're doing. It should only take a few minutes a day if you use an accounting software package. (See sidebar for a brief outline of the most popular systems.) Check with your accountant to see if he or she has a preference as to the type of software you should use. There is nothing wrong with using expense books and ledgers, but you will want to be particularly well versed in accounting and bookkeeping practices when doing it this way.

Bookkeeping and Accounting — What's the difference?

Bookkeeping is the act of keeping your financial books — that is, the record of the accounts and transactions of a business. Accounting includes bookkeeping, but is much more than that. It entails understanding, explaining, analyzing, justifying, and interpreting what the business is doing based on the reports and ratios that are generated from all your bookkeeping data. Most importantly, it involves making crucial decisions based on the financial information that you derive from your business.

By all means, do your own bookkeeping if you want to, but leave the "real" accounting to the professionals.

Software for Accounting

Before you buy accounting software, I suggest you speak to your accountant. You may want to select the same program that he or she uses so that you can send electronic files at the end of the year.

Simply Accounting <www.simplyaccounting.com>: An excellent, well-rounded package. The Basic version will handle almost anything you need to do, from standard income and expense reporting to more complex things such as budgeting and advanced reporting. The Professional version is often used by professional bookkeepers and accountants. While the software is intuitive, it does help to have some basic accounting knowledge. There is an option within the program to use either accounting or non-accounting terminology.

QuickBooks <quickbooks.intuit.com>: This product comes in Basic, Pro, and Premier versions. The Basic version does not include budgeting features or cash flow projections but will allow you to record business transactions and do your payroll. The Pro version allows more advanced functions, such as budgeting, vehicle mileage tracking, and customization of forms. The Premier version does everything that the Basic and Pro versions do and more, and also allows you to create a business plan.

2. BOOKKEEPING BASICS

Whether you use a manual system or a software package to manage your business finances, it helps to understand some accounting basics. I'll give you a quick introduction to accounting terminology and then describe some typical reports that you'll be generating after you enter your day-to-day transactions such as sales and expenses.

2.1 Cash versus accrual accounting

There are essentially two accepted accounting methods for recording business revenue and expenses: the cash system and the accrual system.

In the cash method, a sale is recorded when the cash is received and an expense is recorded when the cash is paid out. It doesn't matter when the sale or expense occurred, only when the money comes in or leaves your business.

In the accrual method, a sale is recorded when the money is earned — that is, on the day the work is invoiced — and an expense is recorded when the expense is generated, not when it is paid. It doesn't matter when you get paid or when you pay invoices. If you use the accrual method, you must keep track of who owes you money (accounts receivables) and who you owe money to (accounts payable). Accrual accounting is generally the preferred method of keeping books, used by all professionals and by most, if not all, accounting software packages.

To illustrate the difference, suppose you clean up Ms. Jones's yard for $400 on September 29. Unfortunately, she is out when you finish up, so you leave an invoice in her mailbox. Using the accrual system, you record $400 worth of revenue for that day *and* you enter a $400 receivable for Ms. Jones. Using the cash system you record nothing.

Ms. Jones is prompt in paying for your service, and you receive her check in the mail on October 2. In the accrual system, you simply enter a payment for Ms. Jones to remove her receivable from your books and give her a clean slate. With the cash system, now that you have the cash, you record the $400 as revenue.

The cash method is simple, and you may wonder why you would bother with the accrual method. But the accrual method allows you to more accurately monitor your business and your defined goals. Continuing with the above example, let's say that you set a revenue goal of $5,000 for the month of September. When it comes time to review your goals, how will you know how much money you earned in September? You may know how much money came in. but how much of that was payment for services completed in previous months? How much work did you do in September that you did not receive payment for in that month (like Ms. Jones's $400)? The same question applies to expenses. Looking at your summary reports, you would not know in which month the expenses actually occurred. This makes it more difficult to track the finances of your business.

Further, when it comes time to file your income tax return, you may be required to use the accrual system (check with your accountant). If you use the cash system, this means you will need to do extra work to adjust your numbers to meet this requirement.

If you use accounting or business software packages, much of the complexity of

the accrual system occurs in the background. However, if you have your heart set on using the simple cash method, I include instructions for doing this in section **5**.

2.2 Single-entry versus double-entry bookkeeping

Double-entry bookkeeping, which all the professionals use, records every transaction twice: once as a debit and once as a credit. With double-entry accounting, each transaction balances, so it's easy to catch mistakes.

With a single-entry system, you enter transactions once, either as an expense or as revenue. It is easier to make a mistake because there is no check to see if the transaction balances. Entries could be recorded incorrectly, more than once, or not at all. As well, it is more difficult to accurately track and balance bank and cash accounts.

The single-entry system is easier, so you may be inclined to use it. But in the long run you will benefit from using double-entry accounting. If you use an accounting software program, it simplifies things considerably.

2.3 Debits versus credits

We all use the words "debit" and "credit" a lot and have been conditioned to believe that credits are good and debits are bad. We are happy when the bank tells us it is putting a credit on our account. We know that when we use our debit card, the balance in our account goes down and that's bad.

It is unfortunate that this view has been reinforced because, from an accounting standpoint, debits are neither good nor bad. In fact, as we just saw, in a double-entry accounting system, each transaction has both a debit and a credit side.

The easiest way to understand debits and credits is to think that when a business *gets* something it is a debit, and where that something *came from* is always the credit. For example, suppose you pay cash for fertilizer. Ask yourself: What did I get and where did it come from? You got fertilizer, so that is the debit side of the transaction: an expense for supplies. Where did it come from? Cash, so that's the credit side of the transaction.

No doubt you will come across some transactions that stump you. That's where having an accountant comes in handy. Flag the transaction so you can ask your accountant about it on your next visit, or have him or her double-check your work and make an adjusting entry if necessary.

Having said that, double-entry accrual accounting is not as hard as you think. Once again, I urge you to see understanding how your accounting system works as part of your job as a business owner. You need to play many parts when you own a small business, and bookkeeper/accountant is one of them.

3. USING BUSINESS FORMS

There are a number of forms that you will use to keep track of the numbers behind your business. If you use a computerized accounting package, it should be able to produce these forms. If you use a manual method, such as the one described in section **5**, you will need to purchase preprinted forms from an office supply store.

3.1 Chart of accounts

The chart of accounts is your map to your bookkeeping system. It is a list of all your accounts and their account numbers, grouped by category. The categories are assets, liabilities, capital, income, and expense. The first three categories are recorded on your balance sheet; the final two categories, income and expense, are reported on your profit and loss statement.

Sample 5 shows a typical chart of accounts for a lawn maintenance company. According to standard accounting practices, account

---

Do I Need a Separate Business Banking Account?

In short, yes. The record keeping for your own business is challenging enough without complicating things by mixing up personal and business money. As well, while most small business owners complain about poor support from banks (since they are considered higher risk), the fact is that a good relationship with your bank and banker is important. You might as well start building that relationship now by opening your own business bank account.

Take care of your credit reputation. Bounced checks look bad on your record, as do late payments to creditors. On the other hand, consistency looks good. Make regular deposits. Stay on top of things by reconciling your account each month. Carry a balance so you are not always hovering around zero. One rule of thumb is to have enough contingency money to run the business for three months with no income. Get a small line of credit or loan that you can pay back easily, and start building great credit. Shop around a little when choosing your bank; some specialize in helping small and local companies. Ask your accountant for a recommendation.

CHART OF ACCOUNTS

DIRTY DEEDS LANDSCAPING
Chart of Accounts

ASSETS

1000	**CURRENT ASSETS**
1050	Petty Cash
1100	Bank Account
1200	Accounts Receivable
1250	Allowance — Doubtful Accts
1300	Prepaid Exp and Deposits
1390	**TOTAL CURRENT ASSETS**
1500	**CAPITAL ASSETS**
1550	Shop Equipment
1600	Motor Vehicles
1650	Computer Equipment
1700	Computer Software
1750	Office Equipment
1890	**TOTAL CAPITAL ASSETS**

LIABILITIES

2000	**CURRENT LIABILITIES**
2100	Accounts Payable
2150	Accrued Liabilities
2200	Customer Deposits
2300	Vacation Payable
2400	WCB Payable
2450	State/Provincial Tax Payable
2550	Tax on Sales Payable
2590	**TOTAL CURRENT LIABILITIES**

2600	**LONG-TERM LIABILITIES**
2620	Bank Loan Payable
2650	Truck Loan Payable
2700	Due to Shareholder
2990	**TOTAL LONG-TERM LIABILITIES**
	EQUITY
3010	Owner's Equity
3500	Retained Earnings
	REVENUE
4000	**REVENUE**
4040	Commercial Contracts
4050	Residential Contracts
4080	Interest Income
4100	Gross Revenue
4390	**TOTAL REVENUE**
	EXPENSES
5000	**COST OF GOODS**
5010	Fertilizers
5020	Landscape Materials
5030	Subcontracts
5040	Direct Labour
5050	Direct Payroll Taxes
5060	Waste Disposal
5070	Equipment Rentals
5080	Small Tools & Equipment
5090	Equipment Expense
5100	Worker's Compensation Expense
5200	Freight Expense
5290	**TOTAL COST OF GOODS SOLD**

5300	**GENERAL AND ADMINISTRATIVE**
5310	Amortization
5320	Advertising
5330	Automotive Expenses
5340	Automotive Insurance
5350	Bad Debts
5360	Bank Charges & Interest
5370	Consulting
5380	Commercial Vehicles — Insurance
5390	Commercial Vehicles — Expenses
5400	Course Fees & Training
5410	Dining
5420	Insurance
5430	Internet Access
5440	Licenses, Fees, & Subscriptions
5450	Management Salaries
5460	Miscellaneous
5470	Office Supplies
5480	Postage
5490	Professional Fees
5500	Promotion & Business Development
5510	Rent
5520	Telephone & Fax
5530	Travel
5540	Utilities
5999	**TOTAL GENERAL AND ADMINISTRATIVE**

numbers are four digits long and are origi-
nally entered in multiples of ten. This lets
you add new accounts in between existing
ones and still maintain a logical or alphabet-
ical order. As well, each number is coded
according to what type of account it is: asset
accounts start with 1; liabilities start with 2;
capital accounts start with 3; revenue or
income accounts start with 4; and expense
accounts start with 5.

Any accounting software package will
start you off with a default chart of accounts
with the appropriate account numbers, so
you don't have to worry about setting it up
properly. Follow the convention as you customize it for the lawn care industry.

3.2 Invoices

Even though your accounting software will
print invoices, you should still buy some
preprinted ones to keep in the truck for ad
hoc jobs. Don't forget to enter the invoice
into the computer when you get home.

For scheduled jobs, you will print out
invoices from whatever software you decide
to use. You'll prepare an invoice for your regular maintenance customers at the end of
the month, detailing all the work you completed during that month. To encourage
prompt payment, make the due date clear.
There may be a spot for it at the top of the
invoice, and in the comments section of the
invoice you could write something such as
"Your prompt payment is important to us.
Thank you" or "Thank you for your prompt
payment." Also include a return mailing
envelope. Use your computer to create
address labels with your business name and
address so that you can stick them on the
return envelopes. Better yet, purchase return

envelopes with all your information preprinted on the front.

For ad hoc jobs, one-time jobs, or jobs
that do not fall under the maintenance
agreement, I suggest leaving invoices with
customers when you have completed the job
to their satisfaction. If the customer is home,
he or she may pay you right away. If not,
then leave the invoice in the mailbox. (Use
discretion with new customers, especially
with bigger jobs. You may want to coordinate it so that the customer is home when
you finish so you can collect payment.)

3.3 The profit and loss statement

The profit and loss (P&L) statement is sometimes called the income statement. It deals
only with two categories of accounts from
your chart of accounts: revenue (or sales) and
expenses. It is an important summary that lists
all your income and expenses for a specified
period. The net result is your profit or loss.

A P&L statement should be completed
each month so you can monitor the status of
the business. As well, at the end of your fiscal year, you or your accountant should prepare a P&L statement that covers the entire
year. Comparative P&L statements are excellent tools. You can compare month to month
or year to year to see if expenses are going up
or revenues declining.

A variety of the P&L statement is the pro
forma statement, which is a statement you
prepare before the fiscal year begins. In it,
you project your revenues and expenses for
the coming period (usually a year). You will
need a pro forma P&L statement for your
business plan, and you should create a new
one each year to gauge how your business is

doing in comparison to the goals on the previous year's pro forma statement.

See Sample 6 for an example of a P&L statement with three main sections: revenue, cost of sales, and general overhead.

Revenue, or income, refers to the money you take in as sales. Note that in the sample, the revenue is grouped by the type of work. It is a good idea to do this so you can discern which services are generating what portion of your income. Alternatively, you may want to separate revenue by crews (if you have more than one) or by geographic location. Use a system that you think will help you provide direction for your company.

The rest of the P&L statement deals with expenses, but it is common practice to divide those expenses into cost of sales (also called cost of goods) and general overhead (or general and administrative expenses). Cost of sales are expenses that are directly related to your sales. These numbers will change in proportion to your sales, as opposed to general overhead, which tends to stay the same even if there is no revenue at all. For example, landscaping supplies, equipment rentals, and your equipment would be listed under cost of sales, because the amount you spend would increase or decrease based on how many sales you have. On the other hand, a truck lease, office or garage rental, and costs associated with administrative staff would be general overhead, because those costs occur whether you make any sales or not.

3.4 The balance sheet

Whereas the P&L statement is a record of business activity over a specified period of time (a month or a year), the balance sheet is a snapshot of the business at a given time. It is a picture of assets, liabilities, and net worth on a particular day. A balance sheet should be part of your business plan and should be completed regularly. Balance sheets are often comparative, so you can easily evaluate how your business is doing. See an illustration of a balance sheet in Sample 7.

The basis of a balance sheet is the age-old accounting principle:

ASSETS – LIABILITIES = NET EQUITY

The balance sheets lists only these three things, and it must *always* balance (which is why it is called a balance sheet).

On the balance sheet, the "assets" category is divided into current and capital assets. Current assets are generally those that will be realized, consumed, or sold within the business cycle (generally a year). Cash is an obvious entry here, as are bank accounts. Don't forget about accounts receivable; they are *almost* cash. Finally, any prepaid expenses or deposits should be listed in this category too.

Capital assets are more permanent. Their value is generally greater than $200, and there should be no expectation that you will liquidate them within the year. They include your vehicle, lawn equipment, computer hardware and software, office equipment, furniture, fixtures, land, and buildings.

The sum of current and capital assets is your total assets.

Liabilities include all the money you owe. As with assets, liabilities are broken into current and long-term liabilities. Current liabilities include accounts payable (the short-term money you owe to vendors), payroll taxes, and other taxes you owe at any

SAMPLE 6
COMPARATIVE PROFIT AND LOSS STATEMENT

Comparative Profit and Loss Statement: 20-- & 20--

GREENER GRASS LAWN AND GARDEN

	20--		20--	
Revenue (Sales)				
Commercial Maintenance	75,463.32		90,367.77	
Residential Maintenance	30,563.36		31,365.98	
Other Maintenance	1,237.00		870.33	
Lawn Renovations	45,663.00		48,987.00	
Other Lawn Care	4,688.14		6,988.14	
Landscaping	6,969.33		15,899.00	
All Other Revenue				
Total Revenue		$164,584.15		$194,478.22
Expenses				
Cost of Sales				
Fertilizers & Other Lawn Treatments	3,563.25		4,502.36	
Landscape Materials	7,589.77		11,188.97	
Subcontracts	4,600.00		4,800.00	
Direct Labor	21,050.00		29,060.00	
Direct Payroll Taxes	2,492.36		3,001.00	
Waste Disposal	1,300.00		1,800.00	
Equipment Rentals	3,846.25		3,525.25	
Small Tools & Equipment	546.25		658.25	
Equipment — R & M	1,950.87		1,780.00	
Equipment Fuel	290.20		310.93	
Workers' Compensation	3,324.87		4,236.00	
Total Cost of Goods Sold		$50,553.82		$64,862.76
Gross Profit		$114,030.33		$129,615.46

	20--	20--
General Overhead		
Advertising	4,560.00	5,100.00
Car — Lease	1,800.00	1,800.00
Car — Gas & Oil	600.00	600.00
Car — R & M	400.00	300.00
Car — Insurance	550.00	550.00
Car — Other Expenses		
Bad Debts	0.00	125.00
Bank Interest & Charges	300.00	300.00
Depreciation Expenses	13,752.00	14,785.00
Truck — Lease	12,000.00	12,000.00
Truck — Gas & Oil	4,800.00	5,900.00
Truck — R & M	1,600.00	2,200.00
Truck — Insurance	3,000.00	3,000.00
Truck — Other Expenses		
Entertainment	280.00	360.00
Business Insurance	1,500.00	1,500.00
Internet Access	360.00	360.00
Computer Expenses	1,250.00	230.00
Licenses, Fees, & Subscriptions	150.00	280.00
Office Supplies	360.00	650.00
Postage	240.00	300.00
Professional Fees	400.00	800.00
Rent/Office Space		
Telephone and Fax	480.00	480.00
Travel Expenses		
Utilities	600.00	600.00
Miscellaneous	258.47	480.88
Total General & Administrative	$49,240.47	$52,700.88
Net Income	$64,789.86	$76,914.58

SAMPLE 7
BALANCE SHEET

GREENER GRASS LAWN AND GARDEN
Balance Sheet — January 1, 20--

ASSETS

Current Assets

Bank Account	$ 2,140.00	
Accounts Receivable	$ -	
Prepaid Expenses	$ 320.00	
Total Current Assets		$ 2,460.00

Capital Assets

Shop Equipment	$ 2,400.00	
Shop Equipment — Accum Amortization	$ -	
Shop Equipment — Net		$ 2,400.00
Truck & Trailer	$ 8,000.00	
Truck/Trailer — Accum Amortization	$ -	
Truck/Trailer — Net		$ 8,000.00
Total Capital Assets		**$ 10,400.00**
TOTAL ASSETS		$ 12,860.00

LIABILITIES

Current Liabilities

Accounts Payable	$ -	
Total Current Liabilities		$ -

Long-Term Liabilities

Trailer Loan	$ 3,500.00	
Total Long-Term Liabilities		$ 3,500.00
TOTAL LIABILITIES		$ 3,500.00

EQUITY

Owner's Equity		$ 9,360.00
Retained Earnings		$ -
TOTAL EQUITY		$ 9,360.00
TOTAL LIABILITIES & EQUITY		$ 12,860.00

given time. These are expenses you expect to pay off within one year.

Long-term liabilities include bank loans, vehicle loans, mortgages on commercial property, and any loan that will exist for over a year.

The sum of current and long-term liabilities is your total liabilities.

Finally, on the balance sheet, is net equity (also called net worth, owner's capital, or owner's equity). It is made up of the owner's initial investment as well as any retained earnings (or losses) that are reinvested into the business.

4. COMPUTERIZED BOOKKEEPING

If you have decided to use your computer to track your sales and expenses, you will need a computer (obviously), an accounting software package and/or a lawn company operator (LCO) software package, and a box of 8" x 11" manila envelopes

4.1 Using the software

I recommend that you use both an accounting software package and an LCO package if you plan on growing your company at all. (If you will be staying small, you can manage with just the accounting package.) The accounting package will let you generate all sorts of reports and summaries, many of which are probably not available from the LCO software. On the other hand, the LCO software will handle industry-specific challenges such as scheduling, routing, and job costing.

There will be some overlap between the two programs you choose, so you'll have to decide which program does what job. Keep in mind that the LCO software is good for tracking anything to do with customers, including names, addresses, and contact information. As well, it will track each customer's individual job history, including what tasks were completed, when, and for how much. It is easy to mark jobs completed, print invoices, and apply customer payments with LCO software. For these reasons, it's best to do anything customer specific in the LCO software. There is no need to duplicate work by entering customer information into the accounting software.

Here is how you can effectively divide the functions of the two software packages:

1. Print invoices from the LCO software. When you print an invoice, the software will remember how much that customer owes (the receivable).

2. When a customer pays, enter the payment in the LCO software to clear the customer's account. Put the payments all together for a weekly (at least) deposit.

3. Track your accounts receivable in the LCO software. Keep a complete list of all the people who owe you money, how much they owe, and how long they have owed it to you. Check it regularly.

4. At the end of each month, enter monthly revenue totals (which you get from the LCO software) into the accounting software. Don't forget to break out the tax, if applicable. (If you want to break down your revenue into groups, as discussed earlier, you would make several revenue entries, but you would still do it only once per

month.) You can create a single "customer" in your accounting software, perhaps called "All Sales." When you enter the revenue totals, enter them as a receivable for this customer. When you are done it will look like one customer, "All Sales," owes the entire revenue balance.

5. Enter the weekly bank deposit into the accounting software. (You have already recorded each individual payment into your LCO software to update everyone's accounts.) Then the entire deposit can be applied to "All Sales."

6. Put everything to do with expenses in the accounting software only.

7. Print out P&L statements and balance sheets from your accounting program. Print out daily work summaries, accounts receivable reports, job-costing reports, and other customer-specific items from your LCO software.

With this system, you have the best of both worlds: LCO software that tracks customer job history, payments owing, and detailed job costing; accounting software that provides an up-to-date bank account and an accurate total for the accounts receivable.

Ideally, you will choose an LCO package that is compatible with your accounting program, making this system easy to use.

4.2 The manila envelope system

Use manila envelopes to collect your expense receipts. Use one envelope per month and write the month (without the year) in big letters on the front. At the end of the year, put all the receipts together into one envelope (staple or paper clip each month's receipts together to keep them organized).

Label that envelope with the year and reuse your 12 envelopes over again for the new year. (You will need to keep your receipts for seven years before throwing them out.)

Put all your expense receipts in these envelopes. Keep a separate envelope in the truck for receipts from incidentals that you purchase on impulse or as needed. Empty it at the end of the month and add it to the envelope in your office so that all your expense receipts are in the same place. Don't forget to write a description of the purchase on the receipt in case it is not obvious. Also note if you paid cash or used a credit card, or write the check number on the receipt. You will need all this information when you enter the transactions in the accounting software.

If you record your expenses every day, it will only take a few minutes. Leaving it until the end of the month makes it more difficult, particularly if something is not clear and you find yourself relying on your memory. For the same reason, it's a good idea to record work as you complete it each day and to record payments as your customers send you money. The LCO packages make these tasks quick and simple.

5. USING A CASH SYSTEM

If you won't be using a computer, you'll need to buy preprinted invoice books (in triplicate), a box of 8" x 11" manila envelopes, a 28-column ledger, and a 4-column ledger.

5.1 Invoice books

Fill in your invoices manually as you complete each job, or do them at the end of the month for your regular maintenance customers. If you buy invoices in triplicate, you can give one copy to your customer, keep one copy in the invoice book until the customer pays (then that copy can be kept in a customer file or attached to the bank deposit slip), and save the last copy for your own records. Generally each copy is a different color, so it will be easy to see who still owes you money by leafing through the invoice book.

5.2 Manila envelopes

Use the manila envelopes as described in section **4.2**.

5.3 The 28-column ledger

You use the large ledger to track daily expenses and monthly revenue. This is called the general ledger. You may need to sit at a large desk or a kitchen table to use it.

You use the columns to record many different types of expenses. Column 1 is for the date, column 2 for a description of the expense (e.g., "deposit from sales"), column 3 for a check number or some other code. After that, the columns are used for amounts. For example, use the next two columns for your bank account: one of the columns for "in" (debits) and the other for "out" (credits).

This ledger is your check register as well as your general journal. Each time money goes out of or is put into your bank account, it should be a line entry in your ledger. You can use this information to reconcile your bank account each month when you get your statement.

The next columns are used in the same way (i.e., double columns) for cash, tax (GST in Canada or state tax where applicable),

and revenue. The remaining columns, or as many as needed, are for expenses, one for each column. You can use your chart of accounts to put all your expenses under headings.

However many categories you have, label the last column "Draws." This is where you would record, for example, a truck payment, where only the interest is deductible and the principal is not. Also, if you write yourself a check as a salary draw, you would put it in here.

5.4 The 4-column ledger

You will use the smaller ledger to create a profit and loss statement and an accounts receivable statement at the end of each month.

Remember that the profit and loss (or income) statement records your income and your expenses for a specific period. All the data you need to complete the income statement will be in the large ledger. Plug the numbers in and subtract your expenses from your revenue to get your profit (I hope!).

It is important to stay on top of customers who owe you money. In a manual system you should list all your receivables each month. To do that, go through your invoice book and, on a page in the 4-column ledger, write the name of each customer who owes you money, the date the work was completed, and the total amount owing to you. Take special note of customers who are being carried forward from the previous month. Perhaps they need a reminder (see section **2** of chapter 11 on collections). Review your receivables weekly so you do not lose track of any of them.

5.5 How to use the system

This is a cash system, which means you record transactions when they enter or leave your bank account, not necessarily on the date that the transaction was completed. Remember, too, that this is a double-entry system, so each transaction or line item in the general journal should have two or more entries that balance.

Let's look at a few examples to see how this system works.

Example 1 — A deposit

You receive a few checks throughout the week, and on Friday you deposit $1,480 in the bank. It's easy to see that your bank account goes up, but how will you apportion this money? Your revenue will go up, but don't forget about tax. You may need to refer to the original invoice to see how much tax you collected. Put the numbers in the ledger. The bank amount should equal the sum of the revenue and the tax.

You can either list each individual customer payment in your ledger or simply post the totals. It depends on how much detail you want. Whichever method you choose, record the names of each customer and the amount of his or her check or cash on your bank deposit slip so that you have something to go back to if you are not sure if they paid. Remember to rip out the middle invoice in your invoice book when a customer's check is deposited.

Example 2 — Purchases by cash or check

When you make a purchase with cash or a check, money is coming out of your bank or the cash account, and the funds are expensed to one of your expense categories. Don't forget to break out the tax.

Example 3 — Payment for home, car, and other split expenses

Some of your expenses are not fully deductible, such as the rental for your home (of which you can deduct a proportion for your office) or the fuel for your car (which you may use sometimes when you drive out to do job quotes). For our example, let's say you paid $90 for your home gas bill. If you use 20 percent of your home for dedicated business purposes, you are allowed to write off 20 percent of $90 or $18. The other 80 percent will be counted as a salary draw, since you are using it for a personal expense. Therefore, the money comes out of the bank and is expensed by splitting it between home office expenses ($18) and draws ($72).

Having said that, if you use an accountant it is much easier for you to record the entire amount as a home office expense and allow your accountant to make a single adjusting entry at the end of the year.

Example 4 — Check to yourself

In a sole proprietorship, the money you take out of the business for yourself is not expensed (as it would be in a limited company). You and the business are the same entity, so the money you take out is counted as your personal draws (and you may be taxed on it). Hence, drawings from the company simply go into the draws column.

A final piece of advice: In your general journal, it is beneficial to have a running total for the year at the bottom of each month. That way you can see how you are doing from month to month. Similarly, there is no law that says income statements must cover only one month or one year. You should also have a year-to-date income statement to see if the business is profitable or not.

8
BUILDING YOUR TEAM: HIRING AND TRAINING STAFF

At some point you'll have to decide whether you want to stay small and remain a one-person show, or if you want to grow and hire more people. My experience is that the landscape maintenance business works well with two people. Once you get to know each other and start anticipating each other's moves, you'll find you can do the jobs more quickly and efficiently. As well, it's always nice to have someone to talk to. My advice, even if you plan on staying small, is to become big enough to keep you and a helper busy. A husband-wife team can work well for couples who don't mind being together 24 hours a day.

Of course, if you plan on growing your business, you will need more than one staff member or helper — you'll need a steady stream of them. If you have seasonal demands, you might hire help on a subcontract basis, but if your needs are long-term, you'll have to hire full-time employees and learn how to be a boss.

1. USING SUBCONTRACTORS

If you don't need permanent help, hiring subcontractors is an option for those times when you are too busy to manage on your own. The advantage to subcontracting is that you don't have to collect payroll tax or do the paperwork that comes with employees. In a subcontract situation, you hire someone for a limited time and he or she invoices you at the end of the job.

You can subcontract on a larger scale when a customer needs specialty work done. For example, you might consider subcontracting such things as tree work, irrigation, chemical applications, and complicated landscaping to other companies that can handle those jobs. You bill the customer for the subcontractor's work, and then you pay the subcontractor directly.

The customer may or may not know that you subcontracted the job. It doesn't matter, because if there are problems, you are the one who will hear about it. You are ultimately responsible for the quality of the work and any issues that arise from it.

If you subcontract a company to do a specific job, you need to decide what markup you will add to its fee when you invoice the customer. The markup will depend on what the job is and how big it is. You should mark up at least 10 percent and probably more in the 20 percent to 25 percent range. This is not money for nothing or an attempt to gouge the customer. It covers the fact that you are left with the responsibilities, costs, and risks of invoicing, carrying the receivable, and dealing with any problems.

Since you are responsible for the final product, choose your subcontractors carefully. Don't necessarily go for the cheapest. Ask other gardeners who they use. Check out companies before you hire them. Look at the work they have done. If you come across an example of excellent service in your travels, find out who did it. If you find reliable contractors, stay on good terms with them. Remember that these relationships are mutually beneficial.

Also remember that your subcontractors will not be covered under your liability and workers' compensation insurance. Make sure they have their own and that their coverage is at least what yours is. Ask them to prove it.

2. THE JOY OF EMPLOYEES

Employees can be a bane or a boon to your business. I was fortunate to have a longtime, faithful staff member, Mark. He loved to work, was passionate about the industry, and was absolutely dependable. In the early days it was just the two of us and we worked together like a well-oiled machine. Later Mark had his own work vehicle, ran his own crews from his home, operated the business for weeks at a time while I took downtime, and did it all with little direction from me.

The Marks of the world are the exception, however. Every employee you hire will be different, with his or her own strengths and weaknesses. Some will work well for you and others will be challenges.

You can avoid costly hiring mistakes if you take your time in the hiring process. Give some thought to where you will look for employees, whether or not you want to advertise, what questions you should ask when you interview potential employees, and how to train them once they are on the job. Of course, you'll also have to learn how to manage your team to keep it happy, and sometimes you'll even have to fire an employee.

All these topics are covered below. I hope my advice helps you find your Mark.

3. WHERE TO FIND GOOD STAFF

It is not uncommon to have interested individuals call you looking for a job. Follow up with them as you already know they are self-starters.

If you get eager workers knocking at your door, your job is much easier. Often, however, you will need to advertise for help. The best place to start is in the classified section of your local paper. Write a brief job description and your expectations. Don't mention a wage or salary in the ad and don't use language that may be construed as discriminatory (i.e., that mentions age or sex). For example, your ad might read:

Enjoy a fun and healthy work environment on a landscape maintenance crew. Must be energetic and hardworking. Experience in commercial gardening an asset. Call 555-5289.

I recommend listing a phone number instead of a mailing address because it makes it easier for respondents to apply and allows you to screen candidates in phone interviews, spending less time in person-to-person interviews.

If you have a website, you can refer interested applicants to it so they can learn about what your company does and what they will be doing. Have a "Contact Us" section or even a special "Jobs" section where you can provide more details about the job. Invite candidates to leave a message or post their résumés.

If you decide to run your ad in a newspaper that has wider distribution, such as a city paper, you may want to mention what area you live and work in. Once they are hired, you will appreciate the benefits of having your employees live in the same area.

Here are some other good sources of employees:

 Check out schools that offer horticultural training. They are a wonderful breeding ground for enthusiastic employees, particularly if you are looking for part-timers.

 Your local industry association may have leads for avid employees.

 Check the classified ads in your paper for people looking for work. Putting an ad in the paper shows initiative, and you can find out if the individuals are suitable for your particular needs by interviewing them.

 File all suitable résumés you receive, even when you aren't looking for help. You never know when you might need to call on someone at the last minute.

Tip:
Don't forget to check local regulations to determine if there is a limit to the number of employees you can hire in a home-based business.

4. INTERVIEWING TIPS

Whether you're hiring a subcontractor, a part-timer, or a full-timer, once you've narrowed down a list of candidates you'll want to interview them to assess their qualifications. Here are some tips for phone interviews and face-to-face interviews.

4.1 The phone interview

Use the phone interview to narrow your search before meeting face to face, following these steps:

1. Prepare. Have a list of questions ready before you expect the calls to start coming in. During the interview, take notes recording the candidates' responses to your questions.

2. Ask about applicants' experience, but remember that attitude is often more important than experience. You can train people, but it's hard to change people. As you interview, let the candidates know that it's okay to say they have no experience. Even so, be aware of weak answers, where they try to pass off casual jobs they have

The Right-Hand Man (Or Woman)

You met Mark early in this chapter. He was a key employee. He knew the business as well as I did and could be relied on to hold the fort if the need arose. Customers knew that if they were talking to Mark, they were practically talking to me. He was my right-hand man.

I believe having a right-hand man or woman in the early days of my business was a key to my success and happiness. Having such an assistant gives you freedom and peace of mind. Without it, a family emergency calling you away for a week could be disastrous, even fatal, to your business. Moreover, having someone intimate with the business side of things is a huge value as you brainstorm and plan for the future. Technically, too, the right-hand person helps you tackle projects that you simply couldn't take on alone.

You may not hire someone with the intention of making them your right-hand person. The role may evolve over time as a particular employee grows with the job. Look for attitudes and qualities that would complement you and the business. Your right-hand person will be passionate and enthusiastic about the industry, sensible, intelligent, prudent, hardworking, motivated, and loyal — just like you!

When you find your right-hand man or woman, treat him or her well. Compensate him or her generously. You may even consider profit sharing of some sort. Above all, make your right-hand person feel an important part of the success of your business — because he or she is.

done as real experience. Cutting Mom and Dad's lawn for $5 does not count as commercial gardening experience.

3. Ask them about the specific tools they have used and how much work they have done with them.

4. Ask about their horticultural training and any related schooling.

5. Pose a technical question or two that they should be able to answer if they have the experience they claim. For example: "Have you applied moss control fertilizer? What do you have to be most careful of when you're doing it?" or "A customer's dog has damaged the lawn in areas. What would you recommend doing?" ("Get rid of the dog" is the wrong answer!)

6. Ask why they are applying for the job. Do they want the money or do they love horticulture?

7. Ask open-ended questions to encourage more elaborate answers. Don't ask "Do you like gardening?" Rather ask "What types of gardening do you enjoy doing?"

8. Be at ease and try to set your interviewee at ease too. Have some fun. Relate a funny experience from the job. Tell them a little about the company. Allow applicants to tell you about themselves.

9. Keep in mind that it is illegal to give preference to prospective employees based on race, sex, religion, marital status, age, disability, or gender. Do not ask any questions over the phone that may be construed as discriminatory.

10. Ask them if they have any questions about the company or the job.

11. Thank them for taking the time to call and tell them when you expect to get back to them. Then follow up on your word. It's rude to leave people hanging when they're hoping for a job.

You should have a good feel for the applicants after your phone interviews. When you have completed them all, make a short list of those you liked best. Call short-listed applicants to set up face-to-face interviews. If you don't already have their résumés, ask them to bring them to the interviews for you to review.

4.2 The face-to-face interview

The main purpose of a face-to-face interview is to meet applicants and try to glean their true personality. You have asked most of the questions on the phone, and you want to check up on some issues and find out more about the individuals. Consider these points:

1. If you have a home office without appropriate space for an interview, consider meeting in a public setting, like a coffee shop. As you don't know these people, you may not want them in your home. Find a quiet corner if you can. If you want to impress, go in early and arrange for the barista to take your coffee order when your applicant comes. Tell him to put it in a "to-go" cup, because the interview may not last as long as the coffee.

2. Review the résumé. If no references are provided, be sure to ask for them. Look for holes in the work or education history. If there is a period of time when a candidate wasn't working or at school, ask what he or she was doing. Query anything on the résumé that interests you.

3. Don't ask or talk about anything to do with politics, religion, or sexual preference.

4. If you like the person, ask about his or her schedule and when he or she could start. Let the candidate know what wage range you are offering (don't be specific until you make an offer) and what opportunities for advancement exist in your company.

Once you have decided which lucky contender gets to work for you, check his or her references to see what former employers or associates thought of the person. Ask specific questions, such as "What were this person's strengths and weaknesses?" Try to read between the lines and take note of what is *not* said about the potential employee.

When you've done your checks, call the successful candidate and offer the job. Be sure to congratulate him or her. Then spell out the employment terms, including wages and benefits. Let the person know there is a three-month probationary period during which time they can quit or be let go if things are not working out for either of you. Send the person an employment acceptance letter (see Sample 8) along with your company employee policy. A sample employee policy is provided on the CD-ROM for you to refer to.

EMPLOYMENT ACCEPTANCE LETTER

Dirty Deeds Incorporated
3005 Awesome Street
Vancouver, BC V7X 1P1
Phone: (555) 555-LAWN (5296)   Toll Free: 1-800-554-LAWN (5296)
Fax: (555) 555-8888   E-mail: dirtydeeds@dirtydeedslandscaping.com

February 24, 200-

Ms Barbara Gordon
1235 Greene Road
Vancouver, BC V7Y 0M1

Re: Employment for Dirty Deeds Landscaping

Dear Barbara:

Thank you for your interest in pursuing employment with my firm. It is with great pleasure that I welcome you aboard. Please take a few minutes to review the information in this letter and in the accompanying Employee Policy. If everything is satisfactory, please sign them both and return them to me on your first day of work. I will provide you with a copy for your records.

I have accepted your application for employment in the position of Landscape Maintenance Technician with Dirty Deeds Landscaping. You will begin work at 8:00 a.m. on March 7, 200-. The position is full time, Monday through Friday. Normal working hours are 8:00 a.m. to 4:30 p.m.

The starting wage for this position is $10/hour. Payday is on the 15th and the last day of each month. You will receive a check with source deductions removed. You will accrue vacation pay of 4 percent of your gross earnings. This may not be carried forward from one year to the next in normal circumstances.

Dirty Deeds Landscaping's policy states that, as a new employee, you will be under employment probation for a period of three months. During this time either you or the company may decide to terminate your employment without notice or just cause. I will evaluate your progress monthly throughout your probation period and quarterly after that and will let you know as soon as possible if I feel the quality of your work or your attitude to work are substandard. I would appreciate the same kind of feedback from you, as I consider my employees to be my most important asset and am very interested in ways I can improve relations with them.

Please accept my sincere congratulations, Barbara. I look forward to working with you in the future.

Sincerely,

Dirty Deeds Incorporated
Joel LaRusic, President

Joel LaRusic, Dirty Deeds Landscaping	Barbara Gordon
Dated: _____	Dated: _____

Finally, be sure to call everyone else you interviewed to let them know they were not successful this time. If there were any candidates that you think might be promising hires in the future, keep their résumés on file.

5. TRAINING MATTERS

Training is essential to the success of your business and must be a high priority for you as you begin hiring people. Improper training or an inability to pass on the high standards that you set for your company will have lasting negative impacts.

When your first employee walks through your door, you have to instill in him or her a strong commitment to customer satisfaction. Explain all the services you offer and all the different duties that occur as you complete these services so that your employees know not just how to do them, but also what the purpose of each duty is and why you offer it to your customers.

Be a mentor to your trainees. The best way to do that is to teach by example. Use on-the-job training to show your staff how to operate equipment, how to work efficiently, and how to conscientiously pay attention to details. Don't do things without explaining why you are doing them. Encourage employees when they take the initiative. Educate them, watch them, correct them, enthuse them, and reward them when they do a great job.

Think of the future. Tell staff to pay attention to how you are training them because one day you may expect them to provide the same quality experience to a green employee. This is key. As your company grows, you cannot be there at every jobsite watching every staff member. You must make sure that everyone, especially crew leads or supervisors, understand and appreciate the quality standards you've set and how to maintain them.

Try to nurture a love of horticulture in your staff. Fully support initiatives such as industry certification and advanced instruction by means of books, videos, magazine subscriptions, night courses, seminars, workshops, or distance learning. (And by support I don't mean just suggest it, but share the financial burden.)

Train on safety issues, too. Bad backs are common in the industry, so show your employees how to protect themselves while moving and carrying equipment. Make sure they know how to safely change the lawn mower blade (remove the spark plug), refuel equipment (not when it's hot), and tie down loads on the truck (so things don't fall off or leave a "trail of crumbs" all the way home). If you use chemicals, special training will be needed (and is probably required by law). Most trade equipment comes with safety precautions that should be observed. And remember: lead by example. If you don't heed the safety precautions, your employees won't either.

Help your staff set measurable goals and develop a career path with you. Do they want to lead a crew? Are they interested in the business end of things? Do they want to branch out into design or landscaping? Help them achieve those goals even if that means an eventual parting of ways. People aren't likely going to work for you forever anyway, and stifling people's dreams and goals to keep them around longer is shameful. On the other hand, if you know their goals, you may be able to continue providing the challenges they are looking for in employment.

Set targets for where they want to be by a certain time and review progress at that time.

6. MANAGING YOUR TEAM

The key to managing your team is to remember that it is made up of people who want to feel appreciated. And you should appreciate them — they are helping your business succeed. You want to promote a sense of self-worth in your employees and make them feel important. That doesn't mean you should avoid giving them the less desirable jobs, especially when they are starting out, but be sure you also offer opportunities to work on more interesting aspects so they can learn from them. You may start by assigning specific tasks, but work toward assigning whole jobs with multiple tasks so the employee feels a sense of accomplishment.

Evaluate your employees often, both formally and informally. You should set aside time for periodic employee reviews, but you should also continually provide on-the-job feedback. You might have a conversation as you work or in the truck on the way home. Use these opportunities to tell them how they are doing, but also to gain insight into how they are feeling. Do they feel stagnant? Poorly paid? Unrecognized? Unfairly treated? Are there personal problems that are affecting their work? Is there anything you can do? Be a good manager and listen.

Build up before you break down. Don't just pick out all the things your people are doing wrong. Start out by telling them what they are doing right and then explain how they can improve.

There will be times when you have to discipline your employees. They may test you, especially in the beginning of their employment, and you must be firm in your response so that your standards are not compromised. Set the tone. Create an employee manual that details the job in writing. Be sure they understand what your standards and limits are.

Finally, don't forget to reward good employees with, for example, a small gift certificate, a pair of tickets to the movies, or lunch for the crew. You might use a property quality assessment form (see Sample 16 in chapter 11) or set up some other kind of bonus system. Reward programs make the job more fun and help build staff loyalty. If you keep your employees happy, your business will do better.

7. DEALING WITH PROBLEMS

It's an unfortunate fact of business life that sooner or later (hopefully later) you will have to deal with problem employees. It is an unpleasant task, but one that you must confront as soon as possible to ensure one employee's poor performance doesn't drag down other employees and your business's bottom line.

What do you do if an employee is habitually late or doesn't show up for work? What if he or she is insensitive or offensive to other employees or even customers? Or what if the person just isn't working to your standards?

The first step is to meet with the person as soon as you have identified a pattern of unacceptable behavior. When you meet, do it face to face, either just the two of you or perhaps with a supervisor. Document what you discuss at the meeting, noting what the problem is, what resolution has been proposed, and when the problem will be considered

Ten Ways to Reward Your Employees

Here are ten suggestions for recognizing and rewarding your employees. Some are suitable for recognizing outstanding achievement, while others are things you should be doing for all employees of your company.

1. Give raises: You should give raises so your employees keep up with the cost of living. Beyond that, raises should be based on performance. Don't wait and make an employee ask for a raise if, in fact, he or she deserves one. If someone does ask for a raise and you feel it is not warranted at the time, explain your reasons clearly, state what needs to be done to get there, and set a goal so he or she can achieve it. Then follow up.

2. Offer benefits: Check out employee benefit packages available for small businesses. You may not be able to afford to pay for a full package, but perhaps you could cover half of it.

3. Consider promotions: Promotions should be based on effort and performance. Give out responsibility sparingly until you have seen how it is handled. A steady increase of responsibility will mean the promotion is not a risky and enormous step for the accomplished staff member, but more like a logical move.

4. Hand out on-the-spot awards: Reward your team on the spot when it shows service excellence, initiative, outstanding workmanship, attention to detail, and other things that are vital to your business. You don't need to have fancy certificates or a lot of pomp and ceremony. Keep free lunch coupons or free coffee certificates on hand and give them out with a thank-you and a hearty pat on the back.

5. Assign special chores: Special treatment makes people feel, well, special. Pull a deserving employee off the job for ten minutes to help you run an errand. Ask your helper if he or she would mind stopping with you on the way to the next job to get their feedback on a quote you are doing.

6. Host pizza Fridays: On the last Friday of the month, have the gang come over to your house, or take them out, for pizza. (Don't be tempted to include beer or other alcohol. You don't want your staff drinking too much and driving home.)

7. Give bonuses: Offer bonuses to recognize top performers. You might give an end-of-year bonus if you feel a staff member has added positively to your company and your bottom line. Call it a Christmas bonus if you wish, but I prefer to say that the bonus is an appreciation of their exceptional service, not a holiday gift.

8. Host a staff picnic, barbecue, or other party. I use the occasion of my business's anniversary to throw a staff party. Try to do something at least once a year. It doesn't need to cost thousands or even hundreds. Ask team members to bring their families. Throw some burgers on the barbecue at your home or in a park. Put up a badminton net or bring a bocce ball or croquet set. Have some fun.

9. Offer an anniversary day off with pay: Giving a day off, perhaps on the anniversary of employment, is a great way to say thank you.

10. Be humble: This one is free. The best way to earn your team's respect is to be humble. Do the menial tasks sometimes. Maybe let your employee prune while you handle cleanup. Or ask a respected staff member how he or she would handle a particular business situation or problem. Asking for help shows your employees that you value their input.

resolved. You can make your notes on an employee status change form such as the one shown in Worksheet 4.

Consider this example: You get a report that one of the employees was telling vulgar jokes within customer earshot. You meet with him and the crew leader and let him know that you are happy with his work (assuming you are), but that this behavior is unacceptable. The only resolution to this is to hear your offending employee say: "It won't happen again." Record the response on the form, adding the employee's name and the date, then check off "First Warning." Allow the staff member to add his comments, which may be his side of the story or perhaps some rebuttal to the complaint. Both of you sign and date it. The form shown in Worksheet 4 allows for three warnings and then a final warning.

Each time you meet with a problem employee, record all the particulars. If you have to fire someone, it is useful to have this documentation to back you up. If you don't have the paperwork, you'll be an easy target for a wrongful dismissal lawsuit.

Try to help your employees with their work problems as much as you can. Don't say, "Let me know if I can help you." Instead say, "What can I do to help you with this problem?" This will encourage your employees to be frank with you about their concerns.

Much as you try to avoid it, the day will come when you have to fire someone. The best course is be professional. Never fire someone on the spot. As much as you'd like to do it, leave that for Hollywood movies. If tempers flare, send the person home for the day and agree to meet again the next morning. If you have been thorough with your

other warnings, a final meeting to terminate employment should be no surprise. Use the employee status change form again, this time checking "Termination," and put the specifics in the description area. Allow the employee to document a protest on the form if he or she wants to. Have the final paycheck ready, and include a termination letter (see Sample 9), a taxation record of employment, any other required government forms, and a copy of the status change form. You may be required to give two weeks' pay in lieu of notice (check with your accountant or lawyer for local laws). However, in most cases this is money well spent to sever all ties with the employee. Once someone is fired, loyalties disappear and so might your equipment and supplies.

8. THE PAPERWORK

Along with employees comes more paperwork. The amount depends on where you live and how much you care to track, but wherever your business is located, you will have to deal with government regulations and requirements.

It's a good idea to keep a folder for each employee, past and present. This is where you should store résumés/applications, annual payroll records, job acceptance letters, written evaluations, records of disciplinary actions, status change forms, and other related items.

You must by law keep accurate and up-to-date payroll information. It's easy to keep track of the hours your staff works if you only have one helper. Just jot the information in your daily planner. If you have a bigger workforce, make your crew leads responsible for verifying hours worked and ask them to pass the information on to you

EMPLOYEE STATUS CHANGE FORM

Employee Status Change Form

Tuxedo Landscape Maintenance Company

Employee Name: _Billy Batson_   Date: _April 18/05_

Reason for Status Change (check one only)

☐ Promotion	☐ First Warning
☐ Demotion	☑ Second Warning
☐ Pay Increase	☐ Third Warning
☐ Pay Decrease	☐ Final Warning
☐ Change in Job Description	☐ Termination
☐ End of Probation	☐ Suspension
☐ Leave of Absence	☐ Name Change
☐ Return from Leave of Absence	☐ Extend Leave of Absence
☐ Other: _____	

Change Information

Effective Date: _April 18, 2005_

Details/Reasons for Change: _Unprofessional conduct in front of a customer. Vulgar language will not be tolerated._

Employee Comments: _I will think before I speak. It won't happen again._

JLaRusic

Tuxedo Landscape Maintenance Company

Date: _April 18, 2005_

Billy Batson

Employee

Date: _April 18/05_

SAMPLE 9
EMPLOYMENT TERMINATION LETTER

Dirty Deeds Incorporated
3005 Awesome Street
Vancouver, BC V7X 1P1
Phone: (555) 555-LAWN (5296)   Toll Free: 1-800-554-LAWN (5296)
Fax: (555) 555-8888   E-mail: dirtydeeds@dirtydeedslandscaping.com

July 20, 200-

Ms Barbara Gordon
1235 Greene Road
Vancouver, BC V7Y 0M1

Re: Employment Termination — Dirty Deeds Landscaping

Dear Barbara:

It is with regret that I write this letter today to inform you of the immediate termination of your employment with Dirty Deeds Landscaping.

Barbara, in the past several months I feel I have made every effort to help you improve your job skills and to instill in you the commitment to customer satisfaction that I demand of all my employees. I feel that these efforts have been futile. Your lack of progress and lackluster attitude on the jobsite are affecting the morale of other employees and the quality of their work. I have spoken with you about this on four different occasions, each time asking how I can help you progress. Still, the same problems exist and continue to affect other employees. Since you seem unable to improve your performance, I must let you go.

Thank you for the work you did provide for Dirty Deeds Landscaping. I wish you every success in your future endeavors. I sincerely hope you find employment to which you are better suited.

Sincerely,

Dirty Deeds Incorporated
Joel LaRusic, President

_____
Joel LaRusic, Dirty Deeds Landscaping

Dated: _____

each day or each week. If you want to be really official, you can purchase time cards from an office supply store.

Every two weeks (depending on your pay schedule) you need to add up each employee's hours and multiply them by the employee's hourly wage to determine gross pay. Then subtract source deductions such as income tax, pension plan contributions, and employment insurance. The result is the net pay, which is the amount you write on the check. Give your employees a detailed pay stub showing the hours they worked, the source deductions, any other deductions or advances, and their net pay. You can buy stubs from an office supply store.

You must keep all this detail in your own books, and you also have to send in to the government the source deductions that you took from your staff each month. The business (that's you) must make a matching contribution for certain things such as pension and/or employment insurance.

The local government agency that handles employee taxation will be able to give you detailed instructions on how to fill out all the forms that are required. Make sure you understand what the law requires for overtime, minimum wages, statutory holidays, vacation pay, sick leave, maternity leave, employment termination rules, record keeping, workers' compensation, and discrimination and sexual harassment policies. This information may also be available on the Internet.

Whatever you do, don't fall behind in your payroll taxes. The government will be contacting you before you know it. If for some reason you are having trouble making payments, take a good hard look at your cash flow situation to understand why. If you are using an accountant or bookkeeper, get him or her to do your payroll. Alternatively, you can investigate local payroll services, which make the process easy.

Advances

One issue that is sure to arise is employees asking for advances. It's a good idea to think about how you will handle this, and perhaps have an official policy in place, before you do your hiring.

I recommend you offer one advance a month, perhaps on the 15th. Since it is a lot of work to do payroll, you don't want to offer advances more often. You can either estimate what the employee has earned and cut a check, or you can ask what amount the employee would like. Many prefer to receive a lesser amount mid-month and the bulk at the end. At the end of the month you would, of course, subtract the advance after you have deducted all the taxes, etc.

At one time I was lenient about giving advances to employees in need because I didn't like to see them dealing with high-interest paycheck loans. Only a few times, when someone asked for an advance two or three times a month, did I refuse. You will have to find your own comfort zone.

9
THE WORKFLOW FROM FIRST CONTACT TO QUOTE

A phenomenal number of things have to occur between the time you answer a potential customer's phone call and the time you sit down to see if you made money on the job. If you think about them all at once, it can be overwhelming. But if you break the process down into small steps, you'll see that everything is manageable. The key is to develop systems and a workflow and stick to them.

In this chapter I'll take you, step by step, from that initial phone call through to a prepared quote. The next two chapters continue with a description of a typical job, covering all the details you need to know to complete your work.

I provide many examples of systems, procedures, and workflows in these chapters. Some may work for you, while others may need adjustment, but I hope they will all serve as a foundation for your own systems.

1. FIRST CONTACT: THE PHONE CALL

A wonderful thing happens after you put your marketing campaign in place. Your phone rings! The first few times it rings, it's pretty exciting. It's been a while now, but I'm pretty sure I did backflips the first time I got a call from a potential customer. After a while the novelty wears off — very rapidly on those days when the phone doesn't stop day or night. That's when you may have to remind yourself that you invited these people to call you.

Whatever your reaction to the phone call, you must realize that it represents the beginning of a job. Have you thought about how you will answer the phone? You want to present a professional image from the first word. A simple, polite answer, giving your name and the company name in a friendly tone, is appropriate. For example, you might say, "Greener Grass Lawn Care, Dave speaking." Stay away from those greetings that seem to go on forever: "Good afternoon. You've reached Greener Grass Lawn Care, specializing in the best customer service. This is Dave speaking. How may I provide you with excellent service today?" Such messages are welcoming, but they can put customers off with their length.

Be sure to maintain a pleasant tone, which tells customers you're happy to hear from them. There's no bigger turnoff than calling a company and feeling that your call is an inconvenience.

Let the customer tell you why he or she has called. If the person wants some work done, you should immediately offer to visit the property and provide a quotation, which of course you do for free. Take the person's name, address, phone number, and information about what he or she would like done, and arrange a meeting at a time convenient to both of you. Keep some quotation worksheets (see section **6** below) near the phone so you can write down the specifics. Thank the customer for calling and be sure to deliver on your promise to quote on the job. (Use the daily drop file described in section **4** of chapter 5.) It goes without saying that a quick response will greatly improve your chance of impressing the customer and winning the job. Try to follow up on quotes within 24 hours.

Try to avoid giving quotes over the phone. If the customer asks for a phone quote, politely explain that you need to size up the property and condition of the jobsite to give an accurate quote. If someone insists that you give a price over the phone, be suspicious. Most genuine customers would be pleased to have a personal visit and a free written quotation. You will have to use your judgment in these cases, depending on how much you need the work, but if the person demands a quote, sight unseen, be prepared to let the job go.

Having said all that, there are some services where it makes sense to provide telephone estimates. I used to offer a lot of aeration and fertilizer deals, and the dollar amount of these jobs meant it was not worth my while to make a special visit to give them a price. In these cases I quoted a price over the phone. However, if you do this, keep the following points in mind:

- Don't commit to a price. Don't even call it a *quotation*. It's an *estimate* based on the information you have received over the phone. You could say something like: "The cost is $65 for an average-sized lawn in your area, and it sounds to me like your lawn falls into that category. I can go ahead and book the job. I don't expect any problems, but if we visit the site and find something unexpected, we'll give you a call before going ahead with the job."

- Listen for hints that indicate an onsite visit is warranted. The customer may call for an aeration, but as an aside she mentions that her lawn is full of moss. Put the brakes on and insist on giving her a free lawn evaluation to make sure that her money is spent effectively — aeration will not solve her moss problem.

Don't forget to ask everyone who calls how they heard about your business. Were they referred by a friend? Did they find you in the Yellow Pages? Did they pick up one of your flyers? Put the information on your quotation worksheet as well as on a referral tracking worksheet like the one shown in Sample 10. Create a new worksheet each month, and at the end of the month tally up the totals and transfer them to an annual summary referral tracking spreadsheet (supplied on the CD-ROM that accompanies this book). This summary information will be invaluable as you consider next year's marketing efforts.

2. THE FOLLOW-UP CHECKLIST

As soon as that first phone contact is complete, you want to have a follow-up system in place. This lets you see where a customer is in your workflow at any given time and, more importantly, it reminds you when action is required on your part. You can use a simple checklist such as the one shown in Checklist 1.

Notice that the list takes you through a typical job from original contact to a thank-you note or card. Not all steps will apply to each customer every time. For example, if someone signs up when you present the quote, then no follow-up is required at all (except for the thank-you). As well, the situation may not justify two follow-ups to the quote, but if it does, the space is provided on the checklist.

Have some blank checklists on hand so that when a customer calls for a quote, you can clip or staple one to your copy of the quotation worksheet. Then record the dates as the potential customer moves through the process of becoming your customer.

This simple system works well and provides you with quick, accurate information about what stage each potential customer is

at. It also means you don't have to rely on your memory to know when to follow up.

3. THE ON-SITE VISIT

Free estimates and quotes are standard in the landscaping business. They're part of the cost of doing business. Here are a few tips to think about as you provide soon-to-be clients with their job quotes and estimates.

First, to be clear, there is a difference between a quotation (or quote) and an estimate. Quotes are a price commitment. Estimates are educated guesses. Most folks want quotes, and you should provide one whenever possible. You will only offer estimates if you are giving a price without having seen the property or if some aspect of the job is uncertain. For example, if there are materials included, such as topsoil, and you are not sure if you will need two or four cubic yards, then you may need to estimate this portion of the job. You could still quote on the job by providing variations based on the different amounts of material that may be used. You might say, for example, "Topsoil is $79 per yard installed, so if we use two yards the cost will be $158. If we use four yards, it will be $316." In short, try to use exact numbers when assessing work, and avoid estimating if possible.

Show up for your appointments on time, and dress suitably. In a perfect world you would have afternoons or even entire days to drive around doing quotes, which would allow you to be perfectly presentable when you knock on the door. In reality, you may have to squeeze quotes into your workday. This is okay. Most people will appreciate your situation, and looking like you're ready to go to work will build confidence. What customers don't want to see, however, is you

SAMPLE 10
MONTHLY REFERRAL TRACKING SHEET

Referral Tracking Sheet March 20—								
Date	Referred by Existing Customer	Yellow Pages	Flyer #1	Flyer #2	Super-market BB	Saw Us Working	Canvassing	Other
Mar. 1								
Mar. 2								
Mar. 3		/						
Mar. 4								
Mar. 5								
Mar. 6		//						
Mar. 7								
Mar. 8		/						
Mar. 9								
Mar. 10								
Mar. 11								
Mar. 12								
Mar. 13		/						
Mar. 14		//////						
Mar. 15		//						
Mar. 16		///						
Mar. 17		/						
Mar. 18								
Mar. 19		////						
Mar. 20								
Mar. 21			/			/		
Mar. 22		/	//					
Mar. 23			///					
Mar. 24								
Mar. 25			//	///				
Mar. 26		/		///	/			
Mar. 27				/				
Mar. 28			/	///// /				
Mar. 29		/	/					
Mar. 30				//				
Mar. 31				/		/		
Totals		23	10	16	1	2		

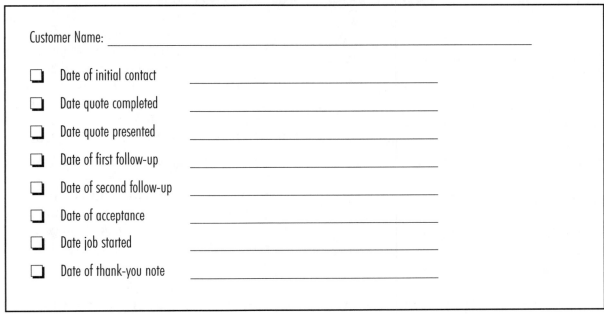

CHECKLIST 1
CUSTOMER FOLLOW-UP CHECKLIST

Customer Name: _____

☐ Date of initial contact _____

☐ Date quote completed _____

☐ Date quote presented _____

☐ Date of first follow-up _____

☐ Date of second follow-up _____

☐ Date of acceptance _____

☐ Date job started _____

☐ Date of thank-you note _____

on their doorstep looking filthy and stinky. Your hands should be clean so you can confidently shake hands (keep hand cleaner in the truck). Try to schedule quotes in the morning before you get too involved in any dirty work.

Greet your customers warmly, introduce yourself, thank them for the opportunity to quote their job, and give them your business card. Listen carefully as they tell you what they want done. Ask questions if you are not clear on anything. For quotes that will only take five or ten minutes, tell customers that you would like a few minutes to wander around and evaluate their property and the job and that you will knock on the door when you are finished. If it is a larger job, or if you have a helper waiting in the truck, you may want to come back later. In this case,

tell your customer that you will leave the quote in the mailbox. Either way, it is better to view the property without your customer looking over your shoulder.

4. PRICING

Before you open your doors for business, you should establish an hourly rate and other pricing methods that you may use in your own operation. The rates you charge will be a big factor in how you market and manage your business.

4.1 Your hourly rate: Promise results, not time

Do not give your customers an hourly rate. Instead, try to quote a total price for the job. In other words, promise results, not time. As long as you do everything you said you would do, and do it well, it should not matter exactly how long it takes to finish.

For example, instead of saying: "We will spend one person-hour per week at your home to cut the lawn and maintain the beds. Our hourly rate is $35 per hour plus expenses," you could say: "We will visit your home once per week, professionally cut and edge the lawn, keep the beds free of weeds and looking fresh, and leave the place neat and tidy. The cost for this is $45 per week."

From the beginning, train your customers not to attach a specific time period to your work. There are a couple of reasons for doing this. First, you are going to get better at what you do. What takes you an hour today may take you 45 minutes next year. If your customers don't attach a specific time to your work, you probably won't have problems if and when the visits get a little shorter (and your profit gets a little larger). Be fair, though; if you find the time has been reduced significantly, it would be prudent to adjust the price. Your customers will love you forever!

Pricing by job also provides you with an incentive to work smart. If you know you are stuck at a job for eight hours and the customer is watching, there is no reason to find ways to work more efficiently. However, if you have promised results and not time, you will work hard to be more effective on the job and you will profit more for it.

There are two things to watch out for. First, the relationship between money and time is deeply ingrained in some people, who will insist you give them a time frame. If you are asked how long a job will take, try to avoid specifics. Say something like: "We'll be here most of the day." Don't put a time estimate on your written quote. If necessary, explain that you prefer to quote on results, not time. Mention the guarantee that you will stay until customers are satisfied, but also ensure you set the expectations precisely. Don't say "General Cleanup — $900," for example. Rather, list all the specific items on your quote, such as: "Cleanup includes cutting the lawn, edging, trimming shrubs, weeding, raking, cultivating, blowing, and final tidying and the removal of all debris."

If a customer absolutely insists on an exact time estimate, be prepared to walk away and leave them for your competition. If you offer exceptional service and high standards, you will not lack business, and you will not be compelled to take difficult customers.

The second thing to keep in mind is that your selling of results works both ways. If you have underestimated the amount of time and effort for a job in your quote, you cannot go back to the customer to ask for more money (unless the scope of the work has changed). Chalk it up as a learning experience and complete the job to the satisfaction of your customer.

Although you shouldn't give an hourly rate to customers, you do need to establish an hourly rate for your own use. You'll need it to figure out your package price and to set prices for specific jobs. There are also some jobs where it makes more sense to charge by the hour — for example, if you have no idea how long a job will take, or if a customer asks for two extra hours on your next visit. You'll also want to establish a minimum charge based on your hourly rate. If a customer wants you for only 15 minutes, you will still incur certain overhead costs when you attend to the job. Many companies charge a one-hour minimum for jobs that take less than an hour.

Finally, avoid lowballing. Lowballing is when companies deliberately quote prices that are way under the industry norm. These companies hurt the industry as a whole. Why would you want to spoil the landscaping business? You wouldn't ... so don't deliberately do it. Instead, combat lowballers (and there will always be lowballers) by teaching your customers and potential customers why they should throw out the lowest bid. Remind them that something has to be cut out for these unscrupulous companies to offer the cutthroat prices they do, and you can bet it's not the profit. That means the standards will likely be low and the service poor.

4.2 Pricing methods

How do you know how much to charge for a job? This is probably the most common question that new business owners have, and I'm sorry to say there is no easy answer — at least not if you want to make a healthy profit and stay in business. If you are sloppy with your pricing, you will find it catches up to you — but it is not always easy to see. It may be too late by the time you figure out your pricing is all wrong. In this section I describe three methods you can use to determine how much to charge for the different services that you offer.

4.2a Use the comparative method

When you are starting out, it may be best to use the comparative method. First, you need to compare your prices to those of your competition. What landscaping companies charge will vary greatly from city to city and

company to company. You could try phoning other companies, but many will not reveal a rate over the phone. Your best bet is to network. Ask around at the suppliers or at gardening business associations. You may also find answers online by asking other commercial gardeners (check out the users forum at <www.mowboy.com>). Be sure you make a fair comparison. For example, if the competitor is using a 54-inch mower and you are using a 21-inch mower, the prices may not be congruent. At this time, the average hourly charge for general labor is about $35 to $40 per hour. Find out what your rivals are charging and set your price accordingly. Next, compare with yourself. Once you have done a few jobs and are confident that you are making a profit, set prices of new customers' lawns based on these jobs. For example, if you can cut Ms. Rogers's 3,000-square-foot lawn in 18 minutes, then you can logically figure out how much time you need to cut a 2,000- or a 4,000-square-foot lawn.

4.2b Use the formula method

The formula method is the best method for pricing many services, especially if they include materials. For example, fertilizer applications, overseeding, or weed sprays can be billed at so much per thousand square feet, and topsoil or mulch can be billed at so much per cubic yard. This is a quick and effective way to price lawn cutting too. You could charge so much per 1,000 square feet of lawn or so much per linear 100 feet of blade or line edging. Note, however, that if your formula is faulty, your prices will be too. There are industry guides that tell you how long it should take to cut 1,000 square feet of lawn or edge 100 linear feet, but the best way to create a formula is through experience. After a while, you will know how long it takes you to complete such duties. Set your formula based on this data. (Remember to account for special circumstances. A lawn with steep slopes, for example, will take longer to cut. Make sure you factor specifics into your equation.)

4.2c Use the textbook method

The principle behind the textbook method is that you should establish a price by taking all your actual costs (overhead, cost of equipment, cost of labor, etc.) as well as your desired profit and adding them together.

To determine how much overhead you need to add on, divide the total annual overhead (from your profit and loss statement) by the total number of hours that you worked during the year. (You should be able to extract something from your schedules and job history.) Don't forget to factor in time spent in the office, too. So if you work full time (40 hours per week), with four weeks off in the winter, you will work 1,920 hours in a year. If your overhead is $15,000, then the overhead portion of your hourly rate will be $7.81 (15,000 ÷ 1,920). If you decide that $30 an hour is a fair rate for you to earn, then your hourly rate will be $37.81.

The drawback to this method is that it doesn't work in your first year because you won't have any historical data to draw upon. For now, as a rule of thumb, take 25 percent of your desired rate and add it on as overhead. In this case it works out to close to the same amount ($30 x 25% = 7.50, giving you an hourly rate of $37.50).

Once you have your hourly labor rate calculated, you need to factor in how much to charge customers for the use of equipment.

You may recall that equipment maintenance and fuel are considered direct costs rather than overhead, which means they are not covered in the hourly rate. There is a formula you can use to calculate a *cost per hour* for your equipment. This hourly rate covers replacement cost, maintenance, fuel, and other related equipment expenses.

To use the formula you need to know —

- the total purchase price of the equipment,
- how many years you expect it to last,
- what the salvage value is (i.e., what it will be worth at the end of its useful life),
- what the total annual costs are (e.g., fuel, oil, maintenance, and repairs), and
- how many hours in the year you expect to run the equipment.

The formula:

1. Subtract the salvage cost from the total purchase price to give you the net cost of the equipment.

2. Divide the net cost by the number of years it will last to give you the net cost per year of the equipment.

3. Add annual equipment costs.

4. Divide the result by the estimated number of hours you plan to run the equipment.

Your final result will be an hourly rate that you should charge whenever you use the equipment.

To save you a bit of time, here are estimates in US dollars based on typical small equipment:

- 🌾 21" Mower — $3/hr
- 🌾 36" Mower — $4/hr
- 🌾 48" Mower — $5/hr
- 🌾 60" Mower — $7/hr
- 🌾 72" Mower — $8/hr
- 🌾 Reel Mower — $5/hr
- 🌾 Line Edger — $3/hr
- 🌾 Blade Edger — $3/hr
- 🌾 Power Rake — $5/hr
- 🌾 Backpack Blower — $3/hr
- 🌾 Hedge Trimmer — $3/hr
- 🌾 Spreader — $2/hr
- 🌾 Aerator — $6/hr
- 🌾 Hand Tools — $0.50/hr

A prudent businessperson will use a combination of all three costing methods — knowing competitors' rates, using convenient formulas, and considering costs. Using all three will ensure you keep yourself out of the red as you operate your business.

5. USING A LAWN AND GARDEN MAINTENANCE QUOTATION WORKSHEET

Since maintenance is your primary business, and also because there is much to consider, it is good to use a separate worksheet to help you calculate the total cost for an entire season of lawn and garden maintenance. Worksheet 5 is an example of such a worksheet; it is also available on the CD-ROM that came with this book.

The worksheet is designed with a *fixed monthly fee* program in mind. However, you may well decide to offer a *cost per visit* program. With this type of program, the customer gets regular cuts billed at a fixed rate (cost per visit). Fertilizers and other extras appear as separate line items on the invoice. As a result, the monthly fees will vary. This type of structure works well for many people, and if you decide to use it, adapt the worksheet as you see fit. (Note that this worksheet may also be used to estimate the price for work that will not be included in the monthly fee but rather billed as an extra. Fill in the numbers but make a notation indicating which services are actually included in the monthly fee and which are not.)

For each category on the worksheet, fill in as much detail as possible, from determining the frequency of your maintenance visits to a careful calculation of the cost of each of the services included. Here are a few tips to help you complete the worksheet:

- 🌾 The services you include in your programs can have a serious impact on your business, so give some thought to what you should include as part of a fixed monthly fee and what to bill as add-on services. One aspect of this decision that many neglect is how it will affect your cash flow. Since the payments for maintenance programs are normally spread out equally over the program length, you will find that some months seem to be more lucrative than others. However, this is an illusion. For example, one month you are spending considerable time and/ or materials on a job and the next month you are just cutting the lawn, but the cash coming in remains constant. The problem multiplies if you

WORKSHEET 5
LAWN AND GARDEN MAINTENANCE QUOTATION

Lawn & Garden Maintenance Quotation

Frequency

☐ One-time Visit ☑ Weekly Visit ☐ Bimonthly Visit ☐ Other: _____

Length of Agreement

☐ Week-to-Week ☐ 8 Months ☑ 9 Months ☐ 10 Months ☐ 12 Months ☐ Other: _____

Services Included   **Total**

Lawn (Rotary): Area _3,000_ Time: _25 min._ x Rate: _$35_ x Visits: _40_ = _$583.33_

Lawn (Reel): Area _____ Time: _____ x Rate: _____ x Visits: _____ = _____

Planted Beds: Area _1,000_ Time: _10 min._ x Rate: _$35_ x Visits: _40_ = _$233.33_

Edging (Lin. ft) _200_ Time: _5 min._ x Rate: _$35_ x Visits: _30_ = _$87.50_

Pruning (Under 15 ft.): Time: _4 hrs._ x Rate: _$35_ x # of trims: _2_ = _$280.00_

Pruning (Over 15 ft.): ☑ Not Included ☐ Subbed Out ☐ Time: ____ x Rate: ____ = ____

Pruning Summary: As part of regular maintenance _280_ As part of fall cleanup _____

Moss Control: Price/1,000 sq. ft: _$12_ x Area: _3K_ x # of apps: _1_ = _$36.00_

Fertilizer Applications: Price/1,000 sq. ft: _$12_ x Area: _3K_ x # of apps: _4_ = _$144.00_

(Lime)/Sulfur App: Price/1,000 sq. ft: _$12_ x Area: _3K_ x # of apps: _1_ = _$36.00_

Weed Sprays: Price/1,000 sq. ft: _$15_ x Area: _3K_ x # of apps: _1_ = _$45.00_

Pest Control: Price/1,000 sq. ft: ____ x Area: ____ x # of apps: ____ = ____

Overseeding: Price/1,000 sq. ft: ____ x Area: ____ x # of apps: ____ = ____

Power Raking: Time: _____ x Rate: ____ x # of times: ____ = ____

Aeration: Price/1,000 sq. ft: ____ x Area: ____ x # of times: ____ = ____

Top Dressing: Price/yard installed: _____ x # of yards: ____ = ____

Topsoil/Mulch: Price/yard installed: _____ x # of yards: ____ = ____

Dumping: Per Visit: _2 x $40_ Pruning: _$30_ Power Raking: ____ Other: ____ = _$110.00_

Cleanup/Curb Sweep: Time: _5 min._ x Rate: _$35_ x Visits _40_ = _$116.67_

Snow Clearing: Area ____ Time: ____ x Rate: ____ x Visits: ____ = ____

Other Materials: Price/1,000 sq. ft: ____ x Area: ____ x # of times: ____ = ____

TOTAL ANNUAL COST .... = _$1,671.83_

TOTAL/MONTH Total Annual Cost ÷ # of Months = $ _185.76_ per month

Other Services/Special Comments: _Easy access. Prominent location! Round down to $180/month._
Lawn renovation needed in back — will bill as separate item.

have a number of customers on similar programs. To avoid this problem, take some services out of the program and bill them separately to balance your income over the course of the season.

🦅 Each service needs to be calculated in a slightly different way. Keep in mind that when quoting for the season-long maintenance program, you are primarily concerned with how much you will charge annually. At the end, you divide the annual cost into the length of program (the number of months) to determine your monthly fee. Each service must be calculated in such a way as to find out how much you should charge for the entire year.

🦅 An effective way to calculate the time and cost for maintaining beds is to use a rotation system, attending to each bed every two or three weeks. Calculate how long it would take you to tend all the bedded areas, then divide by the number of weeks you'll be rotating the job. That will give you the average weekly time spent in the beds. Enter your rate, the number of visits, and finally the total for the year.

🦅 When calculating the costs of pruning, estimate 10 minutes for smaller shrubs and 15 to 20 minutes for shrubs where you need a ladder. Don't forget about plants that may need pruning several times in a year. Make a special note of any hedges or trees that will not be trimmed on regular maintenance visits but will be dealt with on a separate visit, perhaps a fall clean-up. Will you include all the trees and hedges on the site? Personally, I prefer to leave trees and shrubs over 15 feet (the highest I can comfortably reach with my ladder) to tree specialists or arborists who have the proper expertise and equipment to carry out this type of work. Alternatively, you could include them in the program and subcontract the work.

🦅 When you calculate how much dumping will cost you, it helps to separate the different types of dumping that you might have to pay for. How much per visit (multiply by number of visits), how much for special pruning, fall cleanups, etc.?

If there are other services you offer that are not listed on the quotation worksheet, add them in. Once you are done, add up all the annual totals for each item to arrive at a grand total for the year. Dividing this number by the number of months in your maintenance agreement will give you a fixed monthly payment that you can provide to your customer on a quotation sheet.

When you are done with the worksheet, save it in the customer's file folder for future reference.

6. THE QUOTATION SHEET

Don't make the mistake I did in the early days of my business and write your quotes on the back of your business card or on scrap pieces of paper. The quotation sheet is what separates you, the serious businessperson, from the hack (like me when I started). It also allows you to quickly provide your customers with quotations for your work. This is especially true if you use a form customized for the industry, such as the one shown in Sample 11 (also included on the CD-ROM that came with this book).

SAMPLE 11
QUOTATION SHEET

GREENER GRASS LAWN AND GARDEN COMPANY

321 Verdure Street
North Vancouver, BC V7J 1E7
Ph: (555) 555-LAWN • Toll-Free: 1-800-555-LAWN
Fax: (555) 555-1234 • E-Mail: owner@myemail.com

Customer No: _____ Date: *March 4/05* Referred By: *Flyer*

Customer Name: *Mr. Barry Allen* Phone No: *555-1575*

Customer Address: *123 Quick Street*

Comments:

- *Would like package including bed maintenance, trimming, and fertilizers.*
- *Requests Thursday visit.*

Maintenance Programs

- ☐ Year-round ☐ 10 ☑ 9 ☐ 8 ☐ Other ____
- ☑ Lawn Maintenance _____
- ☑ Bed Maintenance _____
- ☑ Fertilizer Program *See Lawn Care Service* →
- ☑ Weed Control Program _____
- ☑ Hedges *and small shrubs* _____
- ☐ Trees/Large Shrubs _____
- ☐ Reel Mower Service _____
- ☑ Dumping Required _____
- ☐ Extra Materials _____
- ☐ Snow Clearing _____
- ☐ Cleanup required: _____

Lawn Care Service

- ☐ Services below packaged as Lawn Renovation
- ☑ Services below packaged with Maintenance Program
- ☐ Fertilizer Application _____
  - ☑ Spring *(Moss Control)*
  - ☑ Summer *3*
  - ☑ Fall _____
  - ☐ Seed Starter _____
- ☑ Lime Application _____
- ☑ Moss Control _____
- ☑ Weed Control Spray _____
- ☐ Power Raking _____
- ☐ Core Aeration _____
- ☐ Top-Dressing _____
- ☐ Overseeding _____
- ☐ Other _____

Other Services

- ❑ General Cleanup _____
- ❑ Clean out beds _____
- ❑ Pruning _____
- ❑ First Cutting _____
- ❑ Establish Edges _____
- ❑ Chemical Application _____
- ❑ Dumping Fee _____
- ❑ Pressure Washing _____
- ❑ Lawn Repair _____
- ❑ Planting _____
- ❑ Other _____

Notes

Total cost of maintenance including all checked items will be $180/month over 9 months.

Thank you!

*Thursday visit will work for me.

Lawn Installations

- ❑ Lawn Removal _____
- ❑ _____ cubic yards topsoil _____
- ❑ _____ square yards _____ turf _____
- ❑ Grass seed installed _____
- ❑ Other _____

Materials

- ❑ Topsoil _____
- ❑ Bark Mulch _____
- ❑ Rock _____
- ❑ Mushroom Manure _____
- ❑ Other _____

I authorize the above work to be completed by Greener Grass Lawn and Garden Company.

Name: _____ Date: _____ Signed: _____

Quotation/Service Agreeement Completed by: _Joel LaRusic_ _____

Of Greener Grass Lawn and Garden Company Signed: _JLaRusic_ _____

Modify the quotation sheet to suit your particular business needs, and then have it printed in duplicate so you can tear off the original to give to your customer and keep the copy for yourself (put it in the customer's file with the worksheet). For example, you might want to add a pager number or your website address at the top with all the contact information. You want to make it as easy as possible for your clients to contact you, so include all this information up front.

Take note of these other specifics on the quotation form:

- Note the "Referred By" space. If you forget to ask potential clients how they heard of your service when you first speak on the phone, be sure you ask when doing the quote. This field should always be filled in so you know if your marketing is working.

- The comments section can be used for any pertinent information. I usually write notes from the initial phone conversation.

- Use the data from the maintenance section of your quotation worksheet. You don't need to price each item individually; simply write your final price in the large box.

- In the lawn care services section, check off the items you are quoting on, and don't forget to check off the appropriate box showing whether you are quoting on a maintenance program, a lawn renovation, or individual jobs (in which case check neither box). If you bundle the lawn care services as a lawn reno or a rejuvenation, you may want to include individual prices for each of the services

so the customer can see the package savings.

- Under Other Services, include those jobs a customer asks for that are above and beyond the scope of the maintenance agreement, jobs for non-maintenance customers, and one-time jobs.

- If you provide lawn installation services, it is convenient to break them down as shown on the sample. Include any other services or tasks that you might want to offer in the new lawn installation. Price these individually and/or put a package price on everything.

7. PRESENTING YOUR QUOTATION

If you are presenting a quote for a typical residential maintenance job, a one-time job, or a non-maintenance job, you can present the handwritten quotation sheet to your customer during your on-site visit. Otherwise, you may want to take it home so you can prepare a more official printed proposal, which you can drop off later.

Make sure you go through the quote with your prospect, explaining what you have quoted and the cost of the job. If there are particular challenges, point them out and describe how you plan to overcome them. For example, you might say: "There's a lot of moss in the lawn, so you can see that I have included two moss control applications, one for spring and one for fall," or "The weeds are coming in fast and furiously in the front bed. It's going to require an initial cleanup, and I'll be giving it a little extra attention for the first few weeks to be sure we're on top of it. Then it can be attended to on our usual two-week rotation." This indicates you are not giving a generic quotation, but have paid particular attention to the customer's property.

Along with the quotation sheet, supply the customer with an information pack and your introductory letter (see below). Then ask the customer if he or she has any questions. Don't be afraid to ask for the job. You can say something like: "I have openings on Wednesdays and Fridays right now. If you like, we could get started as early as next week." Play it by ear. If the customer says he or she is expecting other quotes, just say, "Please don't hesitate to call if you have any further questions." Then follow up later.

7.1 Your InfoPack

The package of information you give potential customers, your InfoPack, should contain general information about all the services you offer, features of these services, and wonderful selling points about them. The InfoPack gives you an opportunity to answer most questions about the work you do. As well, it is a marketing tool that informs your customers about all the services you offer. I have upsold customers more than a hundred times with the InfoPack alone.

There is an example of an InfoPack on the CD-ROM included with this book. Review it and use it as a template to create an InfoPack for your own business based on the services you will offer.

7.2 Your introductory letter

You include an introductory letter with your quotation to briefly introduce yourself and your company to the prospect. In it you want to highlight key points about your business that will help your prospect decide to do business with you. In some circumstances you may also want to include specifics of the job you are bidding on.

Introduce yourself, and perhaps other key players, in the first paragraph. Thank the customer for the opportunity to quote on the job, and mention that you have attached the InfoPack, which should answer any questions they have.

If you have opted to send a printed proposal instead of leaving the quotation sheet, your letter can serve that purpose too. List the specifics of the job in plain English. Include the cost and how and when you will expect payment. You may want to include an outline of all the services included in the program.

Include a paragraph about how good your services are. You don't want to blow smoke; just be real. If you don't live up to the expectations you set here, you will be in for a world of grief. Finally, close by letting the prospect know he or she can call you with any questions, comments, or concerns — or, of course, to book the work.

Create several generic introductory letters and use specific ones to accompany quotes based on key conditions. For example, if you are targeting a specific neighborhood, have one letter tailored for it. You could have one for maintenance programs and one for lawn renos. You only have to write them once, but you can keep using them for years.

Sample 12 illustrates a typical introductory letter.

321 Verdure Street
North Vancouver, BC V7J 1E7
Ph: (555) 555-LAWN Fax: (555) 555-1234

Re: Quotation for services that you requested

Hi. My name is Johnny Green and I am the owner of Greener Grass Lawn and Garden Company. Thank you for your interest in my company. I appreciate the opportunity to help you with your lawn and garden needs.

Please find attached your quotation for the services you requested, as well as an information package that should answer any questions you have about these or other services offered by Greener Grass.

There are three keys to the success of our business that prove themselves day after day. We don't hide these keys like some sort of marketing secret. No, we advertise them because they are the very same reasons people like to do business with us. They are attention to detail, customer service excellence, and happy, helpful, professional employees.

I am sure that you will find, as many have in your neighborhood, that we at Greener Grass take these commitments seriously, not just as words we use in our advertising, but as crucial ingredients to our business success.

If you have any questions, comments, or concerns about the attached quotation, our services, or your property, please don't hesitate to give me a call. I would be happy to provide the information you need. And of course, when you are ready to go ahead with the work, just give me a call and I will gladly schedule it.

Thanks once again for considering Greener Grass Lawn and Garden.

Sincerely,

Johnny Green
Johnny Green
Greener Grass Lawn and Garden

8. THE FOLLOW-UP

Don't make the mistake of thinking that because a person does not call you back right away, he or she is not interested in your services. People get busy, they procrastinate, perhaps they are on the edge of a decision and need a little push. A prompt and friendly follow-up call can be that push.

When following up, all you have to say is that you are calling about the quote you left and were wondering if there were any questions or concerns. You may be able to sense, even on the phone, whether the customer is interested by paying attention to the tone of voice and the words used.

If the customer is noncommittal, you will have to judge whether to try again in a few days with another follow-up call or to give it up.

If the customer isn't interested in your services, thank him or her for the opportunity you had to view the property and wish him or her the best with the selected company. Also let the person know that if he or she needs any help in the future, you would be interested in quoting again. Record the rejection on your follow-up checklist and file the quote in the customer's folder or a folder labeled "rejected quotes." There is a strong possibility that it will come in handy again.

10
THE WORKFLOW FROM ACCEPTANCE TO ROUTING

Are you ready to continue your guided tour of a typical job workflow? You've done the hard work — landing a job. Now it's time to examine what you need to do when accepting a job. You should also think about upselling and face the challenges of scheduling and routing the job.

1. ACCEPTING THE JOB

This is what it's all about — what all the work was for. The customer has accepted your quotation on his or her job. Now what do you do? Obviously it's time to get to work and make some money. Perhaps less obvious are the following steps, which will keep you organized in your office and on the job:

- First, don't forget to thank the customer for his or her business before you hang up the phone.

- If you have not already done so, enter the customer's name and information in your computer software.

- Create a new legal-sized file folder for the customer. In this folder, you will store old quotation sheets and worksheets, letters, and any other customer sundries that you think may be useful down the road.

- If you are using a manual system, staple a 3" x 5" index card with the customer's name on the top inside corner of the file folder so that when you open the folder, you see the card face up. This is your job history card; use it for accepted quotes only. Record on it a brief job description, the dollar value of the work, and the date the work was started.

- On your follow-up checklist, note that the quote was accepted. Don't file the checklist yet; you need it as a reminder to follow up again once the job has been completed. Drop it in your daily drop file.

- If the customer has signed up for regular maintenance, add him or her to one of your existing routes. If the job is non-maintenance, schedule it into your workflow. (See sections **3** and **4** of this chapter for more information on scheduling and routing.) Don't forget to think about what materials you might need to purchase or have delivered.

- Add the customer to the job costing worksheet (see section **6** of chapter 11). If you have a manual system, also add him or her to the customer job time record. Create an equipment usage worksheet too. (These forms are illustrated and discussed in chapter 11.)

- Prepare a new customer kit (see section **1.1** below).

- Depending on the size of the job, you may want to purchase a small thank-you gift.

1.1 New customer kit

A new customer kit is an effective way to thank a new customer for hiring you and to supply important company information. Use a simple file folder with your business card clipped to it, or, if you have the funds, you could have custom folders printed with your business name and logo on the front. Include the following items in your kit:

- Thank-you and welcome letter (see Sample 13)

- New client questionnaire with a stamped, self-addressed envelope for its return (see Worksheet 6)

- An InfoPack (see section **7.1** of chapter 9), if you haven't supplied one to the customer already

- A service contract and policy statement (see section **1.2**)

- Your outline of services included (see section **1.2**)

- An original thank-you card

1.2 Service contract

You have to decide whether you want to use a formal customer contract in your business. A contract is in writing and makes clear —

- the scope of the agreement (what you are saying you will do),

- the cost of the agreement (what your customer is agreeing to pay), and

- any contingency in the agreement (what happens to the agreement in certain eventualities. For example, you might want to stipulate how many days' notice are required to cancel the contract, or under what other conditions the contract may be cancelled).

Contracts can eliminate misunderstandings or possible miscommunications. Also, if you clearly state what services you will perform, the customer can enjoy a measure of confidence that you are actually going to perform them, so a contract can be a selling feature. However, if a contract is too long or is written in legalese, you may scare your

WELCOME LETTER

Tuxedo Property Maintenance Company
123 Premiere Street
Vancouver, BC   V7J 1E7
Ph: (555) 555-1234 Fax: (555) 555-4321

April 4, 200-

Mr. B. Banner
475 Main Street
Vancouver, BC V7U 1P5

Re: Welcome!

Dear Mr. Banner:

Thank you once again for supporting our hardworking company. On behalf of all of us here at Tuxedo Property Maintenance Company, I would like to welcome you aboard.

One thing we value dearly is the feedback we get from our customers. After all, how will we know how we are doing if we don't ask? Please feel free to contact us if you ever have any comments, concerns, or questions about our company, our services, or your property. On that note, I have included a short survey with this letter that I hope you will have time to complete and mail back to me in the self-addressed, stamped envelope. Thank you in advance for your participation.

Also included in your welcome kit is an information pack detailing all our services and providing many interesting facts about what we do. Please read our standard agreement, which covers a few simple policies that we have in place for our landscape maintenance programs.

We appreciate your business and look forward to working with you in the coming months and years.

Sincerely,

Joel LaRusic
Joel LaRusic
Tuxedo Property Maintenance Company

WORKSHEET 6
NEW CLIENT QUESTIONNAIRE

New Client Questionnaire

Greetings and thank you once again for your decision to use Tuxedo Property Maintenance Company. I consider it my personal responsibility to ensure that you never regret your decision. To that end, and in our unending commitment to provide the best customer service possible, we ask new clients to complete the following questionnaire so that we can better serve them. Thank you in advance for your time, and please don't hesitate to call us if you have questions or concerns about your landscape or our service.

1. How did you hear about our service?

    ☐ Flyer ☐ Yellow Pages ☐ Saw our truck ☐ Coupon

    ☐ Referred (Please tell us who referred you): _____

    ☐ Other _____

2. What factors motivated you to call us for a quote?

    ☐ Had a coupon ☐ Liked our ad ☐ Saw us working; was impressed

    ☐ Random choice ☐ Referral was good ☐ No specific reason

    ☐ Other: _____

3. What factors motivated you to select our company?

    ☐ Liked our price ☐ Professional response ☐ Knowledgeable staff

    ☐ Saw our quality work ☐ Based on good referral ☐ Convenient

    ☐ Other: _____

4. What is most important to you as you think about your lawn and garden? Please use a scale of 1 to 5, with 1 as very important and 5 as not very important.

    _____ Having a beautiful, lush lawn   _____ No weeds in lawn

    _____ No weeds in beds   _____ Fresh-looking beds

    _____ Overall property looks neat   _____ Lots of color in garden

    _____ Interesting plants in the garden   _____ Use natural gardening methods

    _____ Know what's going on in garden   _____ Attention to detail

    _____ Understanding technical details about what's happening in the garden

5. Are there any other things that are important to you that were not listed?

    _____

    _____

    _____

6. What aspects of a lawn care/gardening service are most important to you? Please use a scale of 1 to 5, with 1 as very important and 5 as not very important.

    _____ Reasonable prices   _____ Professional service

    _____ Friendly service   _____ Prompt service

    _____ High-quality service   _____ High-quality materials used

    _____ Close attention to detail   _____ Reliability

    _____ Knowledgeable experts   _____ Full-service company

7. Are there any other things that are important to you that were not listed?

    _____

    _____

    _____

8. Which other home services do you currently use or use on occasion?

    ❑ Home cleaning   ❑ Window washing   ❑ Gutter cleaning/repair

    ❑ Pressure washing   ❑ Pool cleaning   ❑ Other

9. Could you tell us some of your favorite things? (If you don't know the proper name, you may use whatever space you need to describe colors, textures, etc.).

    a. Annual bedding plant _____

    b. Perennial _____

    c. Shrub _____

    d. Tree _____

    e. Color _____

    f. Newspaper _____

WORKSHEET 6 — CONTINUED

10. Do you have access to the Internet at home?   ☐ Yes   ☐ No

11. Have you visited us online at www.tuxedomaintenance.com?   ☐ Yes   ☐ No

12. Please use the following space to tell us anything else that will help us provide you with better service.

_____

_____

_____

_____

_____

_____

_____

_____

_____

_____

Thank you for your time. Remember, you don't need a survey to tell us what you think. Please feel free to call us at (555) 555-1234 at any time if you have questions, comments, or concerns about your property or our service.

customer away or at least make it more difficult to close the deal.

One item in the contract that may alarm people is the notice required for cancellation. They may fear that they won't be able to get out of the contract soon enough if things go wrong. Stick to a cancellation notice of 30 days for either party.

You should definitely use a formal contract in the following situations:

- If you are doing work at commercial properties, multi-dwelling properties such as condos, or any property where you are dealing with a property manager

- If your maintenance program is front-end loaded (e.g., many maintenance programs require the bulk of work in the spring, but the customer pays over the year), you need to protect yourself from a customer who quits after the second month, when much of the work has been done but only one-sixth of the fees have been paid. (To address this problem, put a clause in the contract that says the customer will be billed for any unpaid work at the time of cancellation.)

- If a customer is asking you to work on multiple properties

- In any situation where the customer quitting abruptly will cost you money or great inconvenience

- In any situation where you don't feel confident about the customer's ability to pay

You can choose to use a more casual agreement to deal with existing and trusted customers who have one residential property. In some cases it may be enough to merely sign the quotation sheet with the price on it.

Sample 14 shows a simple contractual letter that you can adapt for your own business. An example of a more detailed Outline of Services is provided on the CD-ROM. It lists and briefly describes all the services that you are agreeing to include in the customer's landscape maintenance program, as well as the services that are not included but that you will perform for an extra cost. It is important to set accurate expectations right from the beginning so your customers are not upset when you do not deliver a service that they thought was included. You can include the Outline of Services with your contract or maintenance agreement form if you decide to use one.

2. UPSELLING

How much more does it cost to get new customers than to sell services to existing customers? The numbers vary. Some say it costs five times more, some say ten. No one debates, though, that it does cost more to attract new business. It is interesting, then, that most companies focus the bulk of their marketing efforts on finding new business. Of course, if you are starting out fresh, you have no choice. All your customers are new. However, once you establish a clientele, you should capitalize on what you already have. You have customers who know you, trust you, and may well be willing to spend more money with you ... if only you'd ask.

There are two varieties of upselling: encouraging your customers to buy more of the same, and encouraging your customers to buy different products or services. The

CONTRACTUAL LETTER

Residential Landscape Maintenance Agreement and Policy

This is an agreement between:

Our Valued Customer ('The Customer')

Mr. B. Banner
475 Main Street
Vancouver, BC V7U 1P5

And:

The Hardworking Landscape Maintenance Company ('The Company')

Tuxedo Property Maintenance Company
123 Premiere Street
Vancouver, BC V7J 1E7
Ph: (555) 555-1234 Fax: 555-4321

This is an agreement for The Company to provide lawn and garden services to The Customer for the growing season of 200-.

The services will be carried out at The Customer's address above and will include maintenance of both the front and back yards. For a complete list of all services included, please refer to the attached Outline of Services.

The cost of this program is $1,350 for the season or, in equal monthly payments, $150/month for each of the nine months in the program. We will visit the site each Thursday. If anything prevents us from visiting on that day, we will visit on Saturday or the next possible day.

This agreement may be terminated by either party with one month's notice.

Please keep the following points in mind regarding your lawn and garden service:

- Please keep the lawn free of objects such as children's toys on the day we visit.

- Keep children and pets inside the house during our visits. Our equipment has the potential to harm unsuspecting and unprotected bystanders.

- We do not clean up pet droppings. There are reputable companies that do. Failure to pick up after your pet may result in termination of services.

- If your program includes fertilizer or chemical applications to the lawn or garden, we will take all necessary safety precautions and will notify you both the week before the visit (if feasible) and after the actual service has been completed. We will include any special instructions.

- We will leave invoices in your mailbox on the last visit of the month. Payments are due by the 20th of the following month. Please be aware that cash flow is important to our small business. We thank you for your prompt payments.

As you can see, we like to keep things simple and have few rules. Thank you for your patronage.

additional product or service often complements the existing one, but it doesn't have to.

Ask yourself one simple question: "How can I help my customer?" If you view your business objective as helping your customers, you will have no trouble thinking of new ways to help them. Think about your client's property and imagine creative ways that you could improve it. Consider it your goal, your responsibility, to offer your customers the absolutely best-looking lawn and garden on the block. What would it take to get there? Whatever it is, offer it. Not everyone will buy everything you offer, but you should still offer (see the sidebar on upselling).

Always leave one day each week (or even two, depending on your market) for the "extras." If you have one crew, do maintenance visits three or four days of the week. Save the other day or two for additional jobs for your clients. If you decide to grow your company, someday you could have a special full-time crew, aside from your maintenance crews, that just does extra jobs and improvements.

If you are overly busy with maintenance, it might be a good time to consider adding another crew. You may be surprised at how much income you can generate by asking your loyal customers for more work.

And don't forget that any time is a good time to upsell. Do it when you first sign up a customer, and do it sporadically if you think of an idea for a customer's home. Spend time each spring, before you rev up your business for the season, thinking about innovative ways you can sell your existing customers more services.

Ten Ways to Upsell Your Customers

1. **Encourage them to buy more of what they have already purchased:** If you get a call for a one-time lawn cut, tell the customer that you offer lawn-cutting programs to suit any need or budget. If a customer asks for a fertilizer application or a weed spray, make sure you explain that your lawn care programs include all the weeding and feeding needed.

2. **Add complementary services:** Many services go hand in glove. Lawn cuts with a fertilizer program. Fertilizer programs with weed control. Top-dressing with overseeding. If you think two services complement each other, be sure to tell your customer about it.

3. **Add non-complementary services:** The services you offer as extras do not necessarily have to be complementary. Make sure your customers and prospects have a list of all your services, and don't hesitate to offer some shrub pruning, for example, when you quote on lawn care.

4. **Offer package deals:** This is a way to add complementary services by bundling them at a cheaper price than if the services were purchased separately. Even a 5 percent savings may motivate your customer to buy the package deal.

5. **Add new services:** Since your customers already have a degree of confidence in you, they may be interested in trying out any new services that you choose to offer. Do you have a pressure washer? If you position yourself as a property maintenance company, rather than simply a landscape maintenance company, you could branch out into tasks such as window washing or gutter cleaning.

6. **Add a garden:** Instead of continually combating problem areas in the garden, why not suggest something different. A shade garden under the big oak tree? A fragrant garden by the patio? An island garden to break up the monotony of the back yard? Think about how you can help your customer have the best lawn and garden on the block.

7. **Install a new lawn:** Sometimes a lawn needs so much work that it may be easier to install a brand-new one. But will the customer want to pay for a new lawn? There's only one way to find out ... ask! I have been surprised more than once by how quickly people say yes to a perfect new lawn.

8. **Top up soil and mulch in beds:** Freshly topped up beds look wonderful. Plus, they make your maintenance easier. Make sure you recommend topping up garden beds often. Many customers will pay for it every year.

9. **Sell products:** Are there things you could sell to your customers? I sometimes buy spring flowering bulbs wholesale and sell them to my customers, even if they don't want me to install the bulbs for them. There may be other things that your customers would be happy to buy from you (e.g., hand tools, snips, or rakes) if you offered the same prices as the retailer. Be sure to keep in mind the logistics of supplying what you are selling. It must be feasible to deliver the items while carrying out your normal work routines. (Check with your accountant on the tax implications of selling products without labor attached.)

10. **Remind your customers about your extra services:** Use envelope stuffers, newsletters, flyers, or other advertising. Don't be afraid to offer the extras more than once. Just because your client says no today, it doesn't mean he or she will always say no.

3. SCHEDULING

The logistics of lawn maintenance — how you organize your movement from job to job — are among the most daunting tasks of running your business. You've got lawn cuts to schedule weekly, or perhaps every 10, 12, or 14 days. You don't want to show up too soon or there's not much to cut, but if you come too late the grass will be too long. Mrs. Jones only wants her lawn cut on Fridays; can you oblige? When will you fit in the fertilizing and weed spraying? And what about the extra work you booked outside of your maintenance; when will that be done? Add in rain days or other delays and you face a potential nightmare trying to arrange it all.

I have good news for you. If you decided to computerize and purchased one of the lawn company operator (LCO) software packages recommended in chapter 5, you have made your life a whole lot easier. These packages have been designed with you in mind, and the creators of the software understand the challenges of workflow.

And there's more good news. If you follow some simple rules, the job of scheduling and routing will be more manageable. These rules apply whether you use a computer or not.

The first rule is: *Choose a maintenance rotation and stick with it.* What that rotation schedule looks like will depend on where you live, how fast things grow, whether you have been asked to fertilize the grass, and the demands of your own personal agenda. The most common rotations are weekly, every ten days, every two weeks (biweekly), or "next available day." While you can manage well with a combination of weekly and biweekly maintenance visits, neither of these mix well with the ten-day rotation. Choose one or the other. I recommend weekly/biweekly for the most flexibility.

3.1 Weekly/biweekly rotation

A great feature of the weekly/biweekly rotation is that you give your customers consistency, telling them, for example, that you'll be on the property every Monday, or every other Thursday. This schedule makes things easy for the customer, and easy for you too. The primary disadvantage of the weekly rotation is that there is little room for error. If you get rained out or are down for some other reason on Monday, what will you do? Each job you bump until Tuesday results in the bumping of yet another job to the day after that. This cascading bumping causes a

chain reaction that is difficult to manage. It's time to introduce the second rule of scheduling: *Book your extra workdays strategically.*

I've discussed the idea of leaving certain days available to complete extra work. If you are on a weekly maintenance rotation, make those extra days Wednesdays and perhaps Saturdays. Then, if you get into a pinch on Monday or Tuesday, you can use Wednesday to catch up. Experience downtime on Thursday or Friday, and you can get back on track on Saturday. You may have to reschedule some of your extra work, but it is generally easier to rebook these types of jobs than your maintenance visits.

Perhaps you can leave entire days blank (don't book any extra work) if you know you will need them, say during certain rainy months. Or maybe a combination of both these methods will do the trick.

Some customers may not want a weekly visit. If you use a weekly rotation, you can offer to visit them every other week. However, be careful before agreeing to this plan. I have found that most customers who want a biweekly visit really need a weekly visit; they just don't want to pay for it. We would arrive to find overlong grass, which takes a long time to mow and is tough on your equipment. It is also harmful to the grass. If you run into this problem, you need to be firm with your customers. Tell them they need a weekly cut or will have to pay more for their biweekly cut.

On the other hand, where you live there may be certain times of the year when a cut every 14 days is enough. What should you do if you provide programs with weekly rotation and the grass doesn't grow? Do you skip a visit and reduce the bill? That's one option, but if you have sold your customers on the fact that you are taking care of their property (as opposed to robotically cutting the lawn each and every week), then you could spend some time doing other things such as more bed work, pruning or trimming, dividing perennials, etc. I have found that most customers are agreeable to this arrangement and do not complain if the grass is not cut every week during low season.

3.2 Ten-day rotation

A ten-day rotation allows a little breathing room in your schedule since your customers are not tied to specific days of the week and will not be too upset if they are bumped a day due to downtime. On the downside, you have more days to fill, which means that, overall, it's more administrative work. As well, some customers will insist that you visit on their preferred days. I found Fridays filled up quickly because homeowners wanted their yards to look great for the weekend. On the other hand, commercial properties always seem to want a Monday visit to clean up after the weekend. A ten-day schedule will not work with these types of customers.

3.3 Next-available-day rotation

This method of rotation barely merits discussion since it provides the lowest level of service. Essentially you are saying to your customer: "We'll get to it as soon as we can." It may be a week, it may be ten days, it may be more. I do know of businesses that have used this method, but generally it was because residential maintenance was a sideline for them, not their primary work. While this rotation offers the ultimate flexibility when scheduling, I don't recommend it.

3.4 Scheduling extras

Setting a time for periodic extras, such as fertilizing and weed spraying, is what makes scheduling tough — unless you are using an LCO package. The rule behind scheduling extras is: *Keep all your customers on the same program and do all extras in the same time period.*

It works like this. Try to keep all your customers on a similar lawn care program, which is easier than it sounds. For example, where I live, everyone starts with a lime application first thing in the spring. We hit them with a moss control fertilizer about two weeks later. Then I follow up with the first summer fertilizer about six weeks after that. And so on. Using this method, you finish each task in one or two weeks and then you're done with it for the year.

This system works well because you know that every house you stop at will get an identical treatment. It operates on the same principle as the McDonald's breakfast. Have you ever tried ordering a breakfast at 11:05 a.m.? It's too late because they have changed from their breakfast system to their lunch system. You can't mix the two or efficiency is affected. Compare that to your business. The first customer wants lime, the second needs moss control, and the third needs a regular fertilizer. You can almost hear your profit being sucked up by inefficiency.

Keeping all customers on the same program makes life easier in the office, too. You know, for example, that you lime from March 1 to 15, do moss control from March 15 to 31, and so on. Of course, you will always have exceptions and odd jobs that are out of place. I'm not suggesting you refuse the business as McDonald's would do, but if you get 90 percent of your clients onboard, your scheduling will be much easier than if you use a more haphazard method.

Other extras such as aerations, power raking, or full lawn renovations are easier to schedule. We have already discussed the option of keeping certain days of the week for extras, and this is the best solution for these types of jobs. It's up to you to decide how many extra days you will need.

4. Routing

While scheduling is about planning to do the job on a certain day, routing means thinking about how it will fit in with all the other jobs you have scheduled.

If you have one crew, routing is fairly straightforward. You will probably have a Monday route, a Tuesday route, and so on. If you have several crews, it's a bit more complicated. For example, you could have a midtown route, an uptown route, and a downtown route. I have always found it best to identify routes by the area they service.

The other part of routing, which can be more tricky, is organizing your daily jobs to reduce unprofitable "windshield time" — that is the time spent in your truck, not making money. You should plan routes logically and in advance. If you do it correctly, it will be easy to add, remove, or otherwise edit your routes in the future.

4.1 The wall-map routing system

In chapter 5 I suggested you buy a wall map of your area; here is where it becomes useful. It will help you sort your jobsites into a logical and efficient order. When routing, you want to arrange your jobsites so that as you drive from one to the other, you are not backtracking or driving in circles.

Furthermore, and much more tricky, if you juggle jobs from one route to another, you don't want to have to re-sort them each time. Here is a system that should make it easy:

- Using either thumbtacks or a pencil, mark each of your jobs on the wall map. Now imagine that you are going to visit each site in a single day (you'll also have to imagine that time is not an issue) and wind up back at home base at the end of the day. Which way would you go to complete the route most quickly? Try to arrange it so that you are going in a big circle, with the first job close to your base, say to the west, and your last job in the vicinity of your base in another direction. Experiment with different routes until you find the best one.

- Now assign routing numbers to the sites. Start with the first jobsite on your main route and give it the number 1,000. Then travel along the route in your mind's eye, stopping at each site and giving it a number greater than 1,000, perhaps in increments of 10. The increment value doesn't really matter; you just want to allow enough room for new customers in between without reshuffling and renumbering everyone. The greater the distance between your sites, the larger the increment should be.

- After that, break your market into logical chunks. You can have any number of chunks as long as the system makes sense. Number each chunk, starting with 1 and in increments of 1, as you again follow a route that will take you sensibly through each area and back home again. Take a look at your jobsite numbering again. Customers in the first chunk should be assigned routing numbers in the 1,000 range; customers in the second chunk will get routing numbers from 2,000 to 2,999, and so on.

Logically, when you have completed this task, you should be able to select any set of customers from any area, sort them by their routing number, and have the best route. The system isn't foolproof, and you may need to make minor adjustments, but overall it works well. As you grow, assign numbers to your new customers based on where they fit along the main route.

4.2 Creating routes

Now that you have your main route planned out, it's time to break it into daily routes.

It's best to break your main route into geographic chunks, with each chunk being a different route. Take into account where the job is located (use your routing numbers) as well as how long you expect to be at each job. Don't feel you need to fill an entire day to create a route. For example, your midtown route may only have three customers now, and your uptown route two. That's fine. There is nothing saying you can't do your midtown and your uptown routes on the same day. Or perhaps you want to do your midtown route one morning and deliver quotes for the rest of the day.

Then you have to decide how you are going to handle those customers — all from different routes, of course — who want work done on the same day — usually a Friday. You don't want your Friday route to become a scenic tour of the entire area, defeating the

whole purpose of your routing plan. And don't be tempted to accommodate every customer in the beginning, when you have time to book everyone on Friday. The day will soon arrive when you have to move some customers to other days to improve your efficiency. The customers you move may not take kindly to it.

The best solution is to decide now, before you even begin, what routes will get Friday service. You will not be able to oblige everyone, so you should please as many as you can and hope the others will compromise. Perhaps there is an exclusive neighborhood on your route that you want your business to grow in; you could decide to schedule Friday visits there (consider this a selling feature). There may be some other obvious reason to give a certain area the much-sought-after Friday visit. The bottom line is that it is more important to route your day to avoid unprofitable driving time than it is to meet your customers' demand for preferred days. You will have to tell some customers that Friday is currently booked, but you can provide service on another day and will guarantee their lawns will still look great for the weekend. If you start giving in to every customer's demand for a particular service day, your routing will be a muddled mess and your profit line will show it.

The next step is to enter your newly created routes into your LCO program if you are using one. While every program is a bit different, they all offer the following features:

- They help you create and name your routes. Then you can assign each customer to a route.

- There will be an easy way to book recurring services such as fertilizing and weed spraying. For example, a fertilizer job may be automatically rescheduled every six or eight weeks (whatever you decide).

🍃 You will be able to print out route sheets that list all the jobs for the day and the route in question. You can take these with you on the road, and as you complete your route you can mark off the work that has been done.

If you are not using software, you can use the following manual system. Even if you are using LCO software, you may find components of this system beneficial.

🍃 You will need to buy large 3-, 6-, or 12-month wall calendars. The dry erase type is convenient. As well, if you haven't already purchased a daily planner, you'll need to do so now. Get one of the big ones with a full 8" x 11" page for each day. These will be your route sheets.

🍃 Make lists of the customers on each of your routes — with routing numbers, names, addresses, and phone numbers — and stick them on the wall beside your wall calendar for quick reference. You may need to update your lists each month if you have customers starting and finishing their programs at different times. Keep a copy of this information in your daily planner too.

🍃 On your wall calendar, write the route name on the appropriate day. For example, suppose you have three routes: Uptown, which you service Friday; Midtown, which you service Thursdays; and Downtown, which you service Mondays. For each week on your wall calendar, enter "Uptown" on Fridays, "Midtown" on Thursdays, and "Downtown" on Mondays.

🍃 Assign your recurring jobs to certain weeks. Using either colored pens, pencils, crayons, or dry erase markers, draw a thick rectangle around your first recurring service time frame. Use one color for each service. For example, if you do lime from March 1 to 15, mark a blue rectangle around the entire two-week period. Also in blue, write "lime" somewhere beside the box. Do the same thing, with a different color, for the time frames of all the other services. If you do two services simultaneously — for example, aeration and fertilizer — they can share the time period; just be sure to label your calendar appropriately. Now you can plan ahead and ensure that you have all the supplies you need before each time period.

At the end of this exercise you should have all your extra and recurring services roughed in. When you get closer to the dates, you'll need to fine-tune the schedule, and that's where your trusty daily planner comes in.

It's always a good idea to do your weekly planning on Sunday evening. Refer to your wall calendar and your route lists posted on the wall, then write down in your daily planner the specific jobs that you will need to complete each day. The information you need is the routing number, customer name, and list of the services you plan to complete on that day. If the day falls within your recurring services time frame, then include that service. Leave some space next to each service to enter how long the job took. Your daily planner entry might look something like this:

Monday, March 8, 200-
1000 Ms. Kent
    Regular maintenance visit
    Start: _____   Stop: _____
    Lime application
    Start: _____   Stop: _____

1050 Mr. & Mrs. Parker
    Regular maintenance visit
    Start: _____   Stop: _____
    Lime application
    Start: _____   Stop: _____

1051 Mr. Wayne
    Regular maintenance visit
    Start: _____   Stop: _____
    Lime application
    Start: _____   Stop: _____

Do the same thing for each of your routes, scheduling all your maintenance work for the week. Leave a line or two between each customer in case you need to add more services later.

Now you are ready to go to work! Remember to review your schedule before starting out each day in case you need special equipment or supplies for a particular job. Check your daily drop file for special instructions or tasks that affect your day. As you complete each job during the day, record the start and stop time for each service. This is valuable information that you will use later when you do your job costing (see chapter 11). Also record any extra duties performed or any special requests from your customers in your daily planner. I like to note the weather conditions and who I was working with. Add anything you feel might be relevant.

5. USING JOB EQUIPMENT CHECKLISTS

Part of scheduling is ensuring that you have everything with you when you need it, where you need it. There's nothing worse than arriving at a jobsite, only to realize you have forgotten to bring some essential piece of equipment. Returning home to pick up the forgotten equipment is a huge time-waster. One way to avoid this is to create and use a job equipment checklist.

Make a list of all the equipment that you will need to do a particular job. Create a list for each of the different jobs you do (e.g., regular maintenance, pruning, lawn renovation, etc.). Each list becomes one of your checklists. For example, you might have a pruning checklist that includes hedge trimmers, blower, loppers, orchard ladder, chain saw, shears, etc.

Then, as you review your schedule each day, note which jobs you'll be doing and refer to your job equipment checklists to make sure you have everything you need. You can laminate your checklists for durability and keep them in your shop and/or truck. Remember, make a checklist for every job.

Now you're ready to go!

11
THE WORKFLOW FROM JOB COMPLETION TO JOB COSTING

Your workday in the field is done, but there is still much to do. It's time to think about invoicing, collecting payment, quality assurance, and the all-important job costing, which tells you if you've made any money.

1. INVOICING

If you expect to be paid for your effort on the jobsite, you have to give your customers a bill at the end of the day (or month). If you are computerized, you can produce invoices with your software and print them out on either plain paper or preprinted forms. The invoice should include your contact information, all the job data — including date(s) of service and costs — and any taxes. Your invoices should be sequentially numbered and they should include the payment due date.

Payment terms are an integral part of invoicing. As a business owner, you need to decide what terms to offer your customers. There are only two practical options: "Payment due upon receipt" and "Net 20" (or Net 15 or Net 30).

"Due upon receipt" simply means you are asking that the invoice be paid as soon as it is received. As a general rule, if you are doing jobs for non-maintenance customers, you should let them know when you accept a job that payment will be due upon satisfactory completion of the job, before you leave the site. If possible, coordinate with the customer so that he or she is home when you finish up and can pay you at that time. If the customer is not at home, leave the invoice with "Due Upon Receipt" stamped on it. If it is for a large amount, I recommend that you visit the customer within a day or two to confirm the job was satisfactorily completed and to collect the payment in person.

"Net 20" means that the net (or total balance) is due within 20 days of the invoice date. Use this option for your regular maintenance customers as it is not practical to collect payment from them each week. As well, since they are regular customers and have some history with you, you have a little more trust that they will pay the bill and pay it on time. On the last visit of the month, you can leave an invoice with the month's charges chronologically detailed.

An alternative to using net 20 is to simply put the due date of the payment on the invoice. For example, if you deliver the invoice at the end of February, your due date could be March 20.

When jobs require some outlay of cash to buy materials or tools, or if you are doing large jobs for new customers, consider asking the customer for a deposit, with the balance due on completion.

2. GETTING PAID

There is nothing like opening your mailbox and taking out a stack of envelopes from people sending you money. It's a fulfilling experience and one of the greatest joys of self-employment. Savor it!

When you receive money, simply record it in whichever system you are using. If you are computerized, enter the customer payment into the computer and add the check to a bank deposit, making sure you include the customer's name on the deposit slip for later reference. In a manual system, either enter the individual customer payment in your ledger or get the deposit together and post the entire deposit to your ledger.

But what if those envelopes don't arrive in your mailbox? How do you stay on top of past-due accounts? First of all, remember that your systems must be in place, as discussed in chapter 7. If you use the systems recommended there, you will be on top of who owes you what. If you do not have a system in place to monitor your receivables, you will be faced with much grief.

Here are some suggestions for handling collection issues:

- Take note of past due accounts *before* sending invoices out. If a regular customer has not paid a previous month's bill, stick on the invoice/statement a conspicuous label that reads: "Please pay overdue balance today." If you are especially sensitive to payment tardiness, you could also put a note in with the bill that says something like "Thank you for your continued support of Dirty Deeds Landscaping. Consistent cash flow is imperative for a small business. Please help me by paying your balance each month. Thanks again."

- If the customer is not a regular, or if it is his or her first year of a maintenance contract, take the additional step of putting a note in your daily drop file to follow up in one week with a phone call. Non-regular or new customers are high risk. In the 10 years I've been in business, no maintenance customer who has been with me over a year has defaulted on payment.

- After 60 days it's time to turn up the heat. Phone the customer and ask if there is a problem. Try to ask a specific question, such as "When will the check be ready?" Tell him or her that you can come by to pick it up.

- Be professional, polite, and diplomatic when you phone and write. But be firm. Make a record of each attempt to collect.

- Follow up with another statement, showing aged receivables, and another letter, this one more strongly worded than the last. At this point you should consider restricting services to cash only or suspending them altogether.

- If worst comes to worst and your attempts are ignored, write a letter threatening legal action. Depending on the size of the debt, you have recourse through small claims court or a third-party collection agency.

- If you give up on the bill at any time, don't forget to write it off as a bad debt business expense.

What is more important than developing collection methods is knowing how to avoid the need for them in the first place. You'll have fewer problems if you implement the following policies:

- Make your monthly invoices look like statements, so the entire balance, including past due, is clear. Make sure there are aged receivables (e.g., 30–60 days, 60–90 days, and (horror!) 90+ days overdue) so both you and your customer can see how much of the debt is current (e.g., from the past 30 days).

- When dealing with new customers, don't front-end load your maintenance contracts. If you include a pricey lawn renovation in your program and complete it in the first month, it is going to take you all year to recoup the costs (assuming the customer is paying a fixed monthly fee). It's better to bill for it at the end of the month. To take it a step further, include only core maintenance tasks in the monthly fee and bill for everything else each month. This way you will never get too far ahead of yourself.

- Accept credit cards with the stipulation that the money is taken from the account on the first day of the month. I have used this system with great success. Yes, it will cost you a couple of percent, but I felt it was worth it to know that I had guaranteed income in the bank on the first of every month.

- It bears repeating: New customers are high risk. Use caution. Insist on payment on completion. Consider having a special policy for first-year customers. For example, if a job is worth more than a few hundred dollars, ask for 50 percent up front with the balance due on completion. Do not extend credit over that few hundred dollars if you can't afford to lose it.

3. END-OF-DAY PROCEDURES

You've worked hard all day, and now you are back at the office. Did you make money today? I hope so, but you won't know for sure unless you take care of a few end-of-day tasks. So before you get back to your personal life, take a few minutes to keep your system running and your work life organized.

At the end of the day, you should complete four important tasks:

1. Record the work that you completed, including the length of time it took to do each job.

2. Organize any special requests you received or quotes you wrote up during the day.

3. Prepare for the next day.

4. Make a few follow-up calls.

3.1 Recording work

Using your LCO software, you can mark a scheduled job as completed. At the same time, use the data you collected throughout the day to record the start and stop times (or the total time) for the job. The job will then be added automatically to the customer's bill, which you will print out at month end.

If you are using a manual system, you will need to record your job times on a worksheet, such as the one shown in Sample 15. This customer job times worksheet (also included on the CD-ROM that came with this book) helps you track crucial data that you will use to ensure you are making a profit at the end of the day. You need one sheet for each type of service you would like to track times for.

Along the left side of the page, list the names of all your customers. Each of the narrow columns to the right represents one visit. Simply enter the time, in minutes, that the job took from the moment you got out of the truck to the time the equipment was loaded back on the truck (assuming that you took no downtime and did not perform extra services). Remember to multiply the actual time by the number of people in your crew. So, for example, if a two-person crew visited Mr. Wayne from 9:53 to 10:26, you would calculate 33 minutes in real time, multiplied by 2, to give a total of 66 person-minutes at that site. Enter the number in the next available

box on the sheet. Use another sheet if necessary. Keep these sheets in a safe place.

In a manual system, the best way to indicate jobs are completed and to make sure the customer gets billed for them is to have a running invoice that you add to throughout the month as the customer gets more service. At the end of each day, go through the invoices that you have started and add line items for the jobs you did that day, as well as the associated costs. If the customer pays a fixed monthly fee, do not attach a price to individual services, but do list them as having been completed.

3.2 Dealing with special requests and quotes

Another end-of-day task is to take care of any quotes or special requests from the day. First, check your daily planner for any notes that you scribbled as you went about your route. Perhaps Ms. Adams wanted a quote for four yards of topsoil delivered and installed, and Mr. Parker wants his hedges trimmed in the next two or three weeks. Make notes in your daily planner of future events that you need to remember. If you wrote any quotes during the day, put them in your daily drop file for follow-up in a day or two. At the same time, check your drop file for any follow-ups due today. If you find anything, take care of it now.

3.3 Preparing for the next day

The third step before you finish working is to prepare the next day's work. If you do it now, you'll be ready to walk out the door in the morning and start earning money. Print out your route sheet or write it in your daily planner. Check the drop file again for tomorrow's

SAMPLE 15
CUSTOMER JOB TIMES RECORD

Regular Maintenance Visit

Visit Number (Time in Minutes)

Customer Name	1	2	3	4	5	6	7	8	9	10	11	12	13	14	15	16	17	18	19	20	21	22	23	24	25	26	27	28	29
Mr. & Mrs. Parker	24	35	32	28	21	24	30	28	22	22																			
Wayne Estate	152	141	180	175	140	152	125	160	135	148																			
Mr. Kent	68	59	62	60	68	58	62	57	65																				
Banner	40	45	43	48	42																								
Ms. Prince	110	95	120	92	115	102	120	90	110	95	115	92																	
Mr. Reid	90	90	95	87	95	90	85	80	100																				

tasks. If you are doing any extra work the next day, make sure you have the original quote to take with you, as well as any supplementary information. If you are planning on leaving an invoice when the job is done, prepare it now. Put everything together in a stack so you can grab it in the morning and get on with your day.

3.4 Making phone calls

I highly recommend this last end-of-day procedure: make one or two phone calls. One sure way to make your customers feel they are important to you is to maintain good lines of communication. You can do that by phoning customers after you have completed a big job for them, either a few days or a few weeks later, to see if there are any problems or if they need any more work. Also, you should make a point of calling regular maintenance customers once or twice throughout the season (not including the obligatory call at the beginning). Create a schedule so that you call all customers in rotation. Making one or two brief calls in the evening will take only a few minutes and is time well spent.

4. MONTH-END PROCEDURES

It's month end — payday! The good news is that you get to hand out a bunch of invoices and people will start sending you money. The bad news is that this does entail a few extra steps.

The primary month-end task is invoicing. If you have been using running invoices for the month, it's time to close them off and total them. Either print all your invoices, if you are using a computer, or manually total them and rip the top copy out of the invoice book. Put them in a stack. If you are using

an LCO package (and if you have stayed on top of entering your completed jobs), printing the invoices is as simple as a few mouse clicks.

Put your completed invoices in envelopes along with a self-addressed return envelope and perhaps an envelope stuffer promoting extra services. Seal the envelopes and put them in stacks according to the routes they belong to. On the appropriate day of the week, take your stack of invoices and drop them off as you visit each site.

Month end is a good time to put together an income statement and a listing of all your current receivables (as discussed in chapter 7). If you use a running invoice system for your customers, you could start new invoices for each customer now so you are ready to add services as the month rolls along.

Plan ahead for your month-end tasks. If you know the last day of the month is on a Friday and you never work Friday nights, then plan to do it Saturday or Sunday. It's foolhardy to put it off. If you don't get your invoices out on time, how do you expect your customers to pay on time?

5. QUALITY ASSURANCE

If you work for yourself and by yourself in this business, you don't need to read this section. After all, when the president of the company shows up to do a job, customers know they are getting the best. However, if and when you have employees, quality assurance becomes important.

Use a property quality assessment worksheet, such as the one shown in Sample 16, to help you provide consistent, high-quality service to all your customers. In doing so, you will avoid having customers phone to complain about a noticeable drop in service.

SAMPLE 16
PROPERTY QUALITY ASSESSMENT

Property Quality Assessment

Property Name: *The Estates*   Crew Lead: *Bill*

Date of Visit: *March 30, 200-*   Route: *Midtown*

Lawns: Overall — lawn looks great. I see that you have started alternating the cutting direction, and it is noticeably improved. Good work. The grass at north end of site is very weedy, and the weeds are going to seed already (three days after a cut). Do not mulch this area until weeds are under control. Apply herbicide on your next scheduled visit. Watch your edges along the sidewalk — they are a little scalped.

Beds: Increase rotation on the bed on north side of site until the weeds are under control. I'm going to be recommending fresh mulch for this site within a week or two — just FYI. Edges are nicely defined. The beds look fabulous. Nice work!

Plant material: The winter annuals need to come out ASAP — they are looking pretty poor. Have you noticed that holly near unit 3? It looks infected with mealy bug and black soot. I'll speak with you about a plan for that. The periwinkle by unit 1 is trampled — is that you, or the postman? Perhaps mention to resident there. Shrub by unit 4 is blocking window. Please trim ASAP. Mostly good, Bill, but please pay closer attention to plant material.

Other: Stairs to parking garage need blowing out. I'm going to recommend a power wash too. Curbs are perfectly tidy — excellent! The limestone path is getting weedy — manually weed if at all possible (before it gets really bad). Talk to me before applying weed killer.

Details: Great job on edges everywhere (except as noted above). Watch when you leave the site — you left some debris that fell under the tailgate and it's still here. There are small weeds coming in through paving stones — weed every week or two to keep them down. You forgot a small pile of debris in the back of the big bed, behind the hydrangea. Footprints left in same bed. Careful.

General notes: Bill, you're doing a great job at this property. I'm giving you a B+ overall. Congrats and thank you. Watch that plant material and you'll get an A next time. Thank you and keep up the good work.

You can create your own form that suits your company. Print the form in triplicate so that you can give your staff member one copy, put another copy in the customer file folder, and keep the final copy in the employee's folder.

Take the form with you to the jobsite and make notes on it as you walk around the entire site. Note areas that look great and problem areas. You may need extra paper to write additional notes, or perhaps you could make a note on the sheet that you would like to talk to the employee to discuss the work in more detail. If you do this, you should also outline in your daily planner what you need to talk to him or her about. In any case, when you hand an assessment to staff members, go over it with them. Remember to acknowledge and reward excellent work they have done.

6. JOB COSTING

Job costing is a system of examining individual jobs that you do in order to determine how much of a profit (or a loss) you are making. It is an aspect of the business that the inexperienced start-up entrepreneur often overlooks, yet it is crucial to the long-term success of your company. You must identify the unprofitable jobs on your routes and eliminate them. You must know which are your most profitable jobs and concentrate on getting more like them. In this section I'll show you a system I have used for years to determine the amount of time I should be spending at each jobsite. This particular system is strictly for regular maintenance visits. (I'll discuss costing other types of jobs in section 7.)

May I introduce to you another form: the job costing worksheet, shown in Sample 17

(also available on the CD-ROM that came with this book). It's important that you understand the concept behind this worksheet. You take the total annual revenue from the maintenance agreement and then subtract things like dumping, materials, and wear and tear on equipment. Since this worksheet deals only with the regular maintenance visit, you also want to remove any services that are included in the cost of your program but are *not* part of a regular visit — such as power raking and fall cleanups. What you end up with is how much you *really* earn for a regular maintenance visit to a particular customer. From this you can determine how long you should be spending at the site. Working backward, you can use the worksheet to help determine how much you should be charging to spend a known amount of time at the site and still make a profit.

Let's walk through the sample to see how you can use this worksheet.

- *Hourly rate.* At the top of the worksheet, enter your hourly rate. If you followed the instructions for determining your hourly rate in section 4 of chapter 9, you'll remember that it includes overhead, which is why overhead is not among the cost columns listed on the worksheet.

- *Property name.* Enter your customers' names in the column on the left side of the worksheet.

- *Program length.* Enter the length of the program in months. For week-to-week customers, estimate how many months you expect to be working for them.

- *Income.* The next three columns all deal with what you are charging the customer: your income. You need all three values filled in for the system to work, but you only have to enter one of them yourself. The other two are calculated based on the one value you know. If you charge by the visit, enter that charge in the Rev/Visit column. To calculate the revenue per month, multiply revenue per visit by the number of visits per month. If visits are weekly, multiply by 4.3 (average weeks in a month). Finally, in the Rev/Year column, insert the monthly charge multiplied by the number of months the agreement is for. If you charge by the month, enter the known monthly fee into Rev/Month. For Rev/Visit, divide by the number of visits you do in a month. For Rev/Year, multiply the monthly fee by the number of months in your program. If you charge an annual fee, put that known number into the Rev/Year column and calculate the other two numbers accordingly. (If you use a spreadsheet program such as Microsoft Excel, you can simply enter these calculations as formulas and have the computer do the math. Fields are automatically updated as you change key values.)

🍂 *Dumping.* How much will you spend on dumping charges for each customer? Consider factors such as composts you will use, how often you will mulch, and if there are deciduous trees (with leaves to clean up and take away).

🍂 *Pruning/trimming.* The general rule is that if you cannot complete a pruning or trimming task as part of a regular maintenance visit, you should put it here, in a separate category. Otherwise it will throw your averages off. (For example, you may include a four-day fall pruning in the maintenance plan. If you included those four days as you calculated the average time you spent on site each visit, the number would be skewed. You would be "spending" your four days too soon, and then, come fall, you would have no more time left for the cleanup without losing money. On the sample, The Estates' maintenance program includes a four-day cleanup, and it has been duly noted in the specific column.) The number you enter should be the value of the extra trimming, over and above your regular maintenance. Multiply the number of hours the job will take by your hourly rate. If you used the lawn and garden maintenance quotation sheet (Sample 11) for this customer, you should already have the data you need.

🍂 *Fertilizer, lime, and weed/insect sprays.* You'll use the same method to calculate the figures for the next three categories. Determine the cost for the amount of material that you have used or plan on using. For smaller city lots the calculation can be an estimate. For larger lawns you may need to figure out how much material you will need based on the lawn's square footage. If you spend a lot longer than usual at the site when you perform these services, you should subtract the value of the person-hours. This will probably only be necessary for properties with large lawns.

SAMPLE 17
JOB COSTING

Hourly Rate: $37.50

Property Name	Program Length	Rev/ Year	Rev/ Month	Rev/ Visit	Dumping	Pruning/ Trimming	Fertilizer	Lime	Weed/ Insect Sprays	Power Rake
The Estates	12	$8,900.00	$741.67	$172.48	$270.00	$1,200.00	$140.00	$80.00	$60.00	$425.00
Pay-By-Visit	8	$1,548.00	$193.50	$45.00	$ -	$ -	$ -	$ -	$ -	$ -
Pay-Per-Month	9	$1,665.00	$185.00	$43.02	$45.00	$150.00	$60.00	$10.00	$15.00	$ -
Pay-Annually	12	$3,600.00	$300.00	$69.77	$120.00	$300.00	$70.00	$15.00	$25.00	$ -
Biweekly	8	$560.00	$70.00	$35.00	$40.00	$-	$ -	$ -	$ -	$ -
Reel Mower	9	$1,400.00	$155.56	$36.18	$60.00	$-	$40.00	$60.00	$35.00	$ -

Power raking, aeration, and overseeding. These services are normally completed outside the scope of the regular maintenance visit, so if you have included them in your maintenance agreement, you should eliminate them from this job costing equation. Estimate how long each of these services will take you and put that value in the correct spot. (In the sample, special visits were made, outside of the regular maintenance visits, to complete these tasks, and the value of that time has been noted appropriately.)

Planting materials, other services. If you provide plant material, such as summer color or fall bulbs, take it into account here by putting in both the value of the materials and, if applicable, the value of the time to install them. Any other services that you have included in the annual cost of your maintenance program but that are not specifically listed on this worksheet should go in the Other Services column. Examples of such services might be power washing, gutter cleaning, etc.

Equipment factor. This category takes a bit more work, but it is worth it. Who would you rather pay to replace your equipment when the time comes? You (out of your profits) or your customers (out of fees charged)? To

Aeration	Over-seeding	Planting	Other Materials	Other Services	Equipment Factor	Total Extra	Remaining Revenue	Revenue/ Visit	Avg. Time to Spend (Minutes)
$125.00	$220.00	$300.00	$ -	$ -	$278.50	$3,098.50	$5,801.50	$112.43	180
$ -	$ -	$ -	$ -	$ -	$32.00	$97.00	$1,451.00	$42.18	67
$45.00	$ -	$ -	$ -	$ -	$38.00	$393.00	$1,272.00	$32.87	53
$65.00	$ -	$ -	$ -	$50.00	$68.00	$713.00	$2,887.00	$55.95	90
$ -	$ -	$ -	$ -	$ -	$25.00	$65.00	$495.00	$30.94	50
$ -	$ -	$ -	$ -	$ -	$62.00	$203.00	$1,197.00	$30.93	49

make it easy for you to determine what to charge your customers for equipment use on their properties, I have included Sample 18, the equipment usage worksheet. You will see that the cost of each piece of equipment is calculated based on an hourly rate and the time used. (To calculate the hourly rate, see section **4.2c** in chapter 9.) The cost per visit is derived by multiplying the hourly rate by the time used. Keep in mind that you don't use all of your equipment every week, so you will enter the number of times that you actually use the equipment. Calculate the Total for Program by multiplying the visit charge with the number of times you used the equipment. Once you tally up all your annual totals, you end up with a grand total for all equipment for the entire year. This is the number that you will put on the job costing worksheet. Keep your equipment usage worksheet along with the job costing worksheet in your customer's file. You may need to make minor adjustments from year to year, but once it's completed it will generally serve you for many years.

🕊 *Total extra.* Add up all the values in the row from Dumping to Equipment Factor. This is the total value of the extra services that you will *not* complete during regular maintenance visits and that will be costed separately.

SAMPLE 18
EQUIPMENT USAGE

EQUIPMENT USAGE
Customer: The Estates

Equipment	Hourly Rate	Minutes Used/Visit	Cost per Visit	Times Used	Total Cost for Program
Regular Maintenance Visits					
21" Mower	$3.00	90	$4.50	37	$166.50
String Trimmer	$3.00	30	$1.50	37	$55.50
Blade Edger	$3.00	15	$0.75	20	$15.00
Backpack Blower	$3.00	15	$0.75	52	$39.00
Spreader	$2.00	15	$0.50	6	$3.00
Total for Maintenance Visits					**$279.00**
Other Jobs					
Power Rake	$5.00	480	$40.00	1	$40.00
Aerator	$6.00	120	$12.00	1	$12.00
Hedge Trimmers	$3.00	960	$48.00	1	$48.00
Backpack Sprayer	$1.00	60	$1.00	2	$2.00
Total for Other Jobs					**$102.00**

🪃 *Remaining revenue.* This is what is left after you subtract the Total Extra from Rev/Year. It is also the figure that you will use to determine how long you spend on site performing regular maintenance duties.

🪃 *Revenue/visit.* This is the real revenue per visit. It's how much you make after eliminating all the extras. This is pure maintenance.

🪃 *Average time to spend.* Based on the adjusted revenue per visit and the hourly labor rate that you input, calculate how much time you should be spending on site, on average. Divide that time by the number of crew members to get the actual real-time minutes that you should be spending on site. We can see from the sample that maintenance visits at The Estates for a two-person crew should average 90 minutes. For a one-person crew, a visit should be three hours (180 minutes.)

Now you have a goal that you can work toward, a number you can use to gauge if you are spending too much time on site. When I first created this spreadsheet and applied it to my existing clients, I can tell you it was an eye-popper. I was amazed at how my estimated time for maintenance visits was affected after taking extra services into account. Using the spreadsheet helped me focus on ways to reduce the costs and work more efficiently to get in and out of a property within the prescribed time and increase my profit.

Write your goal time on your route sheets so you and your employees know how long you should be on site. Be careful, though, that you don't instill a warped sense of priorities in your crew. The most important thing is to provide excellent service, and that means not cutting corners to get off the site in the defined time. As well, certain times of the year may be busier than others. You are interested in the *average* time spent over a period of months.

This worksheet will not tell you how much time you should spend at a site until you have been working there for a few months. If, however, you find that you are consistently spending more time at a site, you should examine what you can do about it. Can you reduce the time spent without noticeably reducing quality? Can you work more efficiently? Can you reduce any of the values in any category? Are you mulching when you can? Is there a greenbelt or natural area in the back yard, or a compost where you can do some dumping? Can you raise the price?

If you are comfortable using a spreadsheet (or if you are using the CD-ROM version

of the quotation spreadsheet), you can see its power by playing what-if with the numbers. You can plug in different annual rates to see what you would need to charge to spend different amounts of time on jobsites while making the same — or more — money.

Keep an eye on job costing throughout the year, but spend some time during the slow winter months to thoroughly analyze the data in this worksheet so that if you need to adjust the price, you can do it in the spring.

7. COSTING OTHER SERVICES

It's easy to job cost your other services compared to the complexity of costing your maintenance programs. And what else should you job cost? Everything! You should be doing a check on all your jobs, from a simple yard cleanup to a lawn renovation. Always keep your costing data in the customer folders so that you can refer to it again if you complete the same or a similar job for that customer. It may come in handy as a guide for other customers too.

The same costing principles apply, but remember the following points:

- Include your equipment cost. For your maintenance customers, use the equipment usage worksheet to determine equipment costs for power raking, aeration, overseeding, and the other extras that are excluded from the maintenance program.

- Check your hourly rate from year to year. As your overhead grows, so should your rate. Including overhead in your hourly rate makes job costing much easier because you don't have to consider how much overhead to apply to each individual job.

🦢 When you job cost package deals, remember that the individual prices appear slightly inflated because you gave a package discount. Take this into account when you analyze these types of jobs.

🦢 Remember to remove the cost of materials from your formulas. Don't include that as you job cost labor.

You should job cost other services as you complete them. There is no benefit in leaving it until January. In fact, that will only make it more difficult.

8. ANNUAL PROCEDURES

Remember the first day of school, when you had all your nifty new supplies — the untouched pencils, the eraser with its new rubber smell, the neatly organized geometry set? Remember, too, how neat your handwriting was as you wrote on the first page of your crisp, clean notebook? This year was going to be different than other years. This year you were going to start off right and carry through all the way. Your homework would be on time, your desk or locker would be neatly organized, and all your notebooks would maintain that perfect handwriting right through to June.

Yes, the renewed vigor and optimism that you felt at that time was extraordinary. You should strive to realize that same mental state at least once a year as you captain your landscaping business. The best time to do it is in January. It's the start of a brand-new year, and the growing season is just around the corner. Go ahead, buy some new office supplies if it makes you feel better, like

that first day of school. It's time to take a step back, assess, and then move ahead into the new season with unprecedented confidence and energy.

To that grandiose end, I've gathered some tips to remind you what to evaluate and improve as you prepare for the new season. Be positive. It *will* be different this year. You *will* maintain your systems all the way through. You *will* offer second-to-none service to all. You *will* work smarter and make more money. You really will!

🦢 *Job costing.* January is the perfect time to do your job costing. Take time before the spring to go through all maintenance customers and make sure that what you are charging produces a profit for you. If you are going to raise prices, now is the time to do it. Once the season has started, it is generally unacceptable to raise the cost of maintenance unless the scope of the work has changed.

🦢 *Tax time.* If your fiscal year end is the same as the calendar year end, great. It means you can take care of tax filing during your slower winter months. If you have been diligent about recording all your revenue and expenses and have kept all your receipts, this is going to be unbelievably easy. I will again recommend that you use an accountant to help you with your tax return. Even if you know your way around the income tax return, you are likely to miss something.

🦢 *Create a new marketing calendar.* Take the time to analyze your referral tracking sheet. What worked? What flopped? How will you direct your marketing efforts in the coming year?

Create a new marketing calendar for the coming year.

🌿 *Create pro forma profit and loss statements and cash flow projections.* The projections you made when you started your business were practical tools, and you should now complete new projections for the coming year. Each year you operate adds valuable historical data that can serve as a base for future planning.

🌿 *General business planning.* If you will be hiring new staff this season, start planning early. If you need people starting in March, don't wait until then to begin your search. Think about the staff you already have and how many new people you will need, and hold interviews in February for a March start-up. As well, review the reward and recognition programs that you are using. Can you improve them? Can you improve training, compensation, benefits? Think about your equipment and your vehicles. Will they meet your requirements again this year, or do you need any new equipment? Evaluate the systems you used last year. Did they work for you? If not, is it because the systems didn't work or because you didn't work the systems? Go over all the forms and worksheets that you use. Are they still valid? Have you changed services or policies that might affect these documents? Is your InfoPack up to date?

🌿 *Contact and sign up last year's clients.* Send a letter to each of the previous year's maintenance customers to tell them what improvements you have made for the new year. Have you purchased new equipment, implemented new programs or policies, or introduced new services? Early January is an opportune time to let your customers know about changes. Include any price adjustments to the maintenance program and briefly explain the reason for them. Mention when you will be starting maintenance programs, and give them instructions on what to do. Don't say, "Call us if you are interested again this year," because it's too easy for them to do nothing. Instead try something such as: "We begin our maintenance in the first week of March. If you have any questions or concerns about the program or your property, please feel free to call us. Otherwise I will contact you in February to confirm the details of your maintenance program." An example of such a letter is included in Sample 19.

🌿 *Specialty lawn care recommendations.* Once spring rolls around and you have started your maintenance programs, preferably after your first or second visit, leave the customer a recommended extras form (see Sample 20). This is an opportunity, but it's also your responsibility, as your customer's lawn care expert, to give advice on what services are required to provide an exquisite landscape. Leave the form with the customer and follow up with a phone call in a few days or a week. If you suggest other non-lawn care opportunities, leave a quotation sheet with the customer.

SAMPLE 19
CUSTOMER FOLLOW-UP FOR NEW SEASON

Dirty Deeds Incorporated
3005 Awesome Street
Vancouver, BC V7X 1P1
Phone: (555) 555-LAWN (5296)   Toll Free: 1-800-554-LAWN (5296)
Fax: (555) 555-8888   E-mail: dirtydeeds@dirtydeedslandscaping.com

January 24, 200-

Mr. Bruce Wayne
894 Cave Street
Vancouver, BC

Re: 200- Landscape Maintenance Proposal

Dear Mr. Wayne,

Spring greetings to you from your friends at Dirty Deeds Landscaping. Well, with the end of this harsh winter in sight, we can almost taste those spring flowering bulbs and lush green lawns. We at Dirty Deeds are gearing up for another busy spring, and that is the reason for this letter.

We think things went very well last year. Your positive feedback on our efforts to offer a superior level of service and workmanship has been an encouragement to us. However, that is not to say we did not find any room for improvement. In fact, we have been using our slow winter period wisely to think up creative new ways to keep you pleased with us and delighted with your lawn and garden.

Yes, our brainstorming has resulted in improved quality-control practices and new ideas for paying attention to details (the things that give your property that something extra). Also brand-new this year is *The Bloomin' Facts,* an informative newsletter for all our clients and prospects. Stay tuned for the premiere edition coming up in March.

These are just a couple of areas we have improved in our unending commitment to offer the best service available in a lawn care company! The best news of all is that, with few exceptions, we have had no changes to our program and pricing structures for residential maintenance programs. We have provided below our recommendations for your landscape maintenance for the current growing season.

Last year the cost of your landscape maintenance program was $285/month. We have found, however, that more time was spent onsite than we had projected. Therefore, the cost of your 200- program will increase to $315/month. If you would like any further details about your program or this increase, please feel free to contact us using one of the methods above.

If you have any questions at all about this letter, our company, or your property, please give us a call. We are happy to help out, and remember, our advice is always free. We are set to begin residential maintenance at the beginning of March with lime applications. Let us know if you need anything before that. Otherwise we will be contacting you toward the end of February to confirm the details of your program.

Thank you for your past support. We look forward to working with you again in 200-.

Sincerely,

Dirty Deeds Incorporated
Joel LaRusic

SAMPLE 20
RECOMMENDED EXTRAS FORM

Dirty Deeds Landscaping
3005 Awesome Street
Vancouver, BC V7X 1P1
Phone: (555) 555-LAWN (5296)   Toll Free: 1-800-554-LAWN (5296)
Fax: (555) 555-8888   E-mail: dirtydeeds@dirtydeedslandscaping.com

_____*March 18*_____, 200-

Name: *Richard Grayson*_____

Re: Power raking, overseeding, aeration, top-dressing, and other extra services

Dear *Mr. Grayson,*

Now that we are on our way and I have had a chance to take a close look at your lawns, I am able to make the following recommendations.

Power raking is important in removing moss and thatch from your lawn.

☑ I am recommending power raking for your lawn. The price includes going over all areas at least twice, plus dumping fees.
The cost of power raking is $ *165.–* + GST.

Aeration is an important part of regular maintenance. I recommend that this service be completed at least once each year.

☑ I am recommending aeration for a cost of $ *55.–* + GST.

Overseeding helps keep lawns healthy without chemicals. It is especially important after a power rake.

☑ I am recommending an application of grass seed to your lawn.
The cost of this service is $ *57.–* + GST.

Top-dressing is an excellent way to build a better soil base, which is the key to having a healthy, lush lawn. It also helps level any low spots and provides an excellent medium for seed germination. This service is recommended every one to three years, depending on your existing soil base.

☑ I am recommending top-dressing for your lawn.
The cost of this service is $ *267.–* + GST based on *3* cubic yards of topsoil.

I have noted the following other problems/situations at your property and have recommended accordingly.

[Please see the attached quotation sheet, if any.]

Please refer to your information package for details on any of the above services. If you do not have a package or have further questions, please do not hesitate to call me. Thank you for supporting Dirty Deeds Landscaping.

Sincerely,
Joel LaRusic

PART 3
THE SERVICES YOU OFFER

One of the joys of running a landscape maintenance business is that you can offer a wide array of services. It's unlikely you'll ever get bored. From regular yard and garden maintenance to lawn care specialties to off-season specialties, you can keep busy 12 months of the year if you wish. So pay attention: there is a wealth of valuable, honest advice in this section, which is full of methods, procedures, and tricks and tips of the landscape maintenance trade.

12
THE REGULAR MAINTENANCE VISIT

In the landscape maintenance business, you are likely to spend most of your time on the different components of the regular maintenance visit. These components include cutting the lawn, edging the lawn (both line edging and blade edging), maintaining beds, and cleanup (including using the blower).

Of course, these are not the only services you might offer in your maintenance agreements, but they are the nuts and bolts. Everything else revolves around the regular visits, and if you don't do a good job on these tasks, your business is not likely to prosper. On the other hand, if you are good at these tasks, it may compensate for your inexperience in other areas of the business.

This chapter contains advice on how to do all these jobs professionally *and* efficiently. It also includes safety tips.

1. EVERYTHING YOU ALWAYS WANTED TO KNOW ABOUT CUTTING LAWNS

Many walk blindly into a lawn-cutting job thinking it requires no thought at all. But there's more to cutting a lawn than meets the eye.

1.1 General tips

Most of the following tips will apply to both rotary and reel mowers. Where applicable, any special needs of reel mower cutting are included.

- Before you start, scan the lawn for items that you can't mow over. This includes children's toys, large pebbles and stones, debris such as paper bags, large items such as picnic tables, and

Safety First

- Wear ear and eye protection when operating power equipment.

- Wear sturdy shoes or boots (not sandals).

- The mower can throw objects (like pebbles) with tremendous force. Keep this in mind if there are people around. Stop the blade and let people pass by if need be.

- Your mower should be equipped with a blade brake clutch (BBC). This is a control that stops the mower and/or the blade when you let go of it. Do not override this important safety feature! Use extreme caution when cutting slopes. If you stumble at any time, let go of the BBC control immediately.

- Disconnect the spark plug on the mower before you do extensive cleaning, maintenance, or repairs on the mower.

- Refuel your equipment outdoors, not in an enclosed area. Shut off the engine and wait a couple of minutes for the engine to cool before refueling.

- Line edgers and blade edgers are dangerous to passersby and spectators (kids are particularly curious). Stop what you are doing, let people pass, and tell kids it's not safe to watch.

any pet droppings. If you find that week after week you are having to spend more than a few minutes picking up toys and pet droppings, speak to your customer and ask that the lawn be ready for you to cut before you arrive. You should also make it clear in your service contract that your service does not include picking up after pets.

- Line edge the lawn first. If you are working by yourself, edge the lawn and then mow it. If you are part of a crew, let the line edger go ahead of the mower. The mess made by the edger will be vacuumed up by the mulching power of the mower. If you get ahead of the line edger, make sure you go back and either vacuum or

rake up any leftover debris. Reel mowers have no vacuum power, but they also do a pretty good job of picking up grass clippings.

- With the mower, circumnavigate the lawn twice and then start mowing across in straight lines. Going around the area twice will give you some room to turn around without missing any patches of grass.

- Keep your lines straight. This is a trick of the trade that will take practice to perfect, especially on larger lawns. It helps to start a row by lining up with a fixed object (perhaps a plant or a stake in the garden bed) at the point where you want to be at the end of the row. Keep your eye on that object as you push your mower down the row toward it. Once you have one straight line, it is easier to keep subsequent rows straight by using the previous row as a guide.

It is even more important to cut straight lines with a reel mower because this type of mower leaves a nap in the lawn, called striping. Alternating rows appear to be a completely different color. If done correctly (as it is, for example, on baseball fields) this looks impressive. But if it's not done accurately, the imperfections are painfully obvious. (This is why I recommend leaving the specialty of reel mowing until you have some experience and are proficient with other aspects of the job.) Even with a rotary mower you get a degree of striping, so make sure you reverse your mowing direction from one row to the next. Check with your equipment dealer to see if there are striping kits for your mower.

- When mowing around edged garden beds, stay a couple of inches away from the edge. If you slip into the edge, you will scalp the lawn and it will take weeks to heal. Let the line edger take care of edging around the beds. With a reel mower, stay *at least* two inches away. Falling into the edge with a reel mower will leave a nasty scalp, but worse is the damage it could cause to your finely tuned reel mower.

- For the general health of the lawn, change the cutting direction of your rows from week to week. Cutting in the same direction each week will create ruts in the lawn as your heavy mower compresses the same area time after time. This is especially true at the end of each row where you pivot the mower to turn around. You may not notice it at first, but it will become evident as the season goes on; the effect looks poor and unprofessional. The grass also tends to lean in the same direction as you cut. Alternating the cutting direction will encourage the lawn to grow upright. So cut it lengthwise, cut it crosswise, and cut it diagonally.

- Another way to avoid ruts in a lawn is to overlap the rows by a couple of inches. If the ground is soft, the soil may be displaced by the weight of the mower as you go. Putting your wheel in the same track on the way back will increase the chance of unsightly ruts. To avoid this, position the mower so that you overlap the old track on the way back. This will help to flatten out any rut. This technique also helps prevent the formation of "mohawks," those skinny strips of uncut lawn that are taboo for turfgrass management professionals.

- When mowing steep slopes, walk behind the mower *across* the slope for safety. If you fall, there is less risk of the mower landing on top of you. On a rider mower, always go up and down the slope so the mower does not tip over. You may need to use your trimmer to cut the crest of the slope so that you don't scalp it.

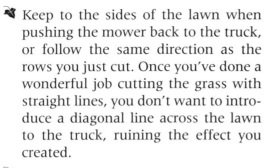

Keep to the sides of the lawn when pushing the mower back to the truck, or follow the same direction as the rows you just cut. Once you've done a wonderful job cutting the grass with straight lines, you don't want to introduce a diagonal line across the lawn to the truck, ruining the effect you created.

Keep your eye on the bag (if you are bagging). When the bag is full, empty it. If the mower is clogged, you will lose your vacuum power even if the bag is not completely full. This may occur if the grass is damp or long. With most walk-behind mowers, you can recognize a clog as soon as it happens because your bag will deflate. When it does, you need to clear out the grass chute and possibly under the mower too. If the grass is wet, you may need to clean the mower many times during the cut. This adds a lot of time to your cut and is a good reason not to cut in the rain. However, if you live in a wet climate, rainy-day lawn cuts are a fact of life. (See sidebar on mowing wet grass.)

Top up your fuel before you start a large lawn or if you think you are running low. Murphy's Law applies to lawn cutting, so it will always be at the point farthest from the truck that you run out of gas. If you do need to refuel in the middle of a cut, *never* do it on the lawn. It's only a matter of time before a spill occurs and causes dead spots in the grass.

Turfgrasses

There are about 7,500 different species of grass, but only a small number, 30 or so, are suitable for turfgrass.

All turfgrasses may be roughly divided into two groups: cool season grasses and warm season grasses. Cool season grasses prefer to grow in the north (throughout Canada) and can tolerate a cold winter. They grow most in the spring and fall, when the temperatures are cooler. Cool season grasses include bluegrass, fescues, ryegrass, and creeping bentgrass. Most lawns in this region are blended lawns and have a mixture of several of these varieties, which is good because if one particular species is susceptible to disease, the entire lawn will not be affected.

Warm season grasses like the sunny, warm climes. They hate the cold and will go dormant if the temperature drops under 60° F (15° C). They are slow to green up in the spring and do most of their growing in the summer months. Warm season grasses include bermudagrass, zoysiagrass, Centipedegrass, St. Augustinegrass, and buffalograss, to name a few. They are not compatible and don't look right growing together, so are rarely blended in lawns. Some grasses, such as buffalograss, zoysiagrass, and creeping bentgrass can survive in both warm and cool regions.

Mowing Wet Grass

If you live in a rainy area, cutting a wet lawn will be a fact of life in your business. Here are some tips for using a commercial push mower on wet grass:

- Clean the chute and under the mower deck often. Try to do this only at the ends of your cutting rows, even if your mower bag is not full or clogged when you reach the end of the row. Avoid cleaning the mower in the middle of the lawn — it is nearly impossible to clean up the area without leaving some evidence of mess. Ideally, you would push the mower off the grass area to clean it, but this may not always be possible. If you must use the lawn area, then at least stay to one side of the lawn. You can then clean that area well when you are finished.

- If you *must* stop mid-row, release the clutch (or stop the mower), remove the bag, clear the chute, and put the grass that you removed from the chute into the bag. Then tilt the mower back and gently shake it so that the loose grass under the deck falls out. Pull the mower out of the way and put this grass in the bag too. Put the bag back on and keep going. When you get to the end of the row you can clear the mower more thoroughly (and make more of a mess).

- Do not expect to push the mower in wet grass as fast as you do in dry grass. If you go too fast, the mower will be clogged long before you reach the end of your first row. It's better to take it down a notch and keep the volume of grass in the chute to a minimum.

- When you are ready to clean out the mower, shut off the engine and remove the spark plug wire. With one hand tip the mower on its side at a 45- to 60-degree angle; scoop out the grass with the other hand (this may not be feasible with your type of mower). Avoid turning the mower completely on its side, and always tip the mower so that the carburetor/air filter side of the mower is up and less likely to leak.

- Regular mower cleaning and maintenance pays off on rainy days. If you don't clean out the undercarriage of the mower regularly, the day will come when you *must* clean it out because it's clogged with wet grass, and it will be a slimy, difficult job. On the other hand, if you clean your mower often, the job will be easy and take only a few seconds.

1.2 How to water a lawn

Grass is like anything else; it's inherently lazy. If you were thirsty and had a glass of water at your desk and another glass of water downstairs, which would you drink? Grass is the same, and you must remember that when you think about watering.

Watering the lawn daily is the worst thing you can do because it discourages a deep root system from forming. Why would the roots go deep if they don't have to? Daily watering also promotes compaction and wastes water. However, underwatering brings its share of problems too.

Creeping Bentgrass Warning

Creeping bentgrass is most often associated with putting greens. Everyone loves these lawns because they are exceptionally fine, textured, and tight, creating an aesthetically pleasing appearance. Some people like them so much they may ask you to give them their own putting green in the back yard. What's worse, if you accidentally get a patch of creeping bentgrass in the lawn, your customer may see it and say, "Oh, I want that!" Be warned: Creeping bentgrass is an extremely high-maintenance grass, is susceptible to a wide range of fungal diseases, and does not fare well under duress. No matter how nice that patch looks, remember that the chances of you getting the whole lawn to look like that (unless you are a trained, professional greenskeeper) are slim to none.

In most cases you can tell your customers to give their lawns a thorough soaking twice a week. They should water so that the moisture reaches a depth of half an inch. The best time to water is morning — the earlier the better. Evening and nighttime watering leave the grass wet for long periods of time, a condition that favors disease. Midday watering is inefficient since it evaporates more quickly. (However, to dispel the old myth, it does not act like a magnifying glass on the lawn and scorch the blades of grass.)

1.3 How much should you cut?

The length at which you cut the lawn depends on several factors, such as the type of turfgrass you are cutting, special circumstances, and your customer's preference, but the most important point to remember is the one-third rule. This simply means that you should never cut more than a third of the plant height away. If the grass is three inches long, don't cut more than one inch off. Cutting it shorter can seriously stunt the grass and affect its health, vigor, and appearance.

Different types of grass have different ideal heights. The following are the best heights for cool season grasses:

- Kentucky Bluegrass 2.0 to 3.0 inches
- Fine-leave Fescue 2.0 to 3.0 inches
- Tall Fescue 2.0 to 3.0 inches
- Perennial Ryegrass 2.0 to 3.0 inches
- Creeping Bentgrass 0.25 to 0.75 inches

The following are the best heights for warm season grasses:

- Bermudagrass 0.5 to 1.5 inches
- Buffalograss 1.5 to 2.5 inches
- Centipedegrass 1.0 to 2.0 inches
- St. Augustinegrass 1.5 to 2.5 inches
- Zoysiagrass 0.75 to 1.5 inches

However, sometimes you need to take peculiarities into account when deciding how much to cut. For example, the season may call for adjustments. Many northern varieties should be cut a little longer in the heat of the summer so they stay green. Some southern varieties should be allowed to get a little shaggy before the winter.

If the lawn is new, or if you have recently renovated it, it should be cut a little higher than normal for the first few weeks until it is established. Then you can gradually reduce it to the recommended height. On the first cut of the season (before the grass has really started to grow) you can mow short to remove dead leaves and rejuvenate the lawn.

Do your homework. Investigate the grasses that grow in your area, find out how they like to grow, and learn their particular nuances. Once you find out how the grass likes to grow, you have to adapt what you know to what your customer wants. You should be prepared for customers who want grass cut shorter than is healthy. Many customers believe that shorter grass looks better, and you'll have to educate them on what is best for their grass. Try not to sacrifice health and vigor to please your customers. Don't let the grass get too short (you'll get the blame if the lawn looks like dirt), and let your customers know that if they insist on your cutting it very short, you do so against your better judgment.

1.4 What to do with grass clippings

You have three choices when it comes to grass clippings: bagging, mulching, or composting.

If you choose bagging, all you have to do is empty the bag when it is full. During the cut you can dump your clippings in either a tarp or a bucket. Set it up before you start cutting. This saves you a lot of time walking back and forth to the truck to dump clippings in there.

Don't be tempted to bag the clippings and leave them at your customer's curb. Most customers will not want to have the bag sitting there until the garbage collector picks it up (if there is curbside pickup where you live), especially if that won't be for a few days.

Mulching is another option. Mulching is what happens when the grass that is normally discharged is cut into fine pieces. Mulching blades work to keep grass clippings circulating underneath the mower, cutting them several times. The power behind the spinning blade also helps to force the resulting tiny bits of grass down to the base of the lawn. You're left with free fertilizer (grass clippings contain lots of nutrients), a faster lawn cut, and savings on your dumping fees. Mulching isn't always the best choice, though. You should not mulch in the following circumstances:

- *When the grass is too long.* It's spring, you fertilized the lawn last week, and you've received a few days of rain since then. This situation begs you to bag. When growth spurts occur, consider bagging. You know mulching is a bad idea when you are leaving trails of clumped grass behind you. It looks terrible, not to mention unprofessional. You could rake up the clumps after your cut, but is it worth the extra time? Probably not, and besides, raking up bits of grass can ruin the look of a freshly cut lawn.

- *When your mower is struggling.* This happens if the grass is too wet or too long. You can tell from the sound of the motor if it's having a hard time. The wear and tear on your mower is, in the long term, more costly than the expense of bagging.

- *When the lawn has weeds that are in seed.* For example, if you run over dandelion seeds while you're mulching, you will be planting the seed in a moist, nutritious medium. Those seeds (and there are thousands, if not millions, in each plant) will germinate quickly, and your weed population will sky-rocket.

🍂 *When you suspect lawn disease.* If there is any kind of disease or fungus, mulching will only spread the problem.

🍂 *When there is debris on the lawn.* In the fall, when leaves are falling, put the bag on. Mulching grass is great; mulching leaves doesn't work. The same is true for flower petals and other debris. One of the great advantages of a rotary mower is that it also doubles as a vacuum. You lose that benefit when you mulch.

Do not leave unmulched clippings on the lawn. If the grass is too long and the clippings are left on the lawn, not only will the lawn look horrible, but its health will be in jeopardy. You could rake the clippings up, but that will take extra time. Even if the grass is short, you should not leave the clippings from a side-discharge mower on the lawn. If you have a mulching blade, by all means mulch the grass.

The third option is composting. If you are fortunate enough to have a compost available to you at your customer's house, use it. It may be a natural area near the house or it may be an actual compost box in the yard. Keep these points in mind:

🍂 Don't overstay your welcome at the compost heap. If it's full, stop adding to it. An overfull compost is unsightly.

🍂 If you have applied a chemical application to the lawn, do not add clippings to the compost for three weeks

after. The residual chemicals can spell disaster when it comes time to use your compost in the garden.

🍂 Offer your customer a compost maintenance program for an extra charge. Composts can be a lot of work. They need to be turned for aeration, and for efficient composting they also need to have other material mixed in. The compost also has to be spread on the garden from time to time.

1.5 Options for cleaning up

Even if you mulch your clippings, you must remove any debris (e.g., clippings, weeds, or pruning trimmings) from the jobsite when you are finished. Here are a few hints for efficient cleanup:

🍂 *Tarps.* Spread a tarp on the lawn or driveway to provide a central location for all your debris. Once the tarp is full, tie the corners together and throw it on the truck. Tarps are easy to stack, allowing you to pack them on the truck. They're also easy to relocate if necessary. The disadvantage of using tarps is that they only last a few months (although they are not too expensive if you buy them in bulk). They can also be difficult in the wind, and you may need to use a weight to hold them down. If you stack tarps of grass clippings on your truck, after a couple of days the grass will start to decompose, with a very strong odor. This is a reason to make more frequent trips to the dump ... and to mulch!

Hint: The best way to tie a tarp is to grab diagonal corners, bunch them, and cinch them up so that you have about 12 inches to work with. Tie a simple knot (the kind you start out with when you tie your shoes) and then another one, but this time do not pull one side all the way through. Double it up and pull it snug to form a loop on one of the ends. This way, no matter how tight the knot gets (and it may tighten as you pick it up), you can untie it simply by pulling one of the ends.

 Bags: You can use garbage bags to collect debris. They, too, are easy to stack and relocate on the truck. You won't have to deal with the odor as you do with tarps, but you may find them more awkward to use generally. It can be difficult to stuff pruning clippings and larger debris into bags.

Buckets: Dumping debris right into the truck is probably the worst option (unless you have a dump truck) because it takes a long time to unload the truck by hand. It is also hard to pack the truck when it's full of loose debris. It can be useful to carry buckets around with you on the jobsite and put debris in them, but I recommend you dump them periodically into a tarp, not straight into the truck.

2. EDGING

There are two types of edging that must be completed, and two different instruments with which to do it. The line edger (also called a string trimmer, weed whacker, or weedeater) uses a nylon line to trim around garden beds and possibly walkway edges. The blade edger uses a metal blade to trim grass from sidewalks.

2.1 Line edging

To use a line edger proficiently and efficiently requires skill, which you will gain over time. If you are just starting out, practice as much as you can on your own lawn. Follow these steps to professional edging.

- Always hold the edger at an angle to the grass, about 30 degrees off the horizontal plane, so that only the tip of the line is touching the ground. Think of the spinning piece of nylon as a solid, spinning disc. If you hold the disc flat, you will likely scalp the grass. Remember that the tip of the line does all the cutting work.

- Walking forward with the edger in front of you is the fastest way to get the job done. It also requires the most skill. For that reason, when you are still learning, it is best to walk backward along the edge so that you are, in effect, pulling the edger with you as you move along. Move slowly and carefully and stop often to see where you are going. As you get better, you will find that you can pull the edger up a little so that you are moving in more of a sideways motion. Work sideways for a while, and then, when you are comfortable, continue to rotate yourself as you move so that the edger is in front of you.

- You must travel in a certain direction when line edging. On most commercial brands it is right to left (as you face the edge from the grass), but it depends on the direction the head spins. You will soon know if you are going in the wrong direction because all the debris will be tossed into the garden bed or the sidewalk, not back on the lawn. You'll have to clean it all up, using valuable time.

- Fence posts and plants present a particular challenge to edging; they are easily damaged. Even a light brush of the edger line against a fence post week after week will eventually wear it down. The best way to avoid this is to install what I call "post savers." Dig an edge one or two inches around each post. If you want, fill the spaces with mulch (*not* pebbles, since they will get picked up by the line and really fly). An alternative is to install sheet metal around the base of each fence post, but this is a more time-consuming task, and some of your customers may not like the look.

- Protect trees by digging "tree circles" (circular beds) around them. *Never* line edge directly against a tree. A small gouge in the bark of a tree will damage it, and even a narrow gap all the way around the tree will kill it.

- Plants offer yet another challenge when they overflow from a bed onto the lawn. If you have a helper, get your partner to stick the handle of a rake underneath the plant and lift it up so you can trim underneath. If you are working by yourself, you'll need to use your ingenuity to figure out how to hold the plant back while you edge.

- Keep the line in the edger cut square. After a few minutes of use, the line becomes tapered from wear and therefore less effective. You should always have your snips handy to trim the line often.

- Use star- or cross-shaped line, available at your equipment dealer. It is much sharper than round line and much more productive.

- The grass along edges should be trimmed to the same length as the rest of the lawn ... not shorter. There is no rule that says you must gradually taper the length of the grass along edges. If you edge too short, the plants will be weaker and more susceptible to heat stress and disease.

- Garden beds need to be edged on both the top and sides. Edging the top involves trimming the grass in areas that the mower cannot reach. To do the sides, you must trim the grass vertically so it does not grow into the bed. You can use a blade edger for this job, but most people prefer to use the line edger, flipping it around so the line is spinning on a perfect vertical plane. Using the line is faster and does as good a job. It is a little awkward at first because, in order to create a vertical cutting plane, you must turn the edger upside down and tilt it up so the engine is near your head. You may want to use a full face shield for this job to protect yourself from flying debris.

🦅 Do not flip the line edger to trim along sidewalks; use the blade edger. The result when using a line edger is not nearly as neat and tidy, even for the seasoned professional.

🦅 Use your line edger to get rid of weeds in sidewalk cracks and between paving stones. (Your line disappears quickly as it wears, but it does a good job.)

🦅 As with all two-cycle equipment, do not run your edger at half throttle all the time. Two-cycle engines are happiest when they are going full bore.

2.2 Blade edging

Your blade edger will probably be one of your least-used pieces of power equipment, but it's an important one. Nothing says "professional" more than a perfect edge along a sidewalk.

Blade edging should be done at least every other week. If you follow this rule, it will only take a few minutes each time. Perfect blade edging is a small detail, but

remember ... this business is all about the details.

3. MAINTAINING BEDS

If you choose to offer bed maintenance in your program, you already have an advantage because many landscape maintenance businesses do not. Some see bed maintenance as a time-consuming, unpleasant task. They imagine themselves on their hands and knees all day, pulling weeds. But if it's done correctly, bed maintenance will take only a small proportion of the time in your regular maintenance visits.

Bed maintenance generally entails the following tasks (though they won't necessarily all be a part of your program):

🦅 Weeding

🦅 Raking (to keep the beds free of leaves, dead plant material, and other debris)

🦅 Cultivating (to keep a fresh, turned-over look)

🦅 Light pruning (but not pruning of large shrubs and trees, which should be kept separate from the maintenance contract)

🦅 Establishing edges (to separate the lawn and the beds, and to improve the overall look of the property)

🦅 Plant care (planting, feeding, cutting, dividing, deadheading, etc.)

The best way to maintain beds is to work them on a rotation basis. The ideal is that each bed should be attended to every other week. Every third week is acceptable in some situations, but if you leave it longer than that, maintenance will take a lot more time.

3.1 Weeding tips

Weeding does not have to be a horrible job. Here are some suggestions for streamlining the task:

🌿 The best way to manage weeds in the beds is to tend them regularly. Keep to your rotation, and once you have the bed looking good, don't stop the regular care. Keep soil and mulch as loose as possible so you can turn the soil over easily.

🌿 Don't let weeds go to seed. It is astounding how many seeds can be produced by a single flower. In some varieties the number reaches the millions. If you see weeds flowering, take immediate action.

🌿 Keep pulling weeds. Even the most tenacious weeds need sunlight to live. If you keep pulling and turning over the soil, eventually they will die.

🌿 Use contact herbicide if necessary. If the weeds are persistent, you may need chemical help.

🌿 Use a pre-emergent herbicide. These are granular herbicides that you sprinkle on the ground to stop new weeds from coming up. Casoron is one of the most popular. Pre-emergent herbicides do not kill existing weeds, and they may affect other tender plants such as annuals and perennials, so they are generally used only on larger beds on commercial properties. Bugs and worms disappear when they encounter these herbicides. Use with discretion.

🌿 Use filter cloth where feasible. This is a type of cloth that is put on a bed and then covered with soil and/or mulch. Water and fertilizers can get through, but weeds can't grow up from underneath. Filter cloth can be effective in larger beds, but it is less useful in smaller beds because you have to cut holes in the cloth for existing plants, and the weeds simply detour to the holes.

3.2 Raking tips

Keep these points in mind as you rake your beds:

🌿 Smaller rakes with the head at a slight angle work best for beds. There are also adjustable ones, which are convenient but don't seem to last as long as the others. Plastic rakes work well on the lawn.

🌿 As you go through the beds, make small piles of debris everywhere, then pick them all up at the end. (Better yet, get your helper to pick up the piles.)

🌿 Make sure you lift low-lying tree and shrub branches once in a while to rake underneath.

🌿 Leave the real estate behind. The soil is precious, and besides, it's too heavy to haul to the truck. If the soil is light and fluffy, rake lightly so you only get the debris. It can be particularly challenging to rake mulch without taking half the bed with you. Experience and a light hand will help. Accept the fact that you will not be able to rake up every pine needle from the mulch.

🌿 Use your blower. After you have raked, a blower can do the final tidying. Use it on low power and scatter any debris you couldn't get so it is not obvious. If you are working beds on a rotation, use the blower to quickly clean beds that you will not be attending in any particular week. This gives the appearance of some activity in the bed. (It's a bit like sweeping the dirt under the carpet until next week.)

3.3 Cultivating tips

A bed looks best when it has been cultivated, which involves loosening the soil, breaking it up, and turning over a couple of inches. Here are some hints for cultivating:

- You don't have to cultivate mulches.

- If the soil is healthy and loose, a rake will suffice to freshen up the beds. On occasion you will also want to use a claw or a hoe to cultivate.

- Be careful when cultivating around shallow-rooted plants such as rhododendrons. Also watch that you don't leave upturned annuals or perennials in your wake.

- If you cannot cultivate because of poor soil, apply new soil or mulch to the beds (see section **3.7** below).

3.4 Light pruning tips

If you will be doing light pruning, be sure to read the section on pruning in chapter 15. You should also study a good pruning book that deals with the plants in your area. Here are some tips to keep the job running smoothly:

- One way to chip away at light pruning is to do it by variety. This week spend a few minutes cutting back the

viburnum; next week work on the rhododendron. This technique makes the job go quickly.

- Carry a bucket when you prune. Put the clippings straight into the bucket so there is less to rake up after.

- Some shrubs, such as rhododendrons and lilacs, must have their spent flowers removed or deadheaded each year. Include this in your light pruning tasks.

3.5 Edging tips

Deep edges help keep the grass out of the beds and the beds out of the grass. As well, they look great.

- Start by standing *in* the bed, facing the edge. Rake back, away from the edge, any loose soil or mulch. Then use a flat spade to establish an edge to a depth of a couple of inches. Your blade should go in perpendicular to the grass. Brush about one inch of the loose soil/mulch back into the edge. Use a string to create or re-establish straight edges; it's almost impossible to get them perfectly straight otherwise. Also, if possible, smooth out any gouges along the way.

- Don't forget to edge tree circles. If there are no tree circles, there should be. Sell them to your customer.

3.6 Plant care

A good garden will contain annuals (plants that complete their life cycle in one year), perennials (plants with a life cycle of more than two years), and perhaps even a biennial or two (plants with a two-year life cycle).

Learn what is popular in your area by visiting retail garden centers, asking questions, and reading books.

Because annuals need to be planted each year, you could offer planting as part of your services. You should be able to find a wholesaler that will give you a good price for bulk buying, or perhaps a retail nursery will offer a 10 percent to 15 percent discount. Depending on your area, you may be able to plant annuals in the spring and the fall.

Here are some tips for taking care of annuals:

- Annuals often need a heavy feeding schedule to do their best. There are slow-release products designed for this purpose. There are liquid fertilizers too, but applying them takes too much time to be practical.

- In order to prolong the life of the annual (so it will last all season), don't let it go to seed. Seeding is the sunset of the annual's life. If you remove the spent flowers, the plant will never go to seed and will have a much longer life.

- At the end of the season, annuals start looking pretty ragged. Take them out of the beds and throw them away.

You may need to offer the following services for perennials as part of your gardening program:

- It's good for perennials to be split every year or every few years. The method of splitting depends on the type, but generally you need to take a spade to the plant. You can be pretty aggressive with them, turning one plant into five or more. If the customer wants the new bounty installed in the garden, you can plant them. If not, keep the split plants for yourself or sell them to another customer.

- Most perennials die back to the ground each year to sleep through the winter. You may have to help your customer cut back dead plant material at the end of the season.

- In the spring, before the perennials come up, is a great time to add fresh humus to the beds.

3.7 Other tips

- Insist on fresh soil and/or mulch in the beds. Weeding in hardpan or clay soil is a never-ending job. Strongly recommend that your customer improve the soil base by installing fresh garden mix and possibly some mulch in beds. (The customer can do this, or he or she can hire you to do it.) Do not install mulch alone. It will not improve the soil sufficiently and will keep weeds down for only a short time.

- If you have high-maintenance beds and the customer is not interested in paying to resolve the underlying problems, consider declining the bed maintenance part of the job. Another option is to tell the customer you will work in the beds, but, because of the underlying problems, you will not guarantee weed-free beds. Make it clear that bed work will be completed on the clock (i.e., you'll spend a set amount of time per visit doing bed work and no more).

🐦 Charge extra for initial cleanup. Once the beds are cleaned up, it is usually easy to maintain them in just a few minutes per week, but the initial cleanup can be a huge job. For new customers, quote on cleaning up the beds outside of the maintenance price and tell them that it is required. They may ask if you could include the cleanup in the maintenance price and work on it bit by bit (to save them money). My advice is to say no. It is excruciatingly difficult to get on top of beds without starting with a clean plate. Apply the same policy when you sign up returning customers in the spring.

🐦 Charge to establish a new edge or to re-establish old edges for new customers. These jobs are labor intensive. Edges should be re-established annually, so include the charge for doing this for returning customers either as an extra or as part of the program.

4. THE CLEANUP: USING YOUR BLOWER

It has been said that success in the landscape maintenance business depends on the details, and that's what makes the cleanup so important. The lawn may look spectacular, the edges meticulous, and the beds immaculate, but if you forget to blow the sidewalk clean, that's all anyone will see.

The primary tool used for the cleanup is the blower. Most of the suggestions in this section deal with your use of this often-misunderstood apparatus.

4.1 The versatility of a blower

Blowers are ideal for clearing grass and leaves off sidewalks and driveways, but there is much more you can use them for.

🐦 In section **1.1** I said that it is best to do line edging before mowing so that the debris gets picked up. However, this is not always feasible. You can use your blower to go around all the edges and blow small amounts of grass clippings into the beds or over the lawn. (Use your judgment: the key is to not leave any evidence of the clippings.)

🐦 Use your blower to make piles of leaves in the fall or piles of moss and thatch after a power rake in the spring.

🐦 Always clear off walkways and patios after fertilizer or lime applications.

🐦 You can keep the curbs in front of your client's home clear with a blower. First blow the debris along the curb and then herd back any debris that has scattered onto the road. This takes some practice.

🐦 Blow entranceways and other confined areas that need to be tidied. Again, this takes some practice. The inexperienced blower operator will often find dust and debris scattering everywhere in a confined space. The trick is to reduce the throttle and then point the blower hose at the wall or door about 6 to 12 inches above the walkway. The wind from the blower will come down the wall or door and gently push the debris toward you

Operating Like a Finely Tuned Machine

Your goal is to have your crews operate like a finely tuned machine. Everyone has a job, they know what it is, and they go right to it. They also know what each of the others is doing, and they anticipate each other's moves. They have a goal — a desired time frame to get the job done — and they know that efficiency is key. When it's done right, a maintenance visit is a beautifully choreographed event. Work hard to instill this mindset in your employees.

A typical stop on a maintenance route should look something like this.

- When the truck stops at the jobsite the team jumps out of the truck. They don't finish listening to the song on the radio and they don't gab for five minutes first. Before getting to work, they record the time they arrived on their routing sheet.

- Within a minute the needed equipment is unloaded and everyone is working. They team knows that moping, moseying, and puttering have no place on the jobsite. People see them working from their homes, and the crew's actions speak volumes.

- At the end of the visit, nobody is waiting around for someone else to finish. If someone finishes early, he or she finds something else to do.

- There are smiles, laughter, and conversation among the crew. They are machines, not robots. They love their job.

and away from the wall. Slowly lower the blower hose so that you can turn around, get yourself behind the debris, and blow it out of the confined area.

🍂 Blow off your own equipment at the end of a job or the end of the day.

4.2 Restrictions on blowers

Some areas have either restricted or banned backpack blowers because of the noise they make. If that is the case in your area, you'll have to clean up without the help of a blower. If blowers are allowed where you live, go ahead and use one, but do it with consideration for others. Here are a few common-sense guidelines to help you keep your business "blower friendly":

🍂 Don't try to blow debris in the wind, which will just redistribute what you've blown. Use a rake or, if the wind is strong, reschedule the job and go on to something that the wind does not interfere with.

🍂 Don't create dust storms. This is a huge issue with the public, and rightfully so. It is annoying to see landscape maintenance workers blowing dusty sidewalks on a hot, dry day and creating huge dust clouds. Put the blower down and grab a broom, or reschedule the work.

🍂 Don't blow leaves from the sidewalk onto the road. Even if your municipality permits it, it looks ridiculous.

❧ Stop blowing when people are near. Turn your blower off and let them pass. (Do *you* like getting dust in your hair?)

❧ If you are blowing around parked cars, keep the blower at a lower throttle. When you are finished an area, quickly blow off the cars to clear any flying particles. Be careful not to bump into any of the vehicles. It's easy to forget about the extra width of the blower on your back.

5. LEAVING THE SITE

At the end of the job, one person should take on the responsibility of doing a final walk through the site to make sure everything has been done and nothing left behind. If you are working with a crew, designate one crew member to do this job, perhaps with the title of crew chief or team leader.

If you are working with a two-person crew, it's a good idea to initiate a crosscheck before pulling away from the site. Both of you should walk around the truck to make sure that everything is onboard, closed up, and, if necessary, tied down. This will avoid embarrassing situations where tools or debris fall off the truck or out of the back of your trailer.

Don't forget to record your start and stop times on your route sheet. This information is gold! Do not include downtime in your total time. For example, if you spent 40 minutes at Mr. Wayne's, but for 15 minutes you were trying to get your line edger started, make a note of the downtime and record 25 minutes for this customer. Also record who was on your crew and any special notes, requests, or comments.

Finally, leave a notice for your customers to let them know that you were on the job that day. Attach any special instructions (see Sample 21).

JOBSITE VISIT NOTICE

Beautiful Lawns & Gardens Visited Your Home Today!

During our visit we carried out the following tasks:

☑ Lawn cut	☐ Lawn fertilizing _____
☐ Line edging	☐ Chemical application _____
☑ Blade edging	☐ Watering
☑ Bed maintenance	☐ Soil amendment

Other services/Special notes:

Removed dead azalea. See quote for replacement.

Thank you.

Please call us if you have any questions or concerns about the work we have done.

Sincerely,

Beautiful Lawns & Gardens

(555) 555-1234

Team leader name: *Matthew*

Beautiful Lawns & Gardens Visited Your Home Today!

During our visit we carried out the following tasks:

☑ Lawn cut	☑ Lawn fertilizer *9-3-6 Moss Control*
☑ Line edging	☐ Chemical application _____
☑ Blade edging	☐ Watering
☑ Bed maintenance	☐ Soil amendment

Other services/Special notes:

Please do not water the lawn for 2 days.

Thank you.

Please call us if you have any questions or concerns about the work we have done.

Sincerely,

Beautiful Lawns & Gardens

(555) 555-1234

Team leader name: *Matthew*

13
LAWN SPECIALTIES

While the regular maintenance visit will likely be the mainstay of your business, you can and should offer many other profitable services to your customers. Lawn specialty services such as power raking, core aeration, top-dressing, and overseeding can make up a large part of your work. Collectively, these services can be offered as a total lawn renovation or rejuvenation package.

1. POWER RAKING

Power raking helps solves two problems that almost every lawn suffers from at one time or another: thatch and moss. If you need to combat either of these problems, you'll need to invest in a power rake (see chapter 4 for more information on the different types of power rakes).

1.1 Thatch

Thatch is the layer of dead plant material that builds up between the soil and the grass in most lawns. Thatch is a healthy condition if it is less than half an inch deep, as it provides a kind of underpadding for your lawn and protects delicate crowns from being flattened by the mower and other lawn traffic. As well, thatch breaks down and provides sustenance for beneficial organisms that live in the soil.

However, if thatch is allowed to build up to an inch or more, the results are less desirable. Grass roots may not be able to reach the soil and will succumb at the first sign of distress. As well, the grass will become more susceptible to disease or pest infestation because the thick layer of thatch provides a hospitable habitat for fungus and unwelcome bugs.

The sponginess of the lawn and its susceptibility to other problems will suggest a diagnosis of excess thatch. You can confirm your diagnosis by taking a core sample of the lawn. (If you don't have a core sampler, get

Lawn diagnosis

Your ability to figure out *why* a lawn isn't healthy and how best to treat it will separate your business from the others, which simply throw on the next "treatment" without getting to the root problem. You need to learn to look at the symptoms of an unhealthy lawn (e.g., moss, weeds, or disease) and diagnose the cause. Fixing the symptoms without addressing the cause will lead to more of the same problems down the road, and that means dissatisfied customers.

For example, if you're called in to examine a lawn with lots of moss, it's not enough to recommend a lawn renovation that includes power raking and aeration. You need to figure out why there is so much moss in the first place — and the likely cause is a heavily shaded lawn. In such a case, a proper course of action might be to eliminate some of the sources of shade, perhaps by thinning or pruning trees or reducing the height of a hedge. You might also suggest overseeding with a shade-tolerant seed. Or perhaps the lawn is always damp, indicating that the customer is irrigating too often. If so, the solution is simple.

Always look for the cause of the symptoms.

one. It's a great tool and will make you look like a real pro!)

1.2 Moss

Moss loves moist, acidic (high pH) soil, and it also thrives in the shade. It is common in the Pacific Northwest and other mild, wet climates.

Moss will slowly choke out grass if conditions are favorable for its growth. It detracts from the overall appearance of the lawn and is a hated beast in the areas where it flourishes. When you look at a lawn, it is obvious if excess moss is a problem. (Note: While there is no benefit to having any moss in a lawn, you don't have to get rid of all of it. Your aim is control. In fact, you may be doing well to remove about 80 percent.)

Power raking will remove a great deal of moss, but it *must* be followed by top-dressing, overseeding, aeration, and removal of anything causing excess shade. Otherwise the moss will waste no time returning with a vengeance.

1.3 Power raking tips

Power raking methods differ greatly depending on the area in which you live. You will have to research the specifics of your location to learn about any particular power raking needs. Here are some general tips for taking on this specialty:

- The best time to power rake cool season grasses is early spring or fall. For warm season grasses it is better to wait until the grass really starts to grow in late spring or early summer.

- Power raking should not be done in the rain as that considerably reduces its effectiveness.

- Before raking, cut the lawn as short as you feasibly can. The shorter the grass, the more effective the power rake. Throw the one-third rule out the window for this job.

- Avoid the dethatchers that attach to your mower. They do not do a good job and will not stand up to commercial use.

- Walk slowly when you are power raking. The greater the quantity of moss/thatch in the lawn, the slower you'll need to move.

- Notice what you are pulling up. If you see dirt, green grass, or chunks of grass, the power rake is set too low and you need to stop and adjust the mower. If you see no debris being pulled up, the power rake may be set too high. If you think you could be pulling up more, set the power rake a little lower and try again. You should see only moss or thatch, which is yellow and looks like dead grass.

- Overlap your rows slightly to ensure a thorough job.

- Depending on the volume of thatch and/or moss, you may want to go over the area more than once. (If you are battling moss, I can guarantee you'll have to rake the area at least twice.) If you do, alternate your direction each time. If you are pulling up large quantities of debris, pick up the loose material between the two passes. Otherwise the power rake will just churn over the same material it pulled up on the last pass.

- Be aware of anything sticking out of the grass, such as irrigation heads and surface tree roots. Stay well away from garden edges.

- In larger areas you may be able to use your blower to gather moss and thatch into a big pile for pickup. The most effective cleanup by far, though, is to rake the debris by hand. Use a lawn rake and apply lots of pressure. This will pull up more loose material and ensure you do the best job possible.

- Finally, use a rotary mower with a bag attachment to vacuum up all the loose bits. I'm always surprised how much more the lawn mower bag can collect after the first round of pickup.

It is usually best to price your power raking service by estimating hours because the labor required from one lawn to another will fluctuate tremendously. Estimate how long the power rake will take, factor in the equipment cost, and add in any hauling and dumping charges.

2. CORE AERATION

Once upon a time, only golf courses aerated their lawns. Today, regular aeration is recognized as a fundamental part of a full lawn care program.

Aeration, also called cultivation or coring, is sometimes incorrectly referred to as spiking. Spiking is a practice in which no core is removed, which adds to problems of soil compaction and generally does more harm than good. When aeration is done properly, hollow tines penetrate the soil to a depth of two or three inches and eject the cores of soil onto the surface of the lawn.

Every hole that the aerator punches works in a number of ways to increase the health of the lawn. First, it immediately relieves compaction by loosening the soil and making it easy for grass roots to spread. Water, oxygen, and nutrients all have direct access to the roots through the holes. As the cores break down, they become a productive top dressing for the turf. This slows the buildup of thatch. Aeration is also beneficial if you are dealing with any drainage problems, such as water runoff or puddling.

Most lawns benefit from regular aeration, and many customers will want their lawns aerated many times a year. Spring aeration is a great start to the year, summer aeration is rescue work for heat-stressed lawns, and fall aeration is an important step in winter prep. This service can be a high-profit sideline for your business, as well as being an important part of a lawn renovation.

Depending on the type of aerating equipment you select, you can produce 8 to 16 holes per square foot. Anything more than this is typically reserved for professional greenskeepers, such as those who work on golf courses.

Here are some specific tips for core aeration:

- Check, and preferably mark, all sprinkler heads in the lawn. A collision with an aeration tine will destroy a sprinkler head, and you will have to bear the replacement cost. (You might ask the homeowner to flag all heads for you.) Make sure you tell your customers that aeration tines penetrate to three inches; if an underground irrigation line is not buried deep enough, damage may occur. Let customers know that you will not accept responsibility for this type of damage since it was due to improper installation.

- Cut the lawn before aerating. Then don't cut it for at least a week.

- Most aerators are wider than 21-inch lawn mowers, so getting one through a narrow gate may be an issue. There isn't much you can do about this. If you can't get into a back yard because of a restricting gate, you and your customer will have to decide whether you will limit your aeration to the area in front.

- Aeration works best when the soil is slightly moist.

- Go over high-traffic areas twice.

- If the customer is agreeable, leave the cores on the grass so that they can break down naturally (in a week or so). If the customer is adamant that they be removed (even after you have explained that they are an important part of the benefit), you should insist on top-dressing the lawn with some quality top-dressing mix. Removing the cores without top-dressing is counterproductive for the lawn.

- If the soil base is poor (e.g., clay), the cores may not break down well and may even, if the sun comes out, turn hard as rock. Rake them up and tell the customer that top dressing is required. The fact that the cores react this way is a sure sign that the soil needs improvement.

- If the cores are slow to break down but crumble easily when lightly crushed with your fingers, then stay the course. Rain and watering will help speed up the deterioration. You do not need to wait until all the cores are gone before cutting. In fact, cutting will quicken the breakdown process.

🌱 Fertilizing and/or adding soil conditioners are perfect complements to aeration.

It's best to price aeration using the cost per 1,000 square feet method (see section **4** of chapter 9). Don't forget to include loading and unloading times, as well as the equipment cost, in your quotes. (You will need to replace tines frequently, so consider that as you cost your aerating equipment.)

3. TOP-DRESSING AND OVERSEEDING

Top-dressing refers to the process of adding topsoil or other humus around the top of a plant. Top-dressing a lawn simply entails spreading the soil over the grass and raking it in.

Overseeding, as you might guess, means spreading grass seed over an existing lawn.

Top-dressing with a quality mix is an easy way to improve the health of a lawn by improving the soil base. It follows the old adage: Feed the soil, not the plant. It is the most natural lawn care there is, and it goes beautifully with overseeding. If you plan to promote natural lawn care, these two services will be your best friends.

As a rule, a good top-dressing mix contains at least 50 percent sand, often more. It may also contain any of peat, soil, manure, or compost. Top-dressing with manure or compost, if these materials are fine and not clumped, works wonderfully on lawns. With the large proportion of sand, it's easy to rake top dressing into the grass, although not necessarily quick.

Here are some tips to help you with top-dressing and overseeding:

🌱 Top-dress from a quarter- to a half-inch deep. This amount of mix can be easily raked into the grass, leaving it in a presentable state. In extreme cases, top dressing can be applied heavily, even one or two inches deep (as part of a major renovation), but it will take some time before the area looks like a lawn again.

🌱 To make the job go faster, use a large scoop, rather than a small spade or shovel, to fan out the top-dressing mix.

🌱 Rake in the top dressing with the back side of a hard rake or the back of a fan rake. (The fan rake method works best, but it puts a lot of wear and tear on the rake.)

🌱 In some instances, spot top-dressing may be suitable (e.g., when you don't want to top-dress the entire lawn, but there are some bare patches).

🌱 Top-dressing can help level out small imperfections in the surface of the lawn.

🌱 In overseeding, seed should be applied at a rate of at least 5 pounds per 1,000 square feet. If you want to impress your client, use double this amount!

🌱 Use a broadcast spreader for large lawn areas. Seed by hand for smaller areas. If you're using a spreader, use extreme caution around garden beds or you'll be picking baby grass plants out of them for months. If your spreader has a baffle, use it. Otherwise, stay away from the edges and do them by hand.

🐦 If you're using a spreader, apply half the seed and then go over all areas again in a different direction (e.g., north to south first, then east to west).

🐦 Rake in the seed by dragging a fan rake back and forth behind you over the whole lawn. Don't apply any pressure to the rake; the force of its own weight will suffice.

🐦 Use a lawn roller after top-dressing and seeding to ensure good seed-soil contact. This will improve the chances of successful germination.

🐦 Apply a seed-starter fertilizer to the lawn immediately after seeding.

🐦 Water the lawn soon after seeding. The lawn must be kept moist for the first 10 to 14 days. However, if you saturate the seed, let it dry up, and then repeat this cycle several times, the seed will die. For best results, water a little bit, several times. Leave watering instructions with your customers.

🐦 If you are quoting an overseeding job for a non-regular client, also quote a follow-up visit three weeks later to asses results and reapply seed to any bare areas.

🐦 Customers sometimes panic if they see birds eating the seed after you have finished and left for the day. Assure them that the birds eat an inconsequential amount of seed, especially since you have been generous in your application. Tell them, too, that if there are any bare patches when you make your follow-up trip, you will reseed them.

Overseeding should be priced as cost per 1,000 (see section **4** of chapter 9). Don't buy cheap grass seed; you'll regret it, and sooner than you think. Just because it says "No. 1 Grade" does not mean it's the best. In my experience, it often means nothing at all. Buy from a reputable company, preferably one that specializes in, or has a large division of, grass seed production.

When you price top-dressing, account for buying the soil, delivery to the site, labor to move the soil from the pile into a wheelbarrow, labor to fan the soil out from the wheelbarrow onto the grass, and labor to rake the soil into the grass. Quote the job as cost/cubic yard installed. My rule is to quote the cost of the soil delivered plus 1.5 hours of labor per yard installed. It's a pricey service, but I have found that people don't mind paying for it. There is equipment to make the job easier, but not for the small-timer. If your business grows and you start doing larger lawns (i.e., an acre or more), the specialty equipment may be an option for you.

4. LAWN RENOVATIONS

A lawn renovation is generally a package consisting of power raking, aerating, top-dressing, and overseeding, with a few other smaller services included. Lawn renovation can be an excellent profit center for your business. In most areas there is a large market in need of these services. For example, someone whose lawn is in a sorry state may be thinking about either installing a new lawn or fixing up the existing one. Enter the lawn reno. Other people don't mind spending a few hundred dollars each spring to give their lawn new life and make it the best it can be. Introduce them to the lawn reno (or possibly the lawn rejuvenation — see section **5**).

First, you need to determine if a renovation is possible or if the customer needs an entirely new lawn. The general rule is that if more than 50 percent of the lawn is moss, heavy thatch, weeds, or destroyed in some other way, then a new lawn is needed. Otherwise, a lawn renovation may be the answer. (Note: Some landscape maintenance companies define lawn renovation as killing the entire lawn with chemicals and then reseeding. This is not the type of lawn renovation we are talking about here. If you have to kill the entire lawn, you should just install a brand-new one.)

Pricing the lawn renovation is as simple as pricing each of the individual services I have already covered. On the quotation sheet, describe exactly what is included in the lawn renovation and include your full list prices for each step. Then take off 5 percent to 10 percent at the end, depending on the circumstances. That way, when you present the quote to your customers, you can explain each step and show them that they are saving by purchasing the bundled deal.

Here are the steps in a total lawn renovation:

1. *Moss control and fertilizer application.* If moss is present, even a little, start the reno by applying a moss-control fertilizer. This will cause the moss to dry up a bit, and the power rake will make quick work of tearing it up.

Allow the moss control to work for four to seven days before coming back.

2. *Lawn weed spray.* If weeds are a problem, treat them before seeding. (You mustn't apply chemicals for four to six weeks after seeding.) Use a systemic broadleaf weed killer to control weeds only. If there are rogue grasses in the lawn, boost your firepower and use a nonselective herbicide. Don't worry if some of the healthy grass is a casualty, since you will be repairing it anyway. Leave the lawn for a week to let the weed killer do its work.

3. *Lawn cut.* Start the actual reno by cutting the lawn as short as possible without damaging it. This is another time when you don't have to follow the one-third rule.

4. *Power rake.* The scope of this step varies significantly. It may be that running the power rake over the lawn a couple of times will be enough to remove the unwanted moss and thatch. If the thatch is extremely compacted, however, you may have to remove portions of the lawn manually. If there are such areas, you'll need a manual thatching rake. (Usually power raking alone is sufficient.) Go over all areas at least twice — more times if you think the lawn needs it. Use a blower and/or manually rake the lawn to pick up all the debris.

5. *Lawn cut.* Cut the lawn again to suck up all the little bits of moss and thatch that you did not get when picking up. Drop the mower as low as you can for this step.

6. *Core aeration.* Aerate the lawn as described in section **2**. Go over all areas twice — more in heavy-traffic areas.

7. *Lime/sulfur application.* If the lawn needs lime or sulfur, this step comes next. However, since you should never apply fertilizer on the same day, plan to come back in two or three days.

8. *Top-dressing.* Apply top dressing as described in section **3**.

9. *Overseeding.* Apply the seed at your desired rate. Use your fertilizer spreader, but make sure it is adequately calibrated. Be sure you don't plant seed in the garden beds!

10. *Roll the lawn.* Use a lawn roller to lightly compact the soil and ensure you have the best seed-soil contact. The roller can be empty.

11. *Seed-starter fertilizer application.* My secret is to double the recommended rate of seed-starter fertilizer. This will make a big impact, especially if you were also generous with the grass seed.

12. *Follow-up visit.* Make a return visit, about three weeks after the seed application, to ensure that seed has germinated and that there are no bare patches. If there are, apply more seed manually. Check for any other problems with the lawn. If weeds are appearing, recommend further action.

(Remember, wait four to six weeks after seeding before applying herbicides.)

Since the lawn renovation demands that you pre-purchase such materials as grass seed, top-dressing mix, and fertilizers, it is prudent to ask non-regular (or new) customers for a deposit of 25 percent to 35 percent. I also recommend leaving your invoice with your customer after you have finished seeding and fertilizing — don't wait for your follow-up visit. (Or perhaps hold back 10 percent of the invoice until your final visit.) Be sure to leave watering instructions so the customer knows what to do.

5. LAWN REJUVENATIONS

A lawn rejuvenation is simply a scaled-down renovation. It may include the same steps that make up the renovation, but not to the same degree. For example, you might power rake portions of the lawn and do a quick once-over to stay on top of moss. Or perhaps no power raking is needed, and top dressing will be applied only in bare areas. In other words, a lawn rejuvenation may include some or all of moss-control fertilization, broadleaf weed spraying, lime/sulfur application, core aeration, overseeding, and fertilization.

You can design your own lawn rejuvenation package or let customers choose their own services. You could call it a spring tune-up, marketing it to your customers as a bundled package of services to get their lawns off to a good start in the spring.

14

THE ART OF FERTILIZING

Many professed lawn care operators do not offer their customers fertilizer applications, preferring instead to limit their work to mowing and cleanup. If this is your thinking, take note. Your customers will appreciate and respect you more if you have a good working knowledge of turfgrasses and how to feed them. As well, as more and more lawn care operators offer their clients a full range of services, the "mow and go" operations will risk losing business. So get serious about learning as much as you can about your trade, including fertilizing. It can be a lucrative profit center on its own.

1. WHY FERTILIZE?

If your answer to this question is "To offer my customer the best-looking lawn on the block," you are right. But there is more to it than that, and it's important to understand the technical reasons for fertilizing.

Your goal as a professional lawn care expert is to produce beautiful, healthy, verdant lawns. To that end, lawns must be supplemented with some or all of the 16 chemical elements essential to the health of a grass plant. If all of these elements are present and available in proper quantities, the lawns you care for will likely be lush, uniformly green, dense, and able to withstand disease, stress, and environmental damage.

2. A CHEMISTRY LESSON

The 16 elements mentioned above can be divided into four groups:

1. *Natural elements.* This group makes up the vast majority of the plant, and the good news is that you don't have to worry about it. Carbon, hydrogen, and oxygen are gifts of creation; the plant "inhales" them either as carbon dioxide

from the air, which we conveniently exhale, or as water from the sky or a sprinkler.

2. *Macronutrients.* This is perhaps the best-known group. Macronutrients — nitrogen, phosphorus, and potassium — are often referred to as the primary nutrients because grass plants use them in fairly large quantities. Collectively, these three elements make up about 6 percent to 11 percent of the dry weight of turfgrass.

3. *Secondary elements.* This group, made up of calcium, magnesium, and sulfur, is used in somewhat smaller amounts by the plant, but is still essential for life.

4. *Micronutrients.* The fourth group is also known as the trace elements. These elements are present in minute amounts, but don't let that fool you; they are as important as the other nutrients because grass plants cannot grow without each and every one of them. They include iron, manganese, zinc, copper, molybdenum, boron, and chlorine.

2.1 The importance of nitrogen

On any bag of fertilizer you will see three numbers (e.g., 25-10-30), which represent the percentage by weight of nitrogen, phosphorus, and potassium, in that order. For example, a bag of fertilizer with a 25 as the first number will contain a quarter pound of nitrogen for each pound of fertilizer.

Nitrogen makes the grass grow fast and turn a nice, lush green. It also contributes to the general health of the plant and helps build up its tolerance of heat, cold, drought, and wear. Under ideal conditions it is fast acting, with the nitrogen that comes out of your spreader being translocated to the plant within 15 to 24 hours of application.

2.2 Understanding nitrogen release rates

Nitrogen comes in many forms, and you need to understand each type before you can choose which is best for your application.

2.2a Quick-release fertilizers

Quick-release fertilizers usually contain nitrogen derived from urea, ammonium sulfate, ammonium nitrate, calcium nitrate, or potassium nitrate, all of which are "synthetic organics" (see section **3.6**) and are water soluble. Quick-release fertilizers offer tremendous growth in a short time. However, this presents some risks: they may cause a tremendous growth spurt, but it will be short-lived and may burn the grass. As well, since the grass cannot possibly take up so much nitrogen, most of it runs off into the local storm sewers. Check the small print on the label to see if any of these synthetic organics are present in large proportions. If so, avoid this type of fertilizer unless you have a specific reason to use it (and the specific reason should not be that it is cheaper).

2.2b Slow-release fertilizers

Most professional lawn fertilizers today can be classified as either slow release or controlled release (some fertilizers use a combination of more than one release method). What both types have in common is that, while some of the total nitrogen is made available to the lawn immediately, some is released slowly over time. The rate of nutrient release is governed by factors such as moisture (hydrolysis), temperature, acidity level in the soil (or soil pH), and/or microbial activity in the soil.

Slow-release fertilizers are generally considered mid- to low-grade. They are better than quick-release but not as good as controlled-release fertilizers. Here are some terms you should be familiar with when looking at slow-release fertilizers:

- *Urea.* Urea is the source of nitrogen in most commercial fertilizers today. It is made by combining nitrogen and carbon dioxide and granulating the solution to form a product with 46 percent nitrogen content. You can think of it as the core nitrogen product. Urea all by itself would be considered quick release, but there are ways to make the urea release its cargo more slowly.

- *Water-insoluble nitrogen.* One of the ways to slow the release of nitrogen in fertilizers is to make a portion of it insoluble in water (i.e., not easily dissolved in water). If this method is used, you will see the generic term "water-insoluble nitrogen (WIN)" on the fertilizer label. It is usually represented as a percentage to tell buyers how much of the total nitrogen is water-insoluble and therefore slow-release. If you see this value on the label, it means that the product probably contains either ureaform or IBDU (see below).

- *Ureaform.* As mentioned, urea is water-soluble and therefore releases nitrogen quickly. In order to make urea release nitrogen over time, manufacturers can change it chemically so that a portion is water-insoluble.

Ureaformaldehyde (ureaform or UF for short) is sometimes called methylene urea or MU on fertilizer labels. It is a form of urea that has been changed in this manner. It is 38 percent nitrogen, 70 percent of which is WIN. It is not often used in lawn fertilizers, but is more often found in plant food such as fertilizer pellets. Microbial activity breaks down the ureaform.

- *Isobutylidene diurea.* More commonly known by its initials, IBDU is similar to ureaform in that a portion of the urea has been altered to help it avoid squandering its nitrogen load. It also is 38 percent nitrogen, but 90 percent of that is WIN. The primary difference between IBDU and ureaform is that the rate at which IBDU spends its nitrogen is governed by moisture and particle size, not by microbial activity. IBDU is often found in mid-grade lawn fertilizers.

2.2c Controlled-release fertilizers

Most high-grade turf fertilizers today fall into the category of controlled release. In these fertilizers, the urea is coated to prevent immediate release of the nitrogen. However, there is still some variety in the different kinds and quality of various controlled-release lawn foods.

- *Sulfur-coated urea (SCU).* The original coating technology is sulfur coating, which has been around since the 1960s. Plain fast-acting urea is sprayed with molten sulfur, and the subsequent particle breaks down gradually over several weeks. The rate of breakdown is largely determined by the thickness of the sulfur coating, and then by the work of soil microorganisms. Since the amount of microorganism activity is dictated by temperature and moisture, the release is fastest when the soil is warm and wet, conditions that favor microbial activity. On the other hand, applying SCU fertilizer in the northern regions in fall will yield little if any results until spring. While still widely used, SCU technology is considered old technology with the advent of polymer-coated fertilizers.

🍃 *Polymer-coated urea (PCU).* This is by far the most dependable method of delivering nitrogen consistently. The urea is coated with a resin membrane made from synthetic materials. As water seeps through the membrane, it dissolves the urea. Then, through the process of osmosis, the nitrogen is forced back out. By varying the thickness of the membrane, producers can ensure the nitrogen is released over a precise period of time (from a matter of weeks to as long as a complete season). This form of fertilizer is more dependable because varying soil temperatures and moisture levels do not affect the rate of nutrient release.

2.3 Phosphorus

Phosphorus is represented by the middle number on the fertilizer package. This element works hard to build a strong and deep root system, which will help make a lawn resistant to dry spells and other stresses. Phosphorus is also connected to seed germination and flower and seed production.

Most lawns need only half a pound of phosphorus per thousand square feet each year to maintain an adequate level. Use more if soil analysis shows there is a deficiency or if you are starting a new lawn or overseeding.

2.4 Potassium

Potassium toughens plants to make them more resistant to cold, heat, disease, drought, and traffic. It also contributes to photosynthesis, the process by which plants turn sunlight into energy.

It's good to apply potassium to the lawn in the fall, which is why you will notice "winter prep" fertilizers have a high last number, which represents the proportion of potassium content. An average lawn requires about one to two pounds of potassium per thousand square feet per year.

2.5 Secondary and trace elements

Calcium, magnesium, and sulfur all play important roles in turfgrass. Dolomite lime, which you may have to apply anyway to correct soil pH, can provide the first two. Sulfur is usually present in adequate levels in the soil, but it is also often applied to lower the pH of alkaline soils.

The same can be said for most other micronutrients. There will be plenty of iron in your soil if you use a moss-control fertilizer. As well, iron is often present in proportions larger than you might think, considering it's a micronutrient in many popular brands. It helps give the grass an appealing deep green color.

If you do a soil test and discover deficiencies, then of course you should take action to rectify the problem. Otherwise, using a complete fertilizer, with a micronutrient package, is a good way to ensure that these often-forgotten heroes are present in ample amounts in the soil.

3. CHOOSING A FERTILIZER

There is a staggering array of fertilizers to choose from, and which one you select will depend on the turfgrass you are servicing and the climate of your area. Fertilizer suppliers can be valuable information sources as you develop your feeding programs because they will be intimate with the local conditions and the varieties of grass used in your area.

I have included some general information and advice to help you in your selection as well.

3.1 Granular versus liquid

Unless you happen to have a tank truck with sprayer attachment, granular turfgrass fertilizers are best for commercial gardening. The granular products can be spread effectively with a broadcast or drop spreader, are easy to stock, and can be measured somewhat accurately. Liquid fertilizers take more time to apply, need to be applied more often, and are more difficult to spread evenly on the lawn.

A term that you may see on granular fertilizer labels is *homogeneous*. This means that each fertilizer pellet or *prill* contains all the nutrients specified. For example, in a homogeneous 28-3-8 fertilizer, each prill will contain that proportion of nutrients, which ensures uniform nutrient coverage on the lawn. This is superior to cheaper fertilizers, which contain pellets of each kind of nutrient. In this case, a 28-3-8 fertilizer would contain 28 percent nitrogen pellets, 3 percent phosphorus pellets, and 8 percent potassium pellets. You would have no guarantee that the different varieties of prills would be distributed evenly on the lawn.

3.2 Complete versus incomplete

A complete fertilizer is one that contains all three of the primary nutrients: nitrogen, phosphorus, and potassium. An incomplete fertilizer will contain only one or perhaps two of these elements (e.g., 0-45-0 is incomplete).

3.3 Moss-control fertilizers

A moss-control fertilizer contains a high proportion (often about 17 percent) of iron (ferrous sulfate). When applied to the lawn, it quickly turns the moss black. You should know that it does not kill the moss permanently. Rather, it stunts the moss and stops it from growing for a while. If nothing more is done to remove the moss, it will eventually recover and be as healthy as ever. If a lawn has a heavy growth of moss, you should at least power rake, and perhaps even renovate, the lawn after applying moss control in order to provide a more permanent solution.

Using a moss-control fertilizer as the first application in the spring is an excellent way to start the year. Even if moss is not a problem, consider applying this type of fertilizer anyway because the ferrous sulfate will make the lawn lush.

Avoid liquid moss controls. They do provide a quick green-up, but they leach into the ground quickly and provide no long-term benefits. As well, they are not as respectful to the environment.

You should use either a moss control that has the iron in powder form mixed in with regular fertilizer, or one that comes as all-in-one particles with the iron and the fertilizer mixed together in each particle.

If you decide to use the powdered form (it's cheaper), you will probably learn to hate the week or two out of the year that you do moss-control applications. The powdered iron stinks, and it sticks to your clothes so you stink as well. The all-in-one variety is nicer to use if you don't mind spending a few more dollars.

The iron in moss control may stain certain surfaces, and it is difficult or impossible to clean. Do not spread moss control in the rain, and do blow off all surfaces thoroughly before leaving the site. Do not, whatever you do, get moss control in swimming pools. You may be faced with emptying and repainting the pool surface to get rid of the orange spots.

Always wear a mask when applying moss control.

Some fertilizers contain smaller amounts (2 percent or 3 percent) of iron to help green the grass. This is not moss control, but it may be substituted if moss is not a problem.

3.4 Micronutrient packages

A micronutrient package contains an assortment of trace elements and is the all-round best product for the lawn because it contains all the nutrition required. The nutrient analysis will vary from product to product. Visit your local suppliers and check what fertilizers they have with micronutrient packages. Consider using these for your summer applications.

3.5 Weed & feed

The application affectionately known as the weed & feed is a marvel of modern convenience. It feeds the lawn with fertilizer and also contains a herbicide that will kill certain kinds of broadleaf weeds. And it does all this at the same time! Be careful, however, as there are varying qualities of weed & feeds. You get what you pay for.

In general, the smaller the fertilizer particle, the more effective the weed control. Consider this a pesticide application more than spreading fertilizer, and don't forget to use all the necessary safety equipment. As well, read the label carefully so you know what the active ingredients are and how many dry days you need for the product to be effective. Check to make sure that the herbicide will control the type of weed that you are dealing with. If the lawn is full of crabgrass or other grassy weeds, weed & feed probably won't work. Also, check the local regulations, as some places require that licensed applicators spread weed & feed, while others demand no special permit. You may be required to post signs, but even if you don't have to, notify your customers both the week before and the week of the service so they are prepared and know to keep children and pets off the lawn for a few days.

There are also fertilizers available with built-in pesticides. If you use these, apply the same rules as for weed killers. In addition, watch your application rate or you'll scare off or kill all the good bugs too. Even at the recommended amount you will probably kill a lot of beneficial organisms, so use such products with prudence.

3.6 Natural fertilizers

Do not confuse natural fertilizers with organic fertilizers. Sometimes chemical fertilizers are labeled organic because they are made up of a combination of organic compounds (e.g., carbon). Technically, therefore, since carbon is an organic compound, anything, even some plastics, could be called organic. Such fertilizers are more appropriately called *synthetic organic* fertilizers. A natural fertilizer, on the other hand, is made up of ingredients that used to be alive, such as animal and plant waste.

Natural lawn care has not succeeded on a large scale. However, you may have customers who do not want to use chemicals on their lawn and who ask for natural products. Here are a few facts about natural fertilizers.

* *Advantages.* Lawns can and do thrive without the use of chemical fertilizers. If you use natural fertilizers, you never have to worry about checking for slow-release nitrogen because there is no other kind with natural organics. The food also keeps on giving for a longer period of time, so you won't have to feed the lawn every week. In fact, timing is not as important with natural fertilizers as it is with chemical applications. You won't ever have to worry again about burning the lawn; even large doses will not injure the grass. And, of course, the biggest advantage is that natural products are kind to our planet. While the synthetic fertilizers produced today are more environmentally friendly than ever before, they are no match for a true natural lawn food. (See sidebar on natural fertilizer products.)

* *Disadvantages.* A natural lawn care program requires a sizable upfront investment. In most cases, the nutrients that natural fertilizers provide are locked up in organic compounds and require microorganism activity to free them. This means that your soil base must contain a healthy population of living things to start with. You may need to expend much time, effort, and organic material to build that population up. Further, those microorganisms don't like to work in the cold. They shut down when it reaches about 55° F (13° Celsius), so they don't work as well in cooler climes. The natural foods are often more labor-intensive to apply. There are some products that can be spread in a broadcast spreader, but at times you may need to mix certain products, such as blood meal, rock phosphate, and wood ashes, together before spreading. And finally, some people don't want to wait for natural fertilizers to work. Natural fertilizers do not provide the same quick green-up that chemical applications do.

You will have to weigh the pros and cons for your customer base. If you are passionate about natural applications, or if you have many customers requesting them, you could consider specializing in natural lawn care. Even if you don't go so far as to specialize, you should be mindful of the concern many people have about chemical applications and use natural products whenever possible. For instance, you could encourage your customers to feed the soil by top-dressing the lawn, fight weeds by introducing more and

Natural Fertilizer Products

There are many natural products available that can be used as fertilizers for the lawn and garden. Here is a list of a few, along with their estimated analysis.

- Alfalfa meal: 3-3-2
- Bat guano: 10-4-1
- Blood meal: 10-1-0
- Bone meal: 0-4-1
- Castor pomace (castor oil meal): 5-1-1
- Coffee grounds: High nitrogen and potassium
- Composted cow manure:1-1-1
- Cottonseed meal: 7-2-1
- Erth-Rite (trade name): 3-2-2
- Feather meal: 11-0-0

- Fish meal: 10-4-4
- Hoof and horn meal: 12-2-0
- Leather meal: 10-0-0
- Milorganite (dried sewage sludge): 6-2-0 (and lots of micronutrients)
- Poultry manure: 4-4-2
- Rock phosphate: 0-3-0
- Seaweed: 1-0-4 (+ 50 important elements!)
- Wood ash: High in potassium and micronutrients

newer species of grass plants with overseeding, and be sensible when applying fertilizer so that they don't apply too much and waste it.

4. HOW AND WHEN TO APPLY FERTILIZER

When should you fertilize? What analysis should you choose? The short answer to these questions is that it depends mostly on what type of turfgrass you are caring for and, somewhat related, where you live. Here are a few tips:

- Do some research to find out what types of turfgrass you expect to look after in your area and what their feeding requirements are. Visit one or two fertilizer suppliers in your area and quiz them on what other lawn care companies are using and when.

- A good rule of thumb is to fertilize every six to eight weeks from spring to fall. Looking at it another way, most grasses should be fed four or five times per year.

- End the season with a fall fertilizer (also called a winter prep).

- Create a fertilizing schedule before you get started in the spring, and try to use the same or a similar program for all your customers. This will make the logistics of delivering your programs less complicated.

Choosing a Fertilizer Supplier

Your local fertilizer supplier should have a wealth of knowledge that you can tap into as you decide on the specific fertilizers you would like to offer your customers. Keep the following points in mind:

- Avoid retail centers if possible. They are not likely to stock a full range of professional-quality fertilizers, may not be able to advise you professionally, and will probably charge you more. Ask other gardeners where they get their supplies.

- Talk to the sales reps at the suppliers you visit to see what they know. They should be familiar with what other lawn care companies are using and what is most popular. They should also be able to help you decide what will suit your needs.

- A supplier should offer high-quality polymer-coated fertilizers as part of its selection. As well, it should offer both chemical and organic/natural alternatives.

Once you find suitable product and a program that works for you, stick with it.

To determine how much fertilizer you need for any one application, you again need to consider the grass type. Every variety of turfgrass has an annual nitrogen requirement/recommendation. It is stated in terms of the number of pounds of actual nitrogen that should be applied to 1,000 square feet (lbs/K) over the entire year. You can use this information to plan your fertilizer programs.

The following list shows the nitrogen application rates for a few of the more common turfgrasses. Keep in mind that if you are maintaining a sand-based turf, you may need to increase these rates.

Cool Season Grasses	lbs/K/year
Kentucky Bluegrass	2 to 3
Fine-leaf Fescue	1 to 2
Tall Fescue	1 to 2
Perennial Ryegrass	2 to 3
Creeping Bentgrass	2 to 4

Warm Season Grasses	
Bermudagrass	1 to 4
Buffalograss	1 to 2
Centipedegrass	2 to 4
St. Augustinegrass	2 to 4
Zoysiagrass	2 to 3

Remember that these values are for the whole year, not a single application. Disperse the total nitrogen requirement into however many applications you will provide. You should not apply more than one pound of nitrogen per 1,000 square feet at one time.

Once you know the suggested nitrogen rate, you can then calculate how much fertilizer to spread on the lawn. This is a two-step calculation:

1. Basically, you need to know how much fertilizer to use to deliver one pound of nitrogen. In other words, if you have a 40-pound bag of 29-3-4 product to apply, you need to figure out how much of that 40 pounds you'll need to apply to 1,000 square feet to distribute one pound of real nitrogen. It's an easy calculation. Divide the nitrogen percentage (which we know is the first of the three numbers of the label) into the number of pounds we want to apply per 1,000 square feet (1 pound ÷ 29 percent, or 1 ÷ 0.29 = 3.45.) So in order to get one pound of real nitrogen onto the lawn, you need to apply 3.45 pounds of the fertilizer bag.

2. Divide the entire area of the lawn by 1,000, and then multiply that number by the value from the first step. So if the lawn is 2,500 square feet, the calculation is 2,500 ÷ 1,000 = 2.5, and 2.5 x 3.45 = 8.6 pounds. You need to apply exactly 8.6 pounds of fertilizer to adequately fertilize the lawn.

Of course, many lawn fertilizers tell you on the label how much product you need to apply per 1,000 square feet to distribute one pound of nitrogen, so you may not need to carry out this calculation.

5. CALIBRATING YOUR SPREADER

To figure out how much fertilizer your spreader spreads, you need to do a test spread. You can try this on your own lawn before going to work on your customers' properties. You'll need a handful of stakes and a measuring scale before you begin.

1. Measure a 1,000-square-foot area and clearly mark it with your stakes.

2. Pour a known amount of fertilizer into the spreader. Make a note of how much, in pounds, you put it.

3. If there are recommended spreader settings on the fertilizer label, set the spreader accordingly. Otherwise, take a guess. Make a note of this setting too.

4. Spread the fertilizer as you normally would over your 1,000-square-foot area.

5. Pour the product remaining in the spreader into a container and weigh it. The difference between this weight and the starting weight is the amount of fertilizer you have applied. Does it match what you calculated to be the correct application rate above? If not, adjust accordingly and repeat. Keep accurate notes.

You should calibrate your spreader annually in the spring before you begin your regular service.

Many fertilizer labels today include a chart of spreader settings for popular name-brand spreaders. Buy a name-brand spreader and use this information. (But do an annual calibration to make sure the setting is still accurate.)

You'll discover over time that fertilizer application is more an art than a science. If you are inexperienced, be vigilant, follow the rules, and take extra steps to ensure that you are not applying insufficient or unsafe quantities. After a while you will know just by looking if you are applying too much or too little fertilizer. This is especially true if you stick to the same brands and types as much as possible.

6. FERTILIZING OTHER PLANTS

Grass is not the only plant in your customer's yard that needs to be fed, although, thankfully, most of the others do not have such high-maintenance feeding programs. When it comes to feeding shrubs and bedding plants, you have an advantage because you can improve the soil by working in compost or manure around the plants. You want to maintain a rich, organic soil base to keep everything healthy.

It is important that you understand the feeding requirements of the plants you look after. To this end, you should do some homework, reading other books to learn what you need to know. Here are a few tips to build on:

- *Shrubs.* Shrubs and some trees are often fed with fertilizer tabs, which are buried under the ground around the root zone of the plant. The tabs dissolve slowly and generally provide feeding for a full season. Alternatively, you can use a coated plant food that works much like the resin-coated lawn fertilizers discussed earlier. They also provide food for the entire growing season.

- *Perennials.* Perennials should not need much feeding if the soil is healthy. If you do feed them, you can use a coated product or a liquid fertilizer.

- *Annuals.* A coated slow-release product works well with annuals as well. A liquid fertilizer will also work if you have the time — unless you are specially equipped, it is labor-intensive. Good, healthy loam is a key here.

- *Bulbs.* Other than a sprinkle of bone meal when you plant them, flowering bulbs should require no special feeding. When you cut them back in the spring, wait until the green has died back. As it dies back, the plant's energy is returned to the bulb. Cutting off the green when it's still green will rob the bulb of needed nutrients, and it will not be as bountiful the next year.

7. SOME FINAL TIPS

Please heed the following tips, tricks, and cautions as you provide your fertilization services:

- *Storage.* As with many products, the more fertilizer you buy at one time, the less you pay per unit. Stocking up saves you a few bucks and is convenient too, but don't get carried away. Don't buy more than you will use in a season. Make sure you have a dry place to store it; if it gets wet, it's garbage. Check with your local fire department to see if there are limitations on the amount of fertilizer you are allowed to store on your property. Even if you are below that limit, the department may want to take note that you have chemical fertilizers on site in case there is an emergency.

- *Before you spread.* Fill your spreader on a hard surface (not on the grass!) so you can easily clean up spills. Keep unused fertilizer in the truck or trailer so kids and pets don't get into it when you are working.

- *Type of equipment.* Drop spreaders provide the best control when spreading your lawn food, but they also take about five times longer. For most residential applications, a broadcast spreader is sufficient for your needs. Some of the better spreaders have baffles so you only spread fertilizer on one side and also have the ability to control the spread of your product. These are useful features.

🌿 *Planning.* Before you drop the gate to start the flow of fertilizer, take a look at the lawn area and decide on a plan of attack. It is easy to forget where you have been and what's still left to do when you are halfway through the job. Planning a strategy will help you avoid getting into trouble.

🌿 *Method.* Try to work in straight lines as much as possible. Some lawns will be uncomplicated, while others will require you to supply many short bursts of fertilizer as you open the gate for a second or two to catch small or awkward areas of the lawn. Avoid 90- and 180-degree turns; instead, complete the row you are on, close the gate, reposition your spreader, and then start spreading again. If feasible, circumnavigate the lawn first and then do rows. If you cannot do this, make sure you feed the parts of the lawn where you were standing as you started fertilizing each row.

🌿 The distribution of fertilizer is directly affected by your walking speed. Walk at a steady speed, about three miles per hour. Note that a broadcast spreader does not disperse its cargo evenly. Of your total spread, only half of it (the center) gets an adequate

quantity of food; the edges on either side get less. The solution is to overlap each row by approximately a quarter of your total spread to provide even coverage. To provide the absolute best coverage of the lawn, apply fertilizer at half the recommended rate and go over all areas twice. The second time, run the spreader perpendicular to the direction you traveled on your first round. This may not be practical for some lawns; use your judgment.

🌿 *Streaking.* If you are using a broadcast spreader, be careful that you don't streak the lawn by applying the fertilizer inconsistently, producing strips of pale grass. Streaking is more likely to occur because of too little fertilizer rather than too much, so when you are overlapping, err on the side of too much.

🌿 *Burning.* What is called fertilizer burn is not really burning at all; it's desiccation. Too much fertilizer in a localized area has the effect of drawing moisture out of the plant, which then dries up and dies. If you are using a high-quality polymer-coated fertilizer, burning will not be an issue (unless you have a spill — see below). These fertilizers do not even have to be watered in, although it's still a good idea. If you use a cheaper fertilizer with more quick-release nitrogen, it may cause burning if it is not watered in.

🌿 *Spills.* Spills will also kill the grass. The best advice is to avoid spills by using common sense and caution when filling your spreader. Don't overfill the spreader and don't try to fill it on a slope or other uneven surface. To clean up a spill, first pick up the majority of the fertilizer with a flat shovel. After that you may rough-rake the remaining prills to spread them around, or use your blower to disperse them. You may also want to dilute the area with water.

Cleanup. Blow all fertilizer off sidewalks, patios, and decks. Make absolutely sure you get every last prill onto the lawn, where it belongs, especially if you have used moss control or a product with herbicides or pesticides in it.

15
OTHER SERVICES

Over time, as your business develops, you may choose to expand the services you offer. In this chapter I describe some of those options, as well as off-season activities and services that can keep you busy.

1. SOIL ANALYSIS

If you are working on lawns that seem to require more care than usual, you may find it helpful to do a soil analysis so you can prepare the most effective lawn program for your customer.

Soil analysis must be carried out by a qualified lab, so you will need to establish a relationship with a lab in your area (check the Yellow Pages) and take your soil samples there whenever needed. You can pass the cost to your customer as part of your service. The soil analysis will tell you the levels of all nutrients (macro, micro, and other) in the soil, the pH level, and the structure of the soil. Some labs will recommend what steps you should take to correct any problems.

If there is no soil analysis lab near you, you can still offer simple soil amendment or conditioning services based on your knowledge of the typical soil in your area. The most common condition that needs correction is the level of acidity (pH) of the soil.

Soil acidity is measured on a scale of 1 to 14, with 7 as neutral, below 7 as acidic, and above 7 as alkaline. The ideal pH level for a healthy lawn is 6.5 to 7 (slightly acidic). If the soil in the lawns you look after is alkaline or too acidic, your fertilizing may be in vain. Nutrients have little effect on plants if the pH is too far below or above the ideal.

To correct acidic soil, add lime. To correct alkaline soil, you can add sulfur. In some cases of alkaline soil, a fertilizer with a good supply of sulfur will suffice. As a general rule, never condition the soil on the same day you fertilize, as the conditioner will render the fertilizer less effective. Allow for a week between the two tasks.

Note that do-it-yourself soil testing kits are available, but I have never found them to be accurate. You will be better off simply doing research on the soil type in your area or, if the service is available, taking a soil sample to a qualified lab.

2. SOIL TOPPINGS

2.1 Topsoil

Unless you expand into a full landscaping service, you will rarely be installing plain topsoil. More likely you will supply your customers with mixes of topsoil and manure, sand, peat, compost, or other materials. Check with your local soil suppliers to see what kinds of mixes they have. You might see some of the following mixes:

- *Garden mix.* A garden mix will contain at least topsoil, manure, sand, and peat. It is ideal for all gardens, not just vegetable gardens. You can add this to annual or perennial beds. If it is chopped up finely enough, you can top-dress lawns with garden mix, but beware: If there are huge chunks of manure in it, raking the mix into the lawn becomes a time-comsuming chore. If you do find a garden mix that you can use as a top dressing, then use it — the lawn will love it.

- *Top-dressing mix.* These usually contain at least 50 percent sand. The other 50 percent is topsoil or possibly compost. If the latter, and it's easy to spread, then this is the best top dressing to use.

- *Manure.* There are many types of manure available, from many types of animals. If you use manure, you have to be sure to turn it well into the dirt; don't toss it on top.

- *Compost.* More and more commercial outfits are taking the green waste that we pay to dump and are composting it so they can sell it back to us. Compost, whether purchased in this manner or from your customer's own compost heap, is one of the best ways to amend your soil base with organic matter. If your customers have a compost heap, consider selling them a compost maintenance package in which you turn the compost regularly, add to it on your weekly visits, and spread it on the beds in early spring.

2.2 Mulches

Mulches benefit the soil by preserving moisture, preventing erosion, helping with weed control, and maintaining a more consistent soil temperature. They are popular, and your customers may ask for them (or you may want to recommend some). They are most often used in commercial properties because they require less maintenance than soil. They do not work well in beds with bedding plants, which prefer a nice garden mix.

One of the benefits of mulches is that they are slow to break down, so they last a long time. However, keep in mind that the organisms breaking down these complex structures use a lot of fuel to do so, and they take that fuel from the soil. When you mulch, it is a good idea to supplement your plants with nitrogen at the same time. Otherwise, your plants may start losing their healthy green appearance. Mulches also work well on pathways, tree circles, or other areas where no plants are needed or wanted.

Typical mulches are made from bark, pine needles, or even pebbles.

2.3 Landscaping rocks

Rocks are often used decoratively in beds and around the lawn. Think about using them instead of a mulch in certain beds. Walkways, driveways, and other unplanted areas are good locations for some sort of rock material. Some rocks, like limestone or blue shale, serve a functional purpose as they make great paths and driveways. Check with your local suppliers to see what kind of rocks you could potentially sell to your customer.

3. PRUNING AND TRIMMING

Think of pruning as a method to encourage plants to grow in the best way possible. Regular pruning can improve fruit and flower production, stimulate sturdy growth, and control the size, shape, and symmetry of a plant. Overall, pruning results in stronger, healthier, and more efficient plants.

Pruning Terminology

Caliper: The diameter of a tree measured at between 6 and 12 inches from ground level.

Dieback: The dying back of branches due to disease, insects, or other damage.

Disbudding: Pinching off most of the flower buds early on so that the plant blooms less abundantly but with more magnificent flowers. Some plants, such as roses, dahlias, peonies, hibiscus, carnations, zinnias, asters, and begonias benefit from disbudding.

Dormant: The time of year when a plant is not growing.

Double leader: When the leader splits near the top so that there are two separate branches growing upward (generally undesirable).

Espalier: To train a plant to grow against a wall using wire or a trellis as well as special pruning techniques.

Heading back: Cutting back the tip of a branch from the terminal bud to a lateral bud in order to stimulate branching out, resulting in a bushier plant.

Lateral buds: Buds that form on the sides of branches. These buds show minimal or no growth unless the terminal bud is removed. In that case, the lateral buds receive more energy and form more vigorously.

Leader: The main branch (usually the trunk) of a tree or shrub. Other branches grow from it.

Pinching: Similar to heading back, but done with the fingers to prevent the need for future pruning, to redirect growth and to increase the bushiness of the plant.

Shearing: Removing all the new growth along with the terminal buds. This directs strength to the side buds, resulting in a denser, bushier hedge or shrub. Shearing is usually restricted to removing soft, first-year growth that is easy to cut.

Suckers: Vigorous shoots originating from the root below the ground.

Terminal buds: Buds that are formed on the tip of a branch. New growth generally develops from these buds.

Thinning: Cutting a branch back all the way to its origin (i.e., to the trunk or other main branch). Results in a less-dense, taller plant.

Water sprouts: Vigorous shoots originating from the branches or trunk of a tree.

3.1 When to prune

One of the primary reasons for pruning is to maximize flower production. Every specimen is different, and you must understand the growing habits of the plants you are caring for before you decide when is the best time to prune them. If you are pruning for fruit production, the rules may be different and you should research them in a book specifically about pruning.

Many plants are best if they are not pruned at all (assuming they were planted appropriately, with lots of space to grow). Here are some examples of trees and shrubs that should need no pruning:

- Camellia
- Daphne
- Japanese maple (*Acer palmatum*)
- Magnolia
- Most conifers
- Pieris
- Rhododendrons and azaleas
- Witchhazel (*Hamamelis*)

Other plants should be pruned in spring, before flowering. The general rule is that if a plant produces flowers from its new growth, it may be cut back in spring before the plant starts growing. Alternatively, it may be cut back after it flowers (likely late summer or early fall). This category includes the following plants:

- Abelia
- Barberry
- Bluebeard (*Caryopteris*)
- Butterflybush (*Buddleia davidii*)
- Clematis (late-flowering species)
- Common heather (*Calluna vulgaris*)
- Fuchsia
- Heather (*Erica*)
- Hibiscus (late-flowering species)
- Honeysuckle
- Lad's Love (*Artemisia abrotanum*)
- Lavender
- Potentilla
- Red-twig dogwood (*Cornus alba*)

- Roses (Hybrid tea and floribunda types)
- Sage
- St. Johnswort (*Hypericum*)
- Sweet bay (*Laurus nobilis*)
- Tree mallow (*Lavatera thuringiaca*)

Some plants bloom from old wood, which means pruning should occur right after the flowers are finished, usually in early to late summer.

- Broom (*Cytisus*)
- Cherries
- Clematis (early flowering species)
- Escallonia
- Forsythia
- Hydrangea
- Indian hawthorn (*Rapheolepis indica*)
- Japanese flowering quince (*Chaenomeles japonica*)
- Mock orange (*Philadelphus*)
- Plums
- Roses (*ramblers and shrubs*)
- Spirea (early flowering species)
- Viburnum
- Weigela

3.2 Pruning techniques and principles

The first and most important principle of pruning is to follow the 3-D rule: remove *dead, diseased,* and *damaged* branches. You may not have to go any further than that. Note that dead, diseased, or damaged branches can be removed any time of the year and should be removed as soon as they are identified.

After you have applied the 3-D rule, prune any branches that are too big, too small, crisscrossing, or ugly. When pruning shrubs, you can use the "rule of thirds": Cut back one-third of the stems to ground level, starting with the oldest or thickest stems. Of the remaining stems, reduce their height by one-third. This keeps the plant young and healthy, as, theoretically, no stem should be over three years old.

When you are cutting or pruning larger branches, you must be careful not to damage the tree as the heavy branch rips away from the trunk. To avoid this, use a procedure involving three cuts. The first cut goes on the underside of the branch about a foot or so away from the truck. Next, cut the branch off, making sure you start farther out from the trunk than where you made your first cut. The third cut is to simply remove the remaining stub, which is much smaller than the whole branch and can be removed without damaging the tree.

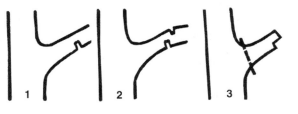

3.3 Practical pruning tips

Many of the rules for pruning involve selecting the correct tool for the task at hand. For example, hedge trimmers are a wonderful tool and make quick work of otherwise intimidating jobs, but you have to know when to put them aside and use snips, loppers, shears, and other hand pruning tools. Here are some practical tips for using the right tool to prune the right plant:

- Broadleaf shrubs, such as rhododendrons, should be pruned with snips and loppers, not shears or power hedge trimmers. If the plants get too large, you can suggest your customer move them or replace them — but don't cut them back with power trimmers. You may want to "raise" shrubs by removing a few of the lower branches so they don't touch the ground. Most people find it looks neater, and it makes it easier for you to tidy fallen leaves under the plant. However, check with the customer first as some prefer to have their shrubbery draped on the ground.

- It is a common misconception that power pruning is faster. This may be true for hedges, but it is not true for specimens like broadleaf shrubs. If you use snips, you can toss the clippings into your bucket; if you use a power pruner, you'll have to rake up the tiny bits of shredded leaves left behind.

- Junipers and similar plants should be hand pruned (if they are pruned at all) with snips and loppers, not sheared. Use thinning and heading back cuts to control size. One common blunder of the lazy gardener is to shear the edges of a juniper to create a "wall" look. The result is plain and uninspiring. Try to maintain the natural form of the plant. If you already have "walled" junipers, use the tip of your

power pruners to make deep, horizontal slashes in the wall. This will leave holes that (I hope) look somewhat natural and add needed texture. These types of shrubs get no new growth from old wood, so don't cut them back too far.

- For shrubs that do get growth from old wood (e.g., forsythia, lilac, rhododendrons), it may be possible to do a shrub renovation. This entails massive thinning cuts, often right to the main stems of the plant. There is no guarantee of success, but if drastic action is needed, it may do the trick.

- Groundcovers need little pruning. Most of the work involves keeping them confined to their rightful spaces. English ivy is particularly invasive; you'll be cutting it back constantly as it tries to take over other plants and even stationary objects (like a house). Cotoneaster sometimes starts looking untidy, with shoots poking straight up. Snip them off with thinning cuts. Try to avoid shearing. Once you start, it only gets worse and you will have to do it more often.

- English laurel is a broadleaf shrub, but when in the form of a hedge, it is often sheared by commercial gardeners. Some may even power prune it, which is acceptable if you cut the shrub close so you're snipping the branches and not cutting leaves. If the leaves get chewed up, the appearance suffers. It will look unsightly, especially in a week or two when the damaged edges turn brown.

When trimming hedges, keep the bottom wider than the top. A common mistake is to do it the other way around, which causes the hedge to suffer because the top blocks the sunlight. As well, it can easily be damaged by heavy snowfall. The best time to shear a hedge is when it is making its fastest growth, which is typically late spring and early summer.

Conifers are primarily pruned to control size. Firs, hemlocks, spruces, cedars, and other fine needle or scale varieties of conifers are often sheared year after year so that they look more like a shaped shrub than a tree. This is a popular technique, and although it does not look natural, it will not harm the tree. This does not work with pines. Control their growth by nipping off the candles of new growth each spring. The more you nip, the less new growth there will be. Don't break or top the leader of a conifer or you will ruin the natural shape of the plant and be left with a high-maintenance atrocity. Put your foot down on this one if you are asked to top a conifer.

Prune water sprouts and suckers as soon as you see them. Remember, it's all about the details.

As you become more experienced, you will find that there are few hard-and-fast rules about what tools and what methods you should use to prune shrubs or trees. For example, forsythia is a spring-flowering shrub that, according to pruning theory, should be cut back after it flowers, using the rule of thirds. However, I have found that most customers prefer to have their forsythia trimmed and shaped a couple of times throughout the season, and then again in the fall so it looks neat and tidy for the winter. Even when I tell them that the plant will provide a dazzling display if they leave it alone, most customers want the neater look. If you want to instill in people the desire to prune correctly, to look past the scraggly shrub to the dazzling display later on, I wish you the best.

Ultimately, your goal is to know the proper method of trimming or pruning a particular plant, and then to understand what people like to see. It will take some time to achieve this balance, but it will come.

4. OFF-SEASON WORK

What you do with yourself and your business in the winter months largely depends on where you live and how busy you want to be. In milder climes, many landscape maintenance companies carry on through the winter, albeit with a reduced set of duties. In those areas that get a lot of snow, some landscapers take up snow plowing to keep them busy in the off-season. Still others, from whatever part of the country, take a well-deserved break.

4.1 Year-round maintenance

If you live in a milder area where there is little or no snowfall, one good way to bring in some income in the slow winter months is to offer year-round maintenance programs. A few residential clients will opt for this service, but you're more likely to find work with commercial contracts.

Here are a some services you might offer:

- *Amending beds.* Get an early jump on spring by amending beds with garden mix or other materials in February.

- *Cleanups.* Many people procrastinate on their fall cleanup and are happy to have someone else come in and do the work.

- *Holiday lighting.* Some companies advertise that they will string holiday lighting around people's homes and gardens.

- *Landscaping.* Some forms of landscaping, such as retaining walls or other construction projects, can be completed in the winter months.

- *Litter control.* A regular visit to pick up litter and keep an eye on the landscape is all some properties need in the winter.

- *Pressure washing.* Many folks want to start off the year clean and will hire you to pressure-wash sidewalks, driveways, and houses. You can provide this service at any time of year, but to keep busy in the slower months, you could market it as a late-winter activity.

- *Pruning.* Depending on where you live, you may be able to complete pruning work in the winter months. For example, hedges could be trimmed in November or December. Some trees can be pruned in the winter months if it's mild. Check the trees, hedges, and shrubs in your area to see if winter pruning is acceptable. If it is, this offers some great winter-time employment.

- *Re-mulching.* Beds, walkways, or driveways may need a fresh application of mulch. Limestone paths could be either roughed up or topped up.

4.2 Snow plowing and clearing

A snow clearing/plowing business is the perfect complement to a landscape maintenance business, assuming you live in an area that actually gets snowfall (the more the better!). It makes sense to capitalize on the opportunity to continue service to your customers. And if you have followed the advice in this book, you are already largely set up for the business. You have a routing, scheduling, and invoicing system ready to go. And you already have a truck, so why not put it to use?

This is not to say that snow plowing is an easy way to make a few bucks in the winter. It's not. The business carries its own challenges and requirements. While your lawn care business infrastructure remains in place, you will need to repeat much of the work you did to set it up to ensure it all applies to your snow-plowing business. There will be different marketing to do, new systems to design, new equipment to purchase, and new routines. Unlike lawn care, there is no scheduling. When it snows, you go. There is no procrastination, and you don't reschedule due to inclement weather, because that's the only kind there is when you're snow plowing. You are working and driving in the worst possible conditions. Although you may have been successful as a one-person show in lawn care, it's more difficult to work alone in the snow-clearing business. You will have to make some alliances so that you can call on other people to cover for you, and they can call on you, when heavy snowfalls occur.

Snow plowing is a competitive business. You will probably have to start with snow clearing — that is, clearing sidewalks and driveways with a walk-behind snowblower. You could start by marketing the service to your existing clients. They already know and trust you and would probably use you if you asked. Do a little market research before you go out and buy equipment. Also research the equipment that you will need, and find out if any additional insurance is required. As in any market, if you are persistent and provide excellent service, your business will grow. In time you can put away your walk-behind and get a brawny blade installed on your four-wheel-drive truck. Eventually, once you have built up your snow business, you should be able to move into the commercial plowing market. That's where the real money is.

If you are still eager to supplement your winter income with such a venture, I suggest that you read a book or two on the subject so you can pick up the tricks of the trade, as you did with lawn care in this book.

4.3 Taking time off

Don't forget that the winter slow months are also when you need to do some relaxing, take some time off, and think and plan for the next season. There's nothing wrong with taking a couple of months off after working hard all the rest of the year.

If you want to work some R&R into your year, you need to plan for it. Don't just expect that you will have enough money to live on for a few months after completing your lawn care season. Use your cash flow forecasts to account for the lack of income. You will have to put away money when you're busy so that you have it when things are slow. It will take vigilance and dedication, but if you succeed, you'll have a most enviable life! You've worked hard for this — now enjoy it!

The following Checklist, Samples, Worksheets, and Resource Lists are included on the CD-ROM for use on your Windows PC.

Checklist

Customer Follow-up

Samples

Employment Acceptance Letter

Employee Policy

Employment Termination Letter

Introductory Letter

Contractual Letter

Outline of Services

Welcome Letter

Business Plan

Business InfoPack

Specific Flyer

New Season Follow-Up

Marketing Flyer

Worksheets

Skills Self-Assessment

My Action Plan

Targeting Your Market

Employee Status Change Form

Annual Referral Tracking Sheet

Lawn and Garden Maintenance Quotation

Quotation Sheet

New Client Questionnaire

Marketing Calendar

Chart of Accounts

Comparative Profit and Loss Statement

Annual Profit and Loss Statement

Balance Sheet

Customer Job Times Record

Property Quality Assessment

Job Costing

Recommended Extras

Monthly Referral Tracking Sheet

Equipment Usage

Jobsite Visit Notice

Resource Lists

Recommended Books

Recommended Websites